HUNTING ALBERTA

WILD COUNTRY PRESS

DUANE S. RADFORD

The Publisher: Wild Country Press is an imprint of Dragon Hill Publishing Ltd.

Library and Archives Canada Cataloguing in Publication
Radford, Duane, 1946–, author
Hunting Alberta / Duane Radford. — 1st edition.
Includes bibliographical references.
Issued in print and electronic formats.

ISBN 978-1-896124-68-1 (softcover).—ISBN 978-1-896124-69-8 (EPUB)

1. Hunting—Alberta. 2. Hunting—Alberta—Handbooks, manuals, etc. I. Title.
SK152.A6R23 2018   799.297123   C2017-907018-5
C2017-907019-3

Project Manager: Marina Michaelides
Editorial: Wendy Pirk
Cover Design: Greg Brown
Front Cover Image: ps50ace/Thinkstock
Back Cover Image: splendens/Thinkstock
Book Layout: Tamara Hartson
Image Credits: Duane S. Radford, except if noted below.
Extra Image Credits: Brian Makowecki, 46; Lanny Amos, 13, 214, 223. From Thinkstock: Betty4240, 34; bobloblaw, 171a; Chilkoot, 87; Debraansky, 148; Denny35463, 142; EEI_Tony, 105, 135; Evgeny555, 192; Eyezaya, 193; GriffinGillespie, 16; HildeAnna, 224; JackVandenHeuvel, 170; James Douglas Stewart, 149; jcrader, 173; Jens_Lambert_Photography, 151; Jupiterimages, 101; kyleperry, 195; Kyryl Gorlov, 157; Lightwriter1949, 175b; MartinM303, 117; megasquib, 144; Mermald, 174; mlharing, 86; photographybyJHWilliams, 153, 159b; RCKeller, 184; river34, 187; SandSandS, 30; SteveOehlenschlager, 163, 167, 179; SWKrullImaging, 130; tmarko, 165; twildlife, 26, 29, 118, 137, 139, 155, 225; UrosPoteko, 161, 162; wmarsik, 152; Yatso, 194. From Wikimedia Commons: Cephas, 169; Grendelkhan, 176; Kevin Cole, 177.
Flourishes and Borders: From Thinkstock: piart, Barbulat.

Produced with the assistance of the Government of Alberta.

Alberta
Government

Under the wide and starry sky
Dig the grave and let me lie.
Glad did I live and gladly die,
And I laid me down with a will.

This be the verse you grave for me;
"Here he lies where he longed to be,
Home is the sailor, home from sea,
And the hunter home from the hill."

–Lines from "Requiem," No. 21 in *Underwoods, Book One: In English*
(1890). The first draft of this poem by Robert Louis Stevenson was
composed in 1880 as an epitaph for his grave marker.

Table of Contents

Foreword

Alberta is blessed with a natural diversity unmatched in Canada. Our landscapes range from the short-grass prairies of the southeast to the rolling foothills, the towering mountains of the Rocky Mountains, the picturesque aspen parklands and on up to the vast boreal forest. This diversity in climate, landforms, soils and plants allows a wide array of birds and mammals to thrive. And for those who hear the hunter's horn, there are few attributes as attractive as the opportunity to pursue a broad variety of species. Alberta offers that in spades.

The first permanent residents of Alberta arrived some 5000 years ago; it's thought they came to the region to hunt large game, specifically bison. And while legendary immense herds of bison no longer traverse Alberta's prairie, our suite of game mammals and birds remains very much as it was when those original hunters set out to feed their families. In fact, thanks to the early 1900s introduction of ring-necked pheasant and Hungarian partridge into Alberta, today's opportunities may exceed those of earlier times.

Hunting has, however, changed over the millennia in several important ways. Born as a community affair, in earlier times it was all about feeding the collective. Through the 20th century, however, killing your own food became less of an imperative, and hunting evolved to become part food-gathering, part outdoor experience and part social interaction. For most hunters today, heading afield remains a blend of collecting their own meat and enjoying the company of like-minded family and friends.

Though, fortunately, hunting is no longer critical to our day-to-day survival, one aspect that hasn't changed with time is the passion we display. Those who hunt do so with an intensity that is difficult for non-hunters to understand. It's in our blood, part of our psychological and physiological make-up, not just something that we do. What might surprise some is that the passion for hunting is growing, or at least it seems to be in Alberta. In 2012 there were slightly more than 111,000 licensed hunters in the Wild Rose province; by 2016 that number had climbed to 127,000, a 14 percent increase in just five years.

Perhaps the growth in Alberta's hunting community reflects the social movement towards consuming more organic food, growing and harvesting your own as a means to a healthier lifestyle. Alternatively, it could simply reflect an increasing desire to find rewarding ways to enjoy an outdoor experience while spending time with like-minded people. Irrespective of individual motivations, the timing couldn't be better for Duane's book *Hunting Alberta*.

A lifelong hunter, I suspect Duane brings more years of experience to educating us about Alberta's hunting opportunities than he'd care to admit. More than the knowledge gained through his many years pursuing large, small and bird game; however, as a professional biologist Duane also brings the understanding of hunting's ecological nuances that only a scientist can recognize.

Beyond the thorough descriptions of proven hunting tactics, seasoned perfectly with anecdotes from his own days afield, Duane provides veteran and novice hunters alike with valuable advice on everything from equipment choices to hunter ethics. Another of his passions, turning birds and big game into table fare that will appeal to all appetites, is handled thoroughly and, well, tastefully.

It's been said that we don't hunt to kill, but rather we kill to have hunted. It's the broader experience of the hunt that we seek and that offers us salvation. This book will serve to both inspire and teach, leading each of us to more rewarding hunting experiences.

You'll likely never have the opportunity to share a campfire with Duane on a crisp, clear October night under a hunter's moon, but absorbing the wisdom offered here will make the fires shared with your hunting companions just that much more enjoyable.

–Ken Bailey, *Outdoor Canada* Hunting Editor

Dedication

I'd like to dedicate this book to my family, starting with my grandfather, Albert Sapeta and his wife, Victoria, who were such great grandparents; my mother, Carrie (Caroline) and father, Sam (Samuel); as well as my wife, Adrienne; daughter, Jennifer; and son, Myles, who have enriched my life in so many ways. This book is also dedicated to the selfless volunteers of the Alberta Fish & Game Association (AFGA) who have given so much of their time, effort and money since 1908 to conserve Alberta's fish and game resources.

I'd also like to say a few words about Stubs (Ludwick von Hachenbach, his kennel name), my late German shorthair pointer, who had no quit. He was so well trained (thanks to my wife, Adrienne) that he was as close to being a human being as a dog could possibly get and an outstanding bird dog in every respect. They don't come any better. To Stubs, thank you for being such a great bird dog and family pet.

Acknowledgements

I'd like to thank my wife, Adrienne, who has always been very supportive of me during our marriage and shared some great hunts for pheasants and waterfowl back in the day. I have also enjoyed many years of hunting with my son, Myles, and with my good friend and fellow outdoor writer Don Meredith. I would also like to acknowledge my brother, Jim, with whom I enjoyed many hunts over the years. My daughter, Jennifer, shared in some wonderful trips in Alberta's outdoors. I'd be remiss if I didn't say thanks to my sister, Jill, who helped clean so many game birds when we were growing up.

Special thanks go out to some dear friends and old hunting partners such as Dennis Amos, Morley Barrett, Eldon Bruns, E.B. (Buck) Cunningham, Dave Donald, Wes English, John and Cindy Gattey, Leo Gudmundson, Lorne Fitch, Duncan Lloyd, Ray Makowecki, Blythe Mattson, Curtiss McLeod, Frank and Donna Murphy, Dennis Reese, Tom Smith, Albert and Johnny Truant with whom I've enjoyed great camaraderie over the years.

I'll never forget sights such as the time Wes, Lorne and I were hunting bighorn sheep on the slopes of Mount Tecumseh near Deadman Pass when we watched a silvertip grizzly as it foraged, its mane rippling in the cool autumn wind. During the same trip there was the irony of watching a black bear trying to wedge its way into the back of my pickup truck at the Allison Creek campsite after we returned from one of our hunting forays.

Special thanks go to Wendy Pirk and Faye Boer who edited this book about a complicated subject to say the least. There's a saying that practically nobody knows all the rules of golf or hunting, and I'm sure they agree there's some truth to this legend. I'd also very much like to thank Faye in particular for advocating publication of this book with the publisher because hunting has an undeserved stigma and is controversial in some circles. Faye and Wendy asked me some tough questions as editors so I hope I've done them a service in getting the book's storyline right. Tamara Hartson and Greg Brown also deserve full marks for an excellent job designing the book's layout and cover and for bringing the subject matter to life.

Introduction

I first started hunting more than 50 years ago just as soon I could legally obtain a hunting licence. I'm still going strong, enjoying big game, upland game bird and waterfowl hunting to this day. Actually, one of the best hunts I've ever been on took place with my son, Myles, when we booked a waterfowl hunt with Black Dog Outfitters in 2014. Blaine Burns runs this business out of hunt camp near Tofield, east of Edmonton. We had some terrific wing shooting for ducks and geese and enjoyed many delicious meals of waterfowl after the hunt was over.

I was born in Blairmore in the Crowsnest Pass of southwestern Alberta and grew up in nearby Bellevue where I lived until my teens when I moved to Calgary. At the time, the Pass was a hot bed of hunting activity, and the surrounding area abounded with both bird game and big game although there weren't many waterfowl hunting opportunities.

My grandfather, Albert Sapeta, was born in 1882 in Austria in an area that is now part of Poland and immigrated to Canada in 1906, settling in Coleman, which is also in the Crowsnest Pass. He was a consummate

Bighorn Ram

———<•●•>———

Don't ever think you're alone in the bush.

—Carl Sapeta, author's uncle, big game hunter, prospector and trapper

———<•●•>———

hunter and amateur taxidermist. I believe that I got my hunting genes from him because my father, Samuel (Sam), was not a hunter, nor was anyone else in his family, although my father and his brothers, Fred and James, were all keen fly anglers. Papa, as we affectionately called my grandfather, was relatively small in stature but had the heart of a giant. He owned several horses and used to pack into the backcountry north and south of the Pass area on his hunts. He'd be gone for weeks at a time in what was then a wilderness area without any roads. He'd often caution me to follow creeks downstream if I ever got lost. Once, while hunting sheep in Gravenstafel Creek in the West Castle area south of his home in Coleman, he told me that a grizzly bear rose from a huckleberry patch scant yards in front of him. He calmly raised his trusty .303 British Winchester carbine and shot it in the neck, killing it in its tracks. Papa willed me this collectable rifle, which has a special place in my gun cabinet. He had many bear rugs, several Boone & Crockett record book bighorn rams, mountain goats and mule deer mounts at his home. My grandmother, Victoria, used to have bear grease in her pantry which she'd use for all manner of cooking and medicinal purposes.

After giving this matter some thought, I'd have to say that Papa was actually more of a trophy hunter in a day of meat hunters. Thanks to my late mother, Carrie (Caroline), my hunting interests were always supported whenever I brought game home for the table. She was a terrific cook, and having come from a home where wild game was a staple in the diet, understood how to cook it well. I think she'd get just as excited as I was when I returned home with wild fowl and deer. I can still recall how I'd savour her roasted ruffed grouse in particular—always done to perfection.

In some respects, hunting for many species in Alberta is better now than it was in the good old days as I've learned from a lifetime in the outdoors. The reason it's better is because, by and large, the biologists hired by the Alberta government have done a great job managing our wild game resources. I worked for the Alberta Fish and Wildlife Division for 34 years and saw many advances in game management during my career. Granted, a lot of wildlife habitat has been damaged and some destroyed during my lifetime, but overall the science of wildlife management is far better than it used to be.

One of the reasons I decided to write this book is because I've had to learn a lot of about hunting the hard way. I didn't really have a mentor to show me the ropes when I was growing up. My uncle, Carl Sapeta, did help me get me off on the right foot, as well as my neighbor, Ted Amos, to whom I'm also indebted, but I'm largely a self-taught hunter. My hope is that my knowledge of the outdoors and experiences will help readers of this book become better hunters. I started my career as an outdoor writer in 1995 and have since written more than 800 outdoor and travel articles, and fish and wild game recipes. I've kept a hunting journal since 1962 when I shot a mule deer doe near Rock Creek on November 1, 1962, this being my first big

Lanny Amos with an outstanding bull elk taken in 2009

game kill. Consequently, I've got accurate records about big game, upland game bird and waterfowl hunting trips in Alberta.

Various chapters in this book cover the range of hunting opportunities that are available in Alberta and key subject matter related to the hunting genre.

Alberta Is a TROPHY Mecca

It may come as a surprise to many hunters, but as of 2016 an astounding 1576 Alberta entries have made the Boone and Crockett Club (B&C) record book, according to the 2016 Alberta's Professional Outfitters Guide, the latest year for which they published this information. The B&C club was established in 1887 to record outstanding big game trophies as one of its goals.

These remarkable figures speak for themselves, validating that Alberta remains a veritable factory for trophy big game animals. Alberta really is a TROPHY Mecca.

To top these remarkable phenomena, some of the finest trophies ever recorded in Alberta have been taken in recent years. A prime example is the outstanding pronghorn antelope that scored an amazing 90 B&C points, which was taken by Tannis R. Piotrowski in 2013 near Manyberries, a new Alberta record. I admired this buck's horns at the 51st AFGA Annual Wildlife Awards Banquet in 2013, and they were truly amazing! Mark my words, this antelope will go down as one of the top entries ever for Alberta. Relatively speaking, it's on scale comparable with the incredible "Broder Buck" that scored 355 2/8 points, along with Guinn D. Crousen's 208 3/8 former world record bighorn, both shot in Alberta. Incidentally, the former Alberta record pronghorn antelope that scored 88 4/8 (taken by Fred J. Streleoff in 2003) was also shot near Manyberries, a go-to location for trophy antelope.

There had been a potential new world record bighorn sheep that was found dead south of Hinton by Fish and Wildlife Officers in 2014. It was initially scored at 209 ⅛ inches. After the mandatory 60-day drying period, the final measurement came in at 205 ⅞ inches.

There has been no letup in the number of big game records set each year, and 2016, the last year for which records are available, was no exception. So why is Alberta such an outstanding place to tag a record book big game animal?

1. For starters, Alberta has a diversity of prime big game habitat that is without equal in Canada, featuring the mountains, foothills, prairies, parklands and boreal forest. It is this remarkable diversity in habitat that spawns so many fine trophies, and as long as wildlife habitat is not impaired, there's no reason why production of trophies should decline.

2. Alberta enjoyed a series of relatively mild winters up until 2010–11, which allowed deer herds to expand. High deer numbers translated into more and larger trophies than normal. I wrote an article about hunting mule deer in Alberta in 2008 (*The Skinny on Alberta's Mule Deer*, see Chapter 8, page 108) for the Alberta Guide to Hunting Regulations when the mule deer provincial population estimate was 185,000. I suggested that hunters should not put off a mule deer hunt but take advantage of their abundance and the exceptional large size of bucks while they last! As things have turned out, hard winters over the past few years have severely reduced the size of the mule deer herd in Alberta, but the numbers are slowly rebounding.

3. Alberta has a lot of sanctuaries that are fodder for trophy animals when they move to their winter ranges, in the case of elk or bighorn sheep in search of ewes. There are several hot spots near national and provincial parks that consistently produce record-book animals as they move out of these sanctuaries. Likewise, large bow-hunting-only zones around Alberta's major municipal centres yield some wall hangers from time to time, notably white-tailed deer.

4. Changes in hunting regulations, especially limited entry draws, must also be credited for allowing better escapement

The world's most outstanding bighorn sheep are found in Alberta.

There's a closed season on grizzlies in Alberta.

of mature animals that have lived longer and grow larger antlers.

5. Lastly, hunters are becoming more strategic in pursuing trophies and are more knowledgeable today than ever before in searching out outstanding animals. They're also better equipped than in earlier days, with fine rifles and optics which help them close the hunt a lot easier than in bygone days.

Bighorn Sheep

Alberta is renowned for its record-book bighorn sheep. An incredible 354 record rams have made the B&C record book. On the night of January 19, 2010, a vehicle on Highway 940 west of Longview, Alberta, struck a bighorn sheep, which is now recognized as the new official Alberta record after finally being scored by officials in 2014. Their measurements yielded a score of 209 ⅘ points, edging out the previous

Alberta record ram shot by Guinn D. Crousen on Luscar Mountain near Hinton in 2000 which scored 208 ⅜ points. The new world-record bighorn is a pick-up from Montana, with an official score of 216 ⅜.

Black Bear

AFGA records indicate that 126 Alberta black bears made the B&C record book. Bear numbers remain high and hunting pressure relatively low, so the chances of shooting a big bruin remain high.

Elk

Alberta's top elk (419 ⅚) was shot by Clarence Brown in 1977 in the Panther River area. Several outstanding bulls have been shot during the last few years, many taken in and around Canadian Forces Base Suffield and in WMU 300 near Waterton Lakes National Park. Sixty-one Alberta elk have been entered in the B&C book.

Pronghorn antelope have excellent vision.

Moose

All time, 164 Canada moose have made the B&C record book in Alberta. With a limited entry draw in most Wildlife Management Units, there's a good chance at taking a large moose in many parts of Alberta.

Pronghorn Antelope

Even though Alberta is at the northern edge of the range of pronghorn antelope in North America, it has been producing some exceptional bucks during the past decade, with record-book bucks being shot fairly routinely; 53 bucks from Alberta made the B&C records. The severe winter in 2010–11 took its toll; however, and no pronghorn antelope made the book in either 2011 or 2012. Things changed in 2013 though with some fine bucks being shot. In the previous dozen years B&C bucks were taken in 2000 (5), 2001 (6), 2002 (3), 2003 (7), 2004 (2), 2007 (5), 2008 (8), 2009 (6) and 2010 (4).

Mule Deer

Alberta has become a go-to destination for trophy mule deer in recent years where 108 mule deer have qualified for the B&C record book. The top spots for trophy mule deer over the past several years were Arizona, Alberta, South Dakota, Texas, and Saskatchewan. Non-residents are not allowed to hunt mule deer in Saskatchewan.

The humongous "Broder Buck," which scored an unbelievable 355 ⅞ points (taken in 1926 by Ed Broder near Chip Lake west of Edmonton) still stands as the number one non-typical mule deer in the world. It's unlikely this record will ever be broken.

White-tailed Deer

AFGA records indicate that 212 non-typical white-tails and 328 typical white-tailed deer qualified for the B&C records up to 2016. The severe winter of 2010–11 reduced the number of record-breaking white-tailed deer bucks. Surprisingly, however, there's been some carryover of big bucks, as evidenced by the 2013 monster shot by Colton Gustafson in Wildlife Management Unit 506 that scored 183 ²/₈.

For information on where Alberta's record big game animals have been taken, readers should check the *Alberta Wildlife Records—Official Records of the Alberta Fish and Game Association 3rd Edition 1963–2010* (2011). Some clues can be found on where to bag outstanding trophies by studying these records, as well as the records for the Boone & Crockett Club, and Pope and Young Club.

———— ❮•••❯ ————

Every Canada goose is a trophy, just like all cock pheasants and antelope.

–George Freeman,
Mr. Ducks Unlimited
Canada

———— ❮•••❯ ————

Alberta is one of the world's top destinations for trophy white-tail deer.

CHAPTER ONE

Getting Started

Big Game Hunting Homework

If you want to tag a big game animal, do your hunting homework, and don't say the dog ate it if you get caught with an unfilled tag at the end of the season. You'll have nobody to blame but yourself. The gist of this chapter is about getting in position for a shot during the hunting season. If you are hunting on private land, you'll need to keep some extra things in mind, but more on that subject later.

I've often said that one of the best ways to ensure you can bag big game animals is to go grouse hunting before the big game season starts. Why? Grouse hunting requires walking over the same ground that big game animals frequent, and you'll notice all sorts of forensic evidence regarding their whereabouts as you search for grouse. This is especially true if you adhere to the "edge" effect and do most of your scouting on the edges of fields and along the perimeter of stands of trees where big game animals find sanctuary. Travel lanes, aka game trails, invariably follow areas of low relief between feeding areas and bedding areas in stands of aspen and conifers, or escape cover in a gully (i.e., draw) and coulees. Clues, such as droppings, beds and tracks, are often located on or near game trails. The same principles apply if you're hunting Alberta's vast prairies for sharp-tailed grouse, the foothills and mountains for blue grouse, the aspen parklands for ruffed grouse or the boreal forest for spruce grouse.

To be successful, it does not matter how much money you have invested in your hunting gear and vehicles to go hunting. More important is how much time you invest in scouting your hunting territory to connect the game sign "dots" and subsequently bag an animal. By advance scouting you'll not only discover all sorts of sign, you'll also get in better shape for that upcoming big game hunt. Furthermore, you'll become a better outdoorsman in the process and a more complete hunter.

You gotta keep pokin' around because moose, deer, elk are where you find them.

–Keith Kivett, veteran moose hunter with regard to not seeing game and wondering whether it's worthwhile investigating areas that you've already looked at

Always check for big game sign during scouting trips.

The autumn of 2009 was one of the most challenging times I've ever had to do pre-season scouting because the deciduous trees near Edmonton did not experience their typical fall colours. Rather, the leaves stayed green well into October and then started to fall and blanket the ground toward the end of the month, effectively hiding most big game sign in the process. Argh! Regardless, if you looked hard enough, the sign was still present—old and fresh droppings, tracks in the mud on game trails, hair snagged on bush, even the odd shed antler here and there, which is always a good sign that males frequent an area late in the season. I've even confirmed an area that bull moose seem to favour in one of my favourite hunting spots near Edmonton where shed antlers are scattered as if in a bone yard. The next time I get a moose tag, guess where I'm going to hunt!

Big game animals prefer secluded areas where they feel safe, and for this reason I always try to concentrate my pre-season scouting in out-of-the-way spots. Scout in areas away from roads and trails that vehicles travel regularly, particularly when scouting for elk, since they like to keep a ridge top or large stand of forest between them and human activities. A "ridge top" is a height of land between two valleys. Granted, in farm country and in forested areas where industry is active, game can become habituated to vehicles, but as soon as vehicles stop, all of their attention is focused on what the occupants intend to do. They will stop feeding and keep their eyes on the vehicle for any sign of danger. The most secure areas might just be on the edge of your hunting territory up against the border with another province, territory or Montana, in any given WMU—places that are far removed from the most accessible spots to go hunting.

Time and space are both factors in the foregoing "secluded areas" dimension. You can capitalize on "space" by hunting the most remote areas in your chosen territory. In terms of "time," spend the most time hunting when pressure is lowest, for example, during the middle of the week or near the end of the hunting season, not on opening or closing day or during or around holidays.

After you've figured out where the most secluded spots are located, either from a topographic map or from previous experience hunting the area, do some serious walking throughout your hunting territory. In addition to actually trying to spot big game, look for all the usual signs: game trails, tracks, beds, areas where game has browsed, droppings, shed antlers, snagged

hair, rubs and white-tailed deer scrapes. Try to make sense of what you see and figure out if there is a pattern to all the signs. Many animals can hide in plain sight, so look everywhere, including behind you, when you're scouting and during the actual hunt.

If you spend enough time scouting (and subsequently hunting) a particular area, you'll eventually have a "Eureka" moment. I recall one such event where white-tailed bucks routinely gave me the slip until I finally figured out their travel lanes between their feeding and bedding areas. In hindsight, it was obvious where I should have located my stand to intercept the deer when they returned from their feeding area enroute to where they bedded down during the day. From then on, I tagged several nice bucks in subsequent years.

However, it was scouting that helped me understand the clues and solve the puzzle.

Moose droppings indicate they're using the area for feeding or bedding purposes.

Deer tend to travel near cover whenever possible, not wide open spaces.

Some hunters may be oblivious to the most obvious of patterns displayed by big game animals. Try to think like your quarry and anticipate their moves.

Another important principle to remember is that big game animals have a home range and are creatures of habit to a large degree as long as they are not unduly pressured by hunters. You can and should expect to see them make the rounds of their home range with a fair degree of predictably, though some animals such as mule deer bucks, which are highly mobile, will travel extensively throughout their range prior to and during the November rut. There's nothing wrong with revisiting areas where you've seen game during previous scouting and hunting trips; in fact, this is a good practice because animals will often be found in the same spots at a later date.

It's of even more importance to do some advance scouting throughout Alberta nowadays because the landscape is forever changing: forest fires ravage the boreal forest; pine beetles destroy cover; what was once a forested area may have been logged; native grasslands might have been ploughed and re-seeded to tame pasture; new roads may have been built or old ones reclaimed and closed; and ranchers may have changed their grazing practices for range management purposes or other reasons.

It's also important to obtain a municipal map for the area you plan on hunting that illustrates property owners and lessees. These maps can be purchased at the various municipal offices within a given municipality. Some of these maps even show the boundaries of the WMUs for the county, improvement district or municipal district. Make sure that you are familiar with the boundaries of the property where you have permission to hunt, and which areas are off limits. Don't expect to bag the trophy of your dreams the first time you hunt in new territory; it seldom happens.

I always call ahead to ask for permission when hunting on private land, even in cases when I know the landowner well and may have hunted on their property for many years. I also check in before I actually go hunting and speak to them in person. One thing I've learned over the years is to listen carefully and pay attention when ranchers talk about places where they've seen game and spots that might warrant a look-see. Alberta's ranchers are generally people of few words. Once, a rancher acquaintance suggested hunting an area that I'd been driving past because it didn't look promising from the road. Was I ever wrong! It turned out to be a jackpot where my party subsequently enjoyed great success over several years.

Doing big game hunting homework might not be up your alley, but it's a must-do if you want to be consistently successful at tagging animals.

The fun ends after the shot.

There's always hard work to do after shooting a big game animal and it often takes a lot of grit to get the job done.

Big Game Calling Cards

Although you don't have to be Sherlock Holmes to interpret game calling cards, you may find yourself thinking like a forensic detective once you start down this road. Here are some questions to think about:

• Do you make a habit of looking for big game sign when you're in the field? Do you subsequently make a mental note of what you see or keep a log in a hunting journal?

• Do you know how to tell the difference between the tracks of the most common species of big game (e.g., moose, elk, deer)? What about their droppings? Can you differentiate between the droppings of common species of big game?

• How about rubs? What tell-tale signs should you look for and where?

• Where do scrapes and wallows fit in?

• Why are game trails significant?

• Are beds important? How do you tell the difference between the beds of various species?

• What about feeding craters or signs of browsing? What might they tell you?

If you don't know what to look for as well as where and why, how can you ever expect to find your big game quarry?

Game animals are largely creatures of habit, and although their distribution changes seasonally, they tend to stay within a defined home range. It's your job to figure out where the boundaries of this home range are located.

By searching out game calling cards, such as tracks, droppings, rubs, scrapes, wallows, trails, beds and feeding craters, you will know which species are frequenting an area, roughly where they are feeding and

Elk antlers sheds in Alberta's aspen parkland

bedding, and where their primary travel lanes are located.

With this knowledge, you can put yourself in a position to spot big game, lay in wait or put on a stalk and make a shot. You'll have a rough idea of their home range and where they are most likely to be found during the hunting season.

The old saying "what goes around, comes around" applies to game sign in more ways than one!

Look and listen!! Although big game calls—the grunts of rutting deer and moose, bleats of female deer, bugling of bull elk, barks and mewling of cow elk and chirps of pronghorn antelope, for example—are not exactly calling cards, it is wise to be ever vigilant of these sounds in the wild.

Likewise, the location of shed antlers is another clue to help narrow down the home range of game animals. Keep an eye open for these sheds.

However, it is the fundamental big game calling cards, such as beds, trails,

droppings and tracks, that will help you determine the primary home ranges of various species, so you can be in the right place to listen for these giveaway calls and figure out the locations where sheds are most likely to be found.

I probably spend just about as much time actually looking on the ground as I do visually searching the forests and fields for big game during a hunting trip.

Let's focus on white-tailed deer calling cards for starters. This deer is the most popular big game animal in Alberta and has a home range that may be less than a square mile in size depending on the carrying capacity of the area. Select a stand within range of rubs, which will normally be associated with scrapes. Rubs are spots where bucks remove the bark from willows and aspen while polishing their antlers and also leave their scent. Rubs also provide a visual clue for does that a scrape is nearby. Scrapes appear in late October before the November rut. Scrapes are areas cleared of vegetation by mature bucks, usually down to bare earth, which are subsequently pawed clear of snow at the onset of winter. They are territorial claim stakes and are also marking posts for receptive does. Receptive does urinate in scrapes to signal bucks that they are ready to mate. A buck will often have several areas of pawed ground along a scrape line, which are commonly found along the edges of stands of aspen or willow. Bucks will monitor these scrapes throughout the rut every few days, usually in the early morning or late afternoon.

You may be surprised by the number of rubs and scrapes inside the sanctuary of cover. This is where the action shifts when hunting pressure escalates. The deer are

Check for deer rubs on alders which are often found near sloughs and indicate that a buck is in the area.

still active, but they move about primarily in the safety of thick cover. If you aren't seeing deer in the open during the rut, you will have to move your stand right into the bush near a rub or scrape to get a shot, at least until the post-rut period when you might spot a buck at any time of the day, almost anywhere within his home range.

If a buck is paired up with a doe in heat, it will not check a scrape line until that doe has been bred. Whitetail does are receptive for about 24 hours. A buck may follow a doe for a day or two before she comes into heat and stay with her for a few days after mating, then look for another doe coming into heat. During the breeding season, a buck may mate with only three or four does. If a doe is not bred, it will come into heat once or twice again at 28-day intervals.

Game trails are always associated with rubs and scrapes. Deer tend to follow these trails out of habit between feeding and bedding areas. You can spot beds by looking for areas of flattened grass, associated deer droppings and hair to confirm that they're actually made by deer, not elk or moose, which are much larger in size. White-tailed deer feeding areas can be hard to judge depending on where you are hunting because they are browsers and feed on tips of shoots as well as grain where it is present. However, by following deer trails, you'll find areas where they stop and feed.

Now you're in business. Start connecting the dots. Where are the rubs, scrapes, feeding and bedding areas? Once you've evaluated the signs, you'll be able to determine the home range of white-tailed deer and make plans to still hunt or stand hunt or both. Sometimes it's hard to interpret all the signs, and you'll have to think outside the box to figure out the puzzle. Other factors also come into play that may throw you off track, such as ups and downs in

Look for deer droppings to see where they're feeding & bedding.

deer numbers resulting from adverse weather and the impact of increasing numbers of predators that prey on deer. These factors cloud the various calling cards.

The same principles apply to mule deer, although they don't make scrapes. Neither do elk or moose, but both of these latter species are fond of wallows, which can usually be scented before they're found. They absolutely reek of the animals' scent and urine! Wallows are wet areas or small ponds, of sorts, that attract both elk and moose during the rut to cool off, mark their bodies with mud, their own urine and other scents from glands to attract females.

In the case of elk, other added variables may compound your strategy, regardless of where you are hunting, because they are herd animals. Bulls tend to become solitary during the rut and then form into bachelor groups after the rut. On a similar note, bull moose tend to gravitate to thick, isolated pockets of cover after the rut to feed and rest up, but they often form groups by November when the weather worsens.

Elk can be exasperating to hunt because of their herd behaviour. It's difficult to sneak up on herd of elk with all those ears and eyes bobbing around, but they are also creatures of habit, and once you get to know their home range the odds tend to tip in your favour. Consequently, you have to beat elk at their own game with stealth and cunning and take the hunt to them whenever possible. This means focusing on where they're most likely to be found at first and last light and being prepared for some split-second shots when opportunities arise. That's not to say that you won't have some standing shots, because you will. During one hunt, for example, I encountered several raghorn bulls that I could have hit with a rock had I wanted to. Raghorns are small bull elk that are larger than spike bulls (which only have a main beam) but smaller than mature bulls, which have at least 5 or 6 tines off a main beam. Elk are often found in fields in the early morning and evening but may be on the move, so your only chance may be a running shot. Just remember the rule of

While elk are most active during the early morning and evening, you might see a bull at any time.

thumb for a running shot: lead big game one body length of a big game animal (i.e., point the barrel of your rifle) at a range of 100 yards and two body lengths at 200 yards, and so on for killing shots

How do you know where to be at first and last light when on an elk hunt? By scouting out their sign. It's all about planning and playing the odds. Look for elk droppings, ragged feeding craters, beds and travel lanes (check for their hair on bushes and fences) to narrow down your options. Listen for their calls, especially at dawn and sundown. If you think elk are in the area, stand hunting can pay dividends. I know of several high-percentage spots where herds tend to gravitate at different times during the season. I've located these spots over the years, sometimes just by happenstance, but usually by watching for big game calling cards.

Spotting Big Game Animals

You've likely heard the saying, "I don't know what I'm looking for, but I'll recognize it when I see it!" When it comes to spotting big game, this saying has a ring of truth because you might actually be looking for several different animal species on a given hunt, and every one of them might be your quarry. Even if you are searching for just one particular species of big game animal; however, you might not actually be able to see all of it, even when it's right in front of you. Most often you'll notice only a small part of an animal before seeing its entire body.

Consequently, job one for all hunters is to be able to recognize big game animals and *parts* of these animals at varying distances and often under less-than-ideal lighting. This means animal side views, front and rear-end profiles, animals in bedded situations and so on. Furthermore, spotting big game in uneven terrain is often akin to a game of whack-a-mole where the quarry appears and just as suddenly disappears. It's at times like these that you may wonder if your mind is playing tricks on you, as an animal appears from out of nowhere and then suddenly disappears.

Hunters must be familiar with the size, shape and colouration of big game species and their habitat preferences, as well as the fundamentals of their behaviour. With this knowledge, you can spot various species in the field.

Sometimes, the clue will be subtle. For example, the only sign in your field of view might be the inside white colouration of the ear of a bedded mule deer off in the distance, or the white throat patch of a white-tailed deer. Maybe you'll see the jaw movements of a bull elk as it ruminates while bedded down on a sunny, south-facing slope on a cold November day, or a bull moose as it shifts in its bed under

similar circumstances. Deer, elk and moose tend to use draws when moving from one piece of cover to another when out in the open, and you might only spot the tips of their antlers as they travel, so keep an eye out for anything out of the ordinary. It's your task to search for these bits and pieces of a bigger puzzle by looking for the key body parts, if you can't see the whole animal.

Most often, the distinguishing clue regarding their whereabouts will be something that looks out of place in your search. Perhaps all you'll see is the glint of a polished antler off in the distance or the white rump patch of a bighorn sheep, mule deer or pronghorn antelope as they feed. The distinctive rump patch of these three big game animal species acts like a beacon under all lighting conditions. You must know where and when to look for big game animals to be successful, particularly hard-to-find animals such as elk, which I'd rate as one of the most elusive species.

Mule deer—note white rump patch.

An often-overlooked tip for spotting big game in forested areas is to look for objects that are out of place in the landscape. For example, search for horizontal objects in a vertical landscape. To illustrate this point, picture a person walking a dog along the edge of a stand of trees. The trees are vertical. The person is vertical. The dog is horizontal. You'll often spot the dog before you notice the person. A horizontal object will stand out like a sore thumb in a vertical landscape.

Alberta's big game animals have some striking features that make them rather conspicuous and should be the focus of your search. Every species has at least one or two classic "calling cards" that you need to be familiar with to spot these animals in the field.

Full curl bighorn sheep ram—note white rump patch.

Bighorn Sheep

Bighorn sheep are notoriously difficult to spot when bedded down, but because of the herd behaviour of rams, if you find one, you'll often find others. You will likely spot their distinguishing white rump patch or strikingly white muzzle first. Patience is the key to spotting rams. They feed during the day and get up from their beds to stretch, and that's when you're most likely to observe them at a distance.

The white rump patch of a bighorn sheep stands out like a beacon, but the white nose patch, though conspicuous, is harder to see. Try to understand something about the biology of bighorn sheep in order to know where to look for the tell-tale rump patch before you can find it and pinpoint the location of a ram. Rams will bed down on cliffs overnight as a defence against predators. They'll be up feeding at the crack of dawn. After they finish feeding, they'll usually bed down again until about noon, when they'll often get up and stretch, perhaps feeding a bit. It is uncanny how often you'll spot a herd of rams as one or more will rise and stretch during the noon hour. When rams are bedded on a talus slope, they're virtually impossible

———————<•••>———————

You can't keep a good
sheep hunting spot secret.

–Bill Michalsky, big game
guide and outfitter and
a founding director of the
Alberta Wilderness
Association

———————<•••>———————

to see from a distance. Consequently, you may only be able to spot the distinctive rump patch on one of perhaps several rams in a herd of a dozen or more animals.

Watch for rams travelling to their favourite waterhole in the evening. I've seen some rams descend a mile or more for a drink, after which they'll return to their bedding area.

Just prior to the rut it's not uncommon to spot single rams on the move from first light until sundown as they search for ewes. Spotting rams is a bit like playing a game of hide and seek. Sure, you know what to look for, but you have to know when and where to look to actually spot them. The sheen on their coats will sometimes give them away if you can catch them at the right angle when the sun is shining. You can also follow tracks in the snow, which will lead to their whereabouts, sometimes in the midst of conifers, where they'll bed out of the wind.

Mule Deer

Mule deer also have a white rump patch, and it's this patch that most often gives them away, although the inside white of their large, erect ears is another unmistakable clue as to their whereabouts.

Because mule deer are early risers, watch for that rump patch after first light. Bucks will bed down in a sunny vantage spot and watch the day go by if they're not disturbed. Bring a good pair of binoculars and set yourself down for some serious glassing if you want to spot mulies. Watch for a bedded deer to stand up, shake itself and stretch. Also look for the glint off a polished antler. I've spotted bucks several miles away by slowly glassing likely bedding areas during the day and catching the glint off a polished antler.

It's not uncommon for hunters to find bachelor herds of mule deer bucks in mountainous alpine areas during September and October, in what you might think

You should expect to see mature mule deer bucks out in the open throughout the day during the rut in late November.

of as bighorn sheep range. They'll stay in the high country until the snow drives them to lower elevations prior to the rut. In their range throughout the foothills, prairies and river breaks in Alberta, also look for bachelor herds during September and October. I've seen more than two dozen bucks in bachelor herds in Colorado during the summer. It is not uncommon to spot half a dozen or more bucks in bachelor herds in Alberta in the early autumn.

Prior to and during the rut in late November and early December, bucks become solitary and are very mobile throughout daylight hours. You should also look for does during the rut because bucks will often be nearby. Mature bucks are not stupid, and they'll often use does as decoys before exposing themselves in open country—following does, not leading them. When a buck and his harem are on the move, the buck will likely be at the tail end of the herd.

Pronghorn Antelope

Pronghorn antelope also have a white rump patch that flares when they're alarmed. It's highly visible. When flared, the rump patch is a warning sign to other antelope that danger lurks nearby. The males' black face patch also stands out on the prairies, as do the white markings on the neck.

Antelope are small creatures, and though they're strikingly marked and colourful, they can be hard to spot because their tan bodies tend to blend in well with prairie vegetation, particularly when they're bedded down. Look for their white rump patch, white underside, white throat bands and dark horns, which tend to catch the sun from a great distance. The best way to spot pronghorns is to find some high ground, sit down and start glassing.

Moose

You'd think that large big game animals such as moose would be easy to spot, but they are difficult to notice unless they are

Look for black horns and patches of white on antelope when spotting on the prairies.

Moose—note black body & light coloured antlers.

in the open. Despite their enormous size, moose blend in very well with their surroundings and can often be difficult to spot. Depending on where and when you're hunting, you'll have your work cut out for you spotting even a large bull. Actually, you'll often hear a bull moose calling before you spot one. Keep your ears open for calling moose and then look for antlers, which, thanks to their light colouration, tend to stand out more so than their bulky bodies in stands of aspen and conifers.

If the weather is inclement, moose will usually feed throughout the day. Their dark coats are conspicuous when wet; look for shiny objects out of place in the landscape under these circumstances.

Bulls also form bachelor groups post rut. I've seen up to half a dozen bulls herded up in November. Also, because of their stilted pace when walking and trotting, they tend to be highly noticeable when in motion.

White-tailed Deer

White-tailed deer are perhaps the toughest of all big game to spot because they blend in so well with their surroundings, whether it's on the prairies or in forests or aspen parklands. There's a reason they're often called the "grey ghosts"; they do tend to appear as apparitions, seemingly out of nowhere. However, their coats are actually reddish, which is quite conspicuous on sunny days and often visible several miles distant. The one signature sign you don't want to see; however, is the windshield-wiper-like wagging of the tail of a white-tailed buck as it heads for the next quarter section! Also, it's not uncommon for white-tailed deer to move about with a raised tail even if they're not alarmed, a dead give-away.

During prime hunting time in mid- to late November, the days are often overcast and characterized by cloud cover with less-than-ideal spotting conditions. Often, ground fog obscures visibility. White-tails tend to move along the edge of forested areas where they can be hard to spot. They also most often travel in low spots when on the move, generally out of sight. During the rut they can be incredibly careless at times, and I've seen them bedded down in the wide open at all times of the day. I've also seen them bird-dogging throughout the day. That's why hunting prior to and after the rut can be the best times to spot bucks, rather than during the peak of the rut when they're paired up with receptive does and tend to be secretive.

Bucks also hang back in cover before entering a clearing, on the lookout for signs of danger before exposing themselves. Make it difficult for white-tails to see you by keeping to the shadows (such as on the edge of cover or behind cover) while you still have fairly open sight lines. Also wear camouflage clothing where permitted by law so you're as inconspicuous as possible and use the same stealth as they do in your quest to bag a trophy buck. This is where still hunting or stand hunting is a good tactic to bag a deer.

Elk

Look for a light-bodied animal when spotting elk, especially bulls that tend to have a lighter coloured coat than cows. Also search for the polished tips of their antlers and a tan rump patch. I also look for the shine off antlers on sunny days and vapour from their nostrils, which stands out like a smoke signal on a cold morning.

Bull elk are downright sneaky—not unlike white-tailed bucks—and rely on stealth to avoid detection. If there's any hint of danger, they'll bolt for cover. They also tend to be fairly nocturnal where there's any amount of hunting pressure, but they can be taken at almost any hour of the day. It happens.

Good luck spotting bulls during the rut when all the elk in parts of their range will be in one spot, so to speak. A bull will have a harem of a couple of dozen or more cows. Some subordinate bulls will be on the perimeter of the harem. These satellite bulls often thwart any attempt to get within shooting range of the herd bull. There's a good chance you'll run into one of the satellite bulls during a stalk, causing them to bolt and scare all the elk out of the area. After the rut, bulls will generally gather in bachelor herds from small groups up to dozens of bulls in some areas. There are some exceptions; however, because I've also spotted single bulls post rut.

To bag a decent bull elk, you have to out-manoeuvre it by getting between its feeding and bedding areas, if you can't pattern them while they're feeding. Undisturbed elk are fairly predictable when it comes to defining their feeding and bedding areas, but this takes advance scouting. During the hunt you can put yourself in a shooting position before the sun rises and wait them out, taking a chance on intercepting them. I've never had a lot of success using spot-and-stalk techniques when hunting elk. More often than not I've outsmarted them

Bull elk in pine forest—note horizontal subject in vertical landscape.

and shot them shortly after first light by putting myself in the right place at the right time. My kills were not just the result of good luck; they were based on calculated odds.

Elk are herd animals so listen for calling elk as well as look for them, especially in stands of aspen, which is one of their favourite habitats. Listen for bugling bulls and the chirping and mewling of cows in a herd, or stray animals. I don't know how many times I've heard elk before I've seen them because there's a lot of conversation between animals in a herd, especially when they're on the way to a feeding area. I've often heard elk calling in herds as far off as a ¼ mile distant as they travel from bedding to feeding areas. When elk herds go for water in the evening, they can also make a real racket as they travel through the timber. Keep your ears and eyes open for the sounds of elk.

I also cue in on the smell of elk when hunting in cover. They have a distinct, pungent odour that is easy to detect.

Bison

A chapter on bison hunting is not warranted in this book because hunting opportunities for them are restricted. Only a limited number of licences are available in a Bison Special Licence Draw for WMU 536 and 539 in northwest Alberta for Alberta residents. In the area west of highway 35 and north of the Chinchaga River and the Keg River Metis Settlement, bison is a protected species. No one is allowed to hunt bison in this area, except under the authority of a Bison Special Licence.

The largest free-ranging herd of wild bison in the world is found in remote areas of northern Alberta bordering Wood Buffalo National Park. Many huge bulls are being taken by bow hunters, cross bow and rifle hunters each winter and spring with Alberta outfitters on the periphery of this park, where a licence isn't necessary to hunt bison.

Where to Look

Where should you focus when looking for big game species—and why—when you're spotting? The answer is just about anywhere and everywhere within their range, and at all times of the day, not just prime feeding times in the early morning and evening. Animals move about all day long; they also get up from their beds to stretch and get water or to search each other out if they're herd animals such as pronghorn, elk or sheep. In heavily hunted areas it's also not uncommon for them to be pushed out of bush into openings, often at close quarters. When animals do travel in the open, they tend to boogie and won't be in sight for long, especially elk and white-tailed deer.

Hunters should definitely be on the lookout during midday when, contrary to popular belief, many animals are on the move, particularly white-tailed deer and mule deer before, during and after the rut. I don't know how many times I've spotted bucks at high noon as I'm taking a break to have a sandwich and coffee. Ditto for bighorn rams, which often get up from their beds around noon for a stretch before bedding down again for an afternoon siesta. Rams also tend to move about in search of ewes prior to the November rut and may be spotted heading for wintering grounds

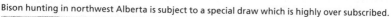
Bison hunting in northwest Alberta is subject to a special draw which is highly over subscribed.

Lorne Fitch spotting big game in Alberta's Rockies.

at this time of year. Likewise, elk often bed down on exposed south-facing slopes following the rigors of the rut when they're recuperating, or they can be spotted when they're on the move from feeding to bedding areas, twice a day. Elk also tend to be quite active just prior to and during storm events, more so than most big game species. Bad weather doesn't seem to bother them, whereas most species will hunker down until a storm passes.

It's essential to use an imaginary grid when spotting for big game. Try scanning from near to far and right to left, opposite to the way you read, so that objects stand out during your search. Then do it again! And again! It's necessary to repeat the process because animals often travel out of sight or may simply shift their position offering a different view.

When snow covers the ground, follow tracks; it's amazing how many times you'll find an animal at the end of a set of tracks. Look for parts of animals instead of the whole creature, which will likely not be visible. Be positive as well as patient. Search an area thoroughly and then search it again, spending several minutes to perhaps half an hour in promising locations. Then move on and repeat the process. It's surprising just how often an animal will appear out of nowhere. If you're not actively glassing an area, you simply won't spot it. So, what's your reward? Perhaps the big game animal of a lifetime, if all goes well.

The Value of Hunting Journals

Most hunters take their sport seriously. They go to great lengths when preparing for hunts, often spending thousands of hard-earned dollars on rifles, hunting gear, equipment and vehicles. They make plans months ahead for most hunting trips to book vacation time for their hunts. They scheme over draw hunting priority scenarios.

However, probably only a small minority of hunters bother to keep a hunting journal. This omission is a mistake, especially for new hunters who stand to benefit the most by keeping records. Things change, often drastically, and you can almost certainly count on having to switch your hunting grounds several times during your lifetime. Furthermore, if you don't keep track of important information as you go along, you'll be missing out on how to fast track your hunting success and minimize making the same old mistakes. For example, when I moved to Edmonton I had to find new areas to hunt deer, elk and moose that were close to home and more affordable than returning to my former hunting haunts. Also, some of the private land in southern Alberta, where I formerly had great success, changed ownership and the new owners didn't allow hunting.

Subsequently, I hunted in several different WMUs to test the waters before deciding on the better spots.

It was by keeping records of what I saw and experienced in these various WMUs that I was able to make informed decisions. Through the process of elimination, I decided on where I was most likely to be successful for various species and when. Remember, all good things must come to an end; make this your mantra as you go forward because I can guarantee that any serious hunter will shift their hunting territory from time to time, if not as a result of changing residences then because of some other circumstance or event. Forest fires may devastate your favourite area; it may become inaccessible when ownership changes; it might be clear-cut by logging; and game populations will crash during harsh winters.

Keep records of where, when, how and why you shot big game animals in your hunting journal.

Note the 5 Ws of any game you shoot in your hunting journal.

I don't actually recall what motivated me to start keeping a big game hunting journal, but I'm glad I followed my instincts. I've been keeping records since my first hunt more than 50 years ago, a smart move that has paid great dividends. My journals are a bit like a dog-eared family scrapbook. The journals have helped me become a better outdoorsman and increase my hunting success. In my journals I describe what species I hunted each year, where and when, as well as family members and friends in my hunting party and their success. My journals also contain information about bird game hunts I've enjoyed.

Many people have poor memories. Only by recording the 5Ws are hunters able to accurately retrieve important factual details about their hunting trips. I keep my entries based on the calendar year. I'll record the dates I hunted various species of animals, such as pronghorn antelope, elk, moose, white-tailed and mule deer, and the WMUs where I hunted these species. I'll note how many animals I spotted and at what time of day, usually on a daily basis, and their location on the lands I hunted. I take fairly detailed notes on any shot animals.

This is a sample notation:

> *Shot a 6-point bull elk about
> 7:30 AM on Monday, November 2,
> at a range of approx. 275 yards with
> a .300 WSM calibre rifle, 180 g bul-
> let—one shot through the lungs; the
> bull was with a harem of five cows.*

If hunting pressure was an issue, I'll also enter details in the journal.

After a period of time, I'll tabulate the results on keystone species. For example, I can search the records regarding which days I've seen the most mule deer bucks in a particular WMU and the dates most deer have been shot. I can subsequently plan a hunt accordingly. This sort of information is a great confidence builder to have in the back of your mind when you go hunting. You know from personal experience what to expect and are mentally ready to capital-ize on your opportunities.

I generally have my big game animals pro-fessionally butchered, and I'll record the weight of the carcass in my journal. The carcass of the 6-point bull elk mentioned earlier weighed 340 pounds, which was a lot smaller than the largest bull I shot, which weighed 469 pounds. Butchers charge by the pound, so these weights are accurate. The anecdotal information in my notes serves as a reminder of what to expect by way of butchered game animals. It's sur-prising how similar the weight has been of most deer I've shot. Mature bucks usually weigh about 125 to 130 pounds, so when I shot a big white-tail buck a few years ago that tipped the scale at 160 pounds, I knew it was exceptional. I had it aged longer than usual and cooked it accordingly.

I've always made it a practice to pace off the distance of killing shots, more out of curiosity than anything else. A few years ago, I decided to tabulate the results over a period of 10 years to see just how far away the various animals had been on

I keep a record of the distances of killing shots in my journal.

average. The mean distance worked out to be 225 yards. It just so happened that I'd sighted in the .270 calibre rifle I'd been using for most of my shooting at 230 yards on the recommendation of a major firearm manufacturer. What a coincidence!

I'll make note of weather conditions during a hunt for future reference, especially temperature, snowfall and wind conditions. Over the past several years, I've clipped out the weather forecast from the local paper or copied online forecasts so that I've got a good record of temperatures and precipitation. If you examine the records, you'll note that big game are often active prior to worsening changes in weather. However, they remain quite active after changes in weather brought on by high-pressure systems. This information can come in handy when gearing up for future hunts because you'll know how to dress and what clothing you should pack for most contingencies. You should always prepare for the worst so that inclement weather doesn't cut your hunt short.

Once your data set grows, you can figure out the best time(s) and location(s) to hunt various species. You'll be able to develop spreadsheets that illustrate important trends. The records are solid, and they'll take the guesswork out of planning and executing hunts. You'll know when deer begin to rut because you'll have a record of when you saw bucks running with does. You'll know when white-tailed deer scrape lines were most active. You'll know when you observed solitary mule deer or white-tailed bucks bird-dogging. You'll have an accurate record of when you (and your hunting partners) shot deer, which will help you focus on the best times to hunt in the future. You'll know when bull elk bugle (during the rut) and when they don't, as well as when elk bachelor groups were sighted, which signals the end of the rut.

You'll know where and when concentrations of pronghorn antelope occurred and under what circumstances. You'll know where and when solitary bighorn rams were on the move in search of ewes, which signals the start of their rut. You'll know where and when you spotted herds of rams and under what circumstances. Because they are creatures of habit, this information can help you locate rams in the future.

Big game hunting journals can take the guesswork out of your hunting plans. They are a practical tool and allow you to use your personal hunting observations to your advantage.

———⋊•••⋉———

It's impossible to spend hours afield, cut off from contrivance and distractions, immersed in everything that is real and vital about the living world that sustains us, without reflecting on the choices we make as hunters. One of those choices is to take personal responsibility for the inevitable deaths that provide us with the meat we eat.

–Kevin Van Tighem, Alberta naturalist, author and outdoorsman, in *Alberta Views*

———⋊•••⋉———

CHAPTER TWO

The Social Norms of Hunting

Hunter Ethics

Poor hunter ethics remains a lingering issue in Alberta despite long-standing efforts by the Alberta Fish and Game Association (AFGA) and the Alberta government to address this concern.

Landowners still complain about game shot being and abandoned, and about hunters who do not ask for permission to hunt on private property. Some of these landowners have closed their land to all hunting as a result of these illegal activities. They really don't need the hassle of dealing with such disrespectful behaviour.

Much has changed on private land during the past couple of decades. Incidents with hunters on top of the financial woes farmers and ranchers face with the cattle market have made them less likely to want to give permission for hunting on their land. During a pronghorn hunt in southern Alberta in 2006—where much of the land is under grazing lease, grazing association or grazing reserve dispositions—I found that hunting was permitted on foot only, and no vehicles were allowed on most ranches. Many gates were padlocked shut that essentially closed large areas to hunting entirely. On the bright side, however, for the first time in more than 30 years of antelope hunting, I did not see any vehicles

pursuing antelope over the prairies. That's one benefit of hunting-on-foot-only stipulations.

In eastern Alberta, I've run into hunters driving over the prairies in search of deer, ruining my stalks in several cases and being an irritant for the ranchers. Some of the local ranchers in the area have asked me whether I think they should opt for hunting on foot only. I told them there would be some benefits based on my experiences with road hunters who refuse to leave their vehicles and spoil other hunters' experiences in Alberta's outdoors.

"Foot Access Only" sign

Besides, if you want to lead a healthy life-style, get out of your vehicle and walk.

I'm not a road hunter, and though I don't want to imply that "road hunting" is improper, I will say that hunters who drive all over private and public land in search of deer give hunting a bad name. They also tend to stir up deer and put them on edge, spoiling hunts for hunters who are not road hunters and often pushing deer out of sight of roads. Where road hunting is common, deer become more and more nocturnal in their behaviour. I would encourage people not to road hunt because it has a downside for all outdoorsmen and women.

I've also noted more than a few shot-up highway signs in my travels, which must leave a bad taste in the mouths of local landowners who drive by them every day. Hunting with or from a vehicle is a particularly stupid and hazardous act and is one of the worst displays of poor hunter ethics. Even if it's pure speculation that hunters actually shot up the signs, they'll be blamed regardless of who actually did the shooting.

Shot up traffic sign

Good hunter ethics boils down to proper behaviour and the need to respect land-owners' rights and public property. It also means abiding by hunting regulations at a time when you're basically on your own in the field. No disrespect intended, but I haven't seen many game wardens on patrol in recent years because they're so short-staffed and over-worked.

Possibly the worst example of inconsiderate hunter ethics I've seen was when a guy took a dump about 75 yards from my white-tailed deer stand just before legal shooting time a few years ago. When I asked him what the h**l he was doing, he said, "When you got to go, you got to go!" Needless to say, I moved my stand.

Promoting Good Hunter Ethics

Here are some suggestions for Alberta outdoorsmen that promote good hunter ethics:

1. Always ask for permission to hunt on private or leased land. Start by purchasing the local county or municipal district map to see who owns or leases the land, and follow up by phoning and/or meeting the landowner.

2. Wherever possible, make face-to-face contact with the landowner during your hunting trip. Thank the landowner for giving you permission to hunt.

3. Abide by the landowner's rules and regulations regarding hunting on his or her land.

4. Leave gates the way you found them, either open or shut.

5. Don't litter. Take garbage bags with you, so that if you do shoot an animal you can dispose of any waste paper, and so on, in the bag to take with you.

6. Don't start fires unless you have permission.

7. Not all landowners will allow you to drive on their land, although many still allow this practice provided you stick to the trails and don't leave the trails except to retrieve a shot animal.

8. Don't drive off established trails unless you have permission to do so.

9. Report illegal activities to the proper authorities, whether it be the local landowner or nearest game warden.

10. Set a good example for other outdoorsmen to follow.

For their part, grazing lessees can oblige hunters by putting their name and phone numbers on government-supplied signage.

A key AFGA objective related to hunter ethics is to "promote outdoor ethics and safety." Maurice Nadeau, Past President of the AFGA, said, "The Alberta Fish and Game Association promotes hunter ethics through its education and recreational programs, hunter education courses, the Use Respect Program, by participating in the Report-A-Poacher program and by example, I hope!" The AFGA also has an award recognizing and encouraging a higher standard of ethical behaviour: The Budd Travers Outdoor Observer Trophy is awarded for contributions made to aiding in the prevention of game law violations. Nadeau said, "Unethical behaviour is becoming ever less accepted by sportsmen; the value of our wild resources is becoming more evident." Nadeau added that practices of the past and the conservation efforts that followed are not forgotten by those who truly appreciate the out of doors, all that lives in it and the ethical

"Use Respect" sign

hunter and angler. "The most positive sign I have recognized is that our youth and new hunters seem to have a greater respect for wildlife, conservation and the hunting regulations. I believe this is a result of the hunter education courses and the high profile given to conservation in today's world," he lamented. Nadeau said, "It offends me personally when the media includes those with the least respect for fish and wildlife as anglers or hunters. Those who would break the rules and laws, taking more than their limits, hunting or fishing out of season, etcetera, are not privileged to be called 'hunters'; they are poachers plain and simple."

Hunting Permission

This section is based on my personal experiences and landowner anecdotes, as well as long-term trends in Alberta, in particular, regarding "Hunting Permission" issues. It also addresses what I see as some possible solutions and trade-offs on both sides of the equation, for both hunters and landowners alike.

Over the past few years, I've detected a growing chill in the air when I've asked for permission to hunt on private land in Alberta. I've also noticed a rise in the number of "No Hunting" and "Hunting by Foot Only" signs during the same period of time. What's going on? What should hunters do when asking permission, and how should they behave to curtail what appears to be a rising tide of anti-hunting sentiment among landowners?

I've always maintained that the worst thing a landowner can say to a hunter who asks for permission to hunt is "no." Being turned down is really no big deal for a hunter because many other landowners will give hunters permission to hunt on their land, if they're approached with courtesy and respect. There's a corollary to

a landowner saying "no," however, that deserves attention. Hunters play an important role in keeping big game numbers in check. Many landowners are frustrated with high deer numbers because they cause crop depredation, and other species, such as elk and moose can damage fences or eat stacked hay and standing crops. It really doesn't hurt to have the odd place where no hunting is allowed because these places act as a sanctuary for big game animals, which don't always stay on posted land and can produce some trophies by default on adjacent land when they move about their home range. However, posted land can really exacerbate crop depredation problems on adjacent property. If land is posted with NO HUNTING signs, this can shift hunting pressure and create isolated game sanctuaries from which animals raid crops and pasture land on adjacent property. Proper game management is important to minimize wildlife crop depredation. Consequently, it is often in the best interests of landowners to allow at least some hunting.

Before you leave home, make sure that you have map that illustrates the land dispositions in the area you intend to hunt. These maps are variously entitled "Map Book" or "Road System and Ownership Maps" and are available for all counties, municipal districts and the Special Areas in Alberta. The Special Areas is a rural municipality in southeastern Alberta granted special status during the depression. Its boundaries outline over 5 million acres of lands. It is a rural municipality similar to a Municipal District, however, the elected council is overseen by three representatives appointed by the province, the Special Areas Board. Land disposition maps illustrate the disposition of all land holdings in these various types of jurisdictions; for example, private or lease lands and the location of provincial parks and their boundaries. They also illustrate roads and trails and the location of private residences, a handy feature in rural areas. Over the past several years the design and layout of these documents has changed from a single rather large map sheet to a binder with a map index that is more portable and much easier to use in the field. These maps can be purchased at private vendors or at municipal offices and are one of the most important tools for hunters in search of a place to hunt. Nowadays, I wouldn't leave home without these maps, although I also usually take a larger scale topographic map. Alberta hunters should check online for a listing of counties, municipal districts and Special Areas online and purchase maps for the areas they wish to hunt. Maps are not cheap, but they're worth every penny.

———✂•••✂———

You don't need to go to the "back forty."

–Frank Murphy, owner of the Murphy Ranch, explaining that deer can be near a farm house and you don't need to go to the back side of a farm (i.e., back forty, meaning "back side of a farm." In the Homestead Acts (1860s–), farmers were granted a quarter section; a section was 640 acres, a quarter section was 160 acres, and the quarter section was itself subdivided into four quarter-quarter sections of 40 acres each: two front forty and two back forty.)

———✂•••✂———

On an elk hunting trip a few years ago, I spotted a cow and calf elk one evening on a ranch where I didn't have permission to hunt, so I tracked down the landowner by checking a municipal map. The land where I spotted the elk was posted "No Hunting." It took me a while to find the landowner's residence because he didn't reside on the land where I'd spotted the elk, which was actually unoccupied land. At first, the landowner said he wasn't letting anybody hunt on his land, but after we got to talking, he changed his mind and said it would be okay for me hunt after all. The next morning I tagged a fat cow elk at first light. I guess the moral of this story is that if I hadn't gone to the trouble of searching out the landowner and asking for permission to hunt, I might have got skunked. However, if I hadn't purchased a landowner map, I wouldn't have known where to find the owner of the ranch where I'd spotted the elk. Furthermore, my guess is that if I'd simply telephoned this particular landowner and asked for permission to hunt on his ranch, he would likely have turned me down flat.

I've found that there's simply no substitute for face-to-face communication when asking for permission to hunt. I make a point of trying to call ahead to see if a landowner is going to be home before I go on scouting trips, and then I drop by their place to formally ask for permission to hunt when I'm out scouting before actually going hunting. If I'm hunting an area for the first time, I'll get in touch with contacts in my network to ask them if they have any suggestions on where to hunt before I venture afield. Afterwards, I hit the road for a first-hand look at the lay of the land. It's a lot harder for a landowner to say no when you're looking them in the eye than over the phone. However, don't wait until just before the season opens to make contact. All sorts of things can go off the rails if you procrastinate. The landowner may be away on business or vacation. He may be getting annoyed with hunters calling to ask for permission and stop answering the phone. He may have already promised other hunters first dibs, so you'll go to the end of the queue until they're finished hunting.

It's important to ask the landowner about any caveats he or she might have with regard to hunting on their land. Almost all landowners will ask you not to hunt in fields where cattle are pastured. It's not a good idea to park your vehicle where cattle or horses are pastured in any case because they've been known to damage such rigs. You also want to stay clear of any bulls, which can be unpredictable at times, and dangerous. Some landowners will ask you not to shoot coyotes, whereas others will ask you to shoot any coyote you see. It's always a good idea for you and your hunting partner(s) to team up when asking for hunting permission. That way everybody knows each other. Tell the landowner what kind of vehicle(s) you'll be driving so there are no surprises when the hunt time rolls around.

Face-to-face communication is also important in developing a personal relationship with landowners. They usually want to know what you look like and what kind of a person you are before they allow you to hunt on their land. Why shouldn't they have these concerns? They can lay out the ground rules for your hunt so that you don't interfere with their business. A side benefit is that they'll often give you some tips on where to hunt on their land and what areas are not worth hunting. They know the lay of the land better than anybody else, and their local knowledge is invaluable. I've often said that many landowners are people of few words; consequently, when they do speak, pay attention because there's often an important message if you read between the lines. Make sure you follow their rules when hunting on their land. If you see suspicious activity, such as poaching, by all means tell the landowners, otherwise they might think you're responsible. In addition, inform authorities such as the local game warden or RCMP of the incident. Sometimes your input will be the clue the warden or police require to take action or close a file.

Sensitive Issues

Although I don't want to stir up unnecessary controversy, I think it's important to raise a couple of sensitive issues. There's no point in trying to avoid these issues because they are major concerns for landowners: drinking alcohol when hunting and shooting roadside signs.

Drinking alcohol or taking drugs while out hunting is strictly taboo and cannot be tolerated because it's totally unsafe. Never drink while you're hunting. Never take any recreational drugs.

In a personal communication, Alberta Justice and Solicitor General spokesperson Brendan Cox provided some statistics with regard to "hunting under the influence charges" in Alberta over the past several years, in the following table. Ideally, there would be no prosecutions or written warnings, which illustrates the important job that Alberta's Fish and Wildlife Officers perform to provide a safe hunting experience.

Fiscal Year	Prosecutions	Written Warnings
2013	10	6
2014	3	6
2015	12	16
2016	2	21
2017	2	14

The senseless shooting of roadside signs is a stupid act of vandalism that serves as a constant reminder of disrespectful hunters whenever a landowner goes for a drive. Shot-up signs are akin to a negative billboard that's always front and centre, every day! Sight in your firearms and target practice at your local gun range. Leave your booze in camp, and for crying out loud don't ever shoot at roadside signs. It's important to report these offences to local authorities.

Be Appreciative

Be sure to show landowners some appreciation for letting you hunt on their land. They look after the wildlife all year long and put up with the damage the animals cause on their property. The very least hunters can do is thank landowners in person, and perhaps provide them with a thank you card, a gift or some token of appreciation. Such gestures will serve to demonstrate that you really do appreciate being able to hunt on their land. Don't take their generosity for granted, and be genuine in showing your appreciation for being able to hunt on their land. Landowners are no different than you and your hunting partners or your neighbour across the street. Treat them the same way you'd like to be treated. Show them some respect!

General Information on Hunting Rules

Hunting rules are complex, so it is imperative that hunters study the Alberta Guide to Hunting Regulations to ensure they understand the hunting regulations for the province. Note that these regulations are subject to change without notice, so check frequently before going out on the range.

There are several dozen different big game licences available for resident and non-resident hunters, including partner and youth licences, calf moose licences,

special licences for various species and special hunts, and so on. There are also licences for bird game and waterfowl. Before purchasing any licence, each hunter must possess a valid Wildlife Identification Number (WIN) and a Wildlife Certificate. WINs are permanent registration numbers issued to each angler and hunter. Persons wishing to hunt with a bow and arrow must also purchase a Bowhunting Permit, which is not required for hunting with a cross-bow. Many licences are only available by a special draw that is subject to a priority system. A person must possess the applicable hunting licence in order to hunt big game or game birds. Non-resident Canadian and non-resident aliens are subject to various licencing restrictions.

First time hunters must be at least 12 years old— Miles Makowecki with a white-tailed buck

Hunters might find the variety of tags and definition of antlered or antlerless animals confusing, some of which are described as follows:

- Antlered—a white-tailed deer, mule deer, moose or elk having an antler exceeding 10.2 cm (4 in.) in length

- Antlerless—a white-tailed deer, mule deer, moose or elk that is not "antlered" (as defined above)

- Trophy Antelope—a male pronghorn antelope that has a horn at least 12.6 cm (5 in.) in length

- Non-trophy Antelope—a female pronghorn antelope or a male pronghorn antelope having horns not more than 7.6 cm (3 in.) in length

- Antlered elk are subject to either antlered and antlerless seasons as well as 3-point or larger, or 6-point or larger seasons.

- A six-point elk is a male elk bearing an antler that is composed of a main beam from which project not fewer than five tines, each of which must be at least 7.6 cm (3 in.) long.

- A three-point elk is a male elk bearing an antler that is composed of a main beam from which project no fewer than two tines, each of which is at least 7.6 cm (3 in.) long.

NOTE: A non-typical animal has horns or antlers that do not conform to the usual configuration for various species. Such animals are rare but must conform to the minimum legal requirements for each species to be harvested.

Numerous "general regulations" apply to hunting and must be adhered to, in addition to "general," "big game," and "game bird" prohibitions. Some of the prohibitions are designed for reasons of public safety. Others are necessary to ensure the principles of fair chase—humane and socially acceptable hunting practices are enshrined in law. While by no means all-inclusive, a brief review of some of the key general regulations follow.

Administrative General Prohibitions
Some of these are related to compliance with licencing provisions:

- It's against the law to carry or use another person's licence or tag or allow someone else to use your licence or tag.

- You must carry your licences and produce them when requested to do so by a wildlife officer.

- It's against the law to harass, injure or kill wildlife with a vehicle, aircraft or boat.

- Use of arrows with explosive heads is prohibited.

- Use of lights to hunt wildlife is against the law.

- Silencers are prohibited.

- Spring guns are illegal as are poisonous substances or immobilizing drugs.

- It's illegal to allow flesh suitable for human consumption to be wasted of any game bird or big game animal (except cougar or bear) or allow it to become unfit for human consumption.

- Hunters may not carry loaded firearms in vehicles or discharge a weapon from boats (except under prescribed conditions) and aircraft.

- It's illegal to discharge firearms within certain distances of occupied buildings or along or across specified highways and roads.

- You must have permission to hunt on private land.

- It's illegal to hunt while impaired by alcohol or drugs.

- It's illegal to discharge a firearm between one-half hour after sunset and one-half hour before sunrise.

"Big Game" Prohibitions

- It's illegal to use

  - ammunition of less than .23 calibre;

  - ammunition that contains non-expanding bullets;

  - an auto-loading firearm that has the capacity to hold more than 5 cartridges in the magazine;

  - a shotgun of .410 or less;

  - bait, except as permitted for the hunting of black bears;

  - unauthorized bows and arrows;

  - a muzzle-loaded firearm of less than .44 calibre.

- It's against the law to discharge a weapon at a big game animal while it's swimming.

- You cannot allow the skin of any bear or cougar to be wasted, destroyed or spoiled.

- It's against the law to remove the evidence of sex and species from the carcass of a big game animal until it's taken to a licenced abattoir or to a person's usual residence for butchering.

- A tag must remain on an animal until it has been butchered and/or otherwise processed.

- Immediately after killing a big game animal, the appropriate tag(s) must be affixed and securely locked to the animal.

- For trophy sheep and goat, one tag must be put through the nostril, and as soon as the skin is removed from the skull, one tag around the lower bone of the eye socket.

- Moose, elk, deer, antelope, bison and non-trophy sheep must be tagged through the space between the bone and tendon of a hind leg directly above the hock and around either the bone or the tendon.

- Evidence of sex and species must be on the leg bearing the tag.

- Bear and cougar must be tagged on the skin.

Game Bird Prohibitions

- It is against the law to remove evidence of sex and species until they're transported to the usual residence of the person who killed it.

- Migratory birds cannot be hunted using a firearm loaded with a single bullet, shot, other than non-toxic shot, a crossbow and a shotgun that is of a large size than 10 gauge.

- It's illegal to exceed the daily or possession limit for any game bird.

- You must make every effort possible to immediately retrieve a migratory game bird that a person has killed or wounded.

Registering Animals

It is compulsory to register the following animals at a Fish and Wildlife office within a specified period of time; however, it is not necessary to register other big game or game bird kills.

- Goat—the incisor bar must be submitted.

- Male sheep over one year of age—the complete unaltered skull with horns and eyes intact must be submitted.

- Wolves taken in any of WMUs 300–318, 324–330, 339 or 400–434 under any authority.

- Cougar—the skull and skin must be submitted, complete with the evidence of sex attached and visible. A premolar tooth will be retained for aging.

- Bobcat—the skin must be submitted complete with the evidence of sex attached and visible.

- Deer—It is mandatory to submit the heads of deer harvested from specific WMUs for Chronic Wasting Disease (CWD) testing and research purposes within 30 days of when it was killed. Hunters should check the regulations for details related to the WMUs where this applies.

According to the "Alberta Guide to Hunting Regulations":

Compulsory registration provides information about the relative numbers of males, females and young in big game populations. It also provides the dates and locations of the harvest. Age structure and sex ratios provide an indication of population productivity (how many young survive to become adults) and status (increasing, decreasing or stable). The population and harvest data can then be used to determine the harvest goals or quotas for following years. This valuable information, provided by hunters, is essential for managing cougar, goat, trophy sheep and wolves in Alberta.

It's incumbent on hunters study Alberta's hunting regulations to ensure they're compliant with the law.

CHAPTER THREE

Hunting Essentials

Hunting Apparel

I've spent a lifetime researching and testing outdoor apparel and compact, lightweight gear to maximize my mobility and comfort while hunting in Alberta's great outdoors. The key to a successful hunting trip is to stay dry and warm. However, when you're not overloaded with bulky and heavy clothing, your outdoor adventures will be even more rewarding.

Synthetics have revolutionized outdoor apparel, starting with boots that are not only light but also waterproof, warm and durable. Next come socks, which provide warmth and cushioned soles for added comfort. New polyester and wool base layers (i.e., underwear) are not only warm but also practically weightless. Then there are synthetic outdoor pants that shed burrs and are waterproof and windproof.

Three key synthetic products have revolutionized the outdoor apparel market:

- Gore-Tex®,
- polar fleece and
- Thinsulate®.

Gore-Tex® is a waterproof/breathable fabric characterized by a porous form of polytetrafluoroethylene. Windproof and waterproof outdoor jackets made of Gore-Tex® are the norm in today's outdoor apparel marketplace.

From microfleece to heavyweight, polar fleece is made from synthetic fibres. It's a soft, highly breathable, lightweight, warm and comfortable fabric. It is hydrophobic, holding less than one percent of its weight in water, and it retains much of its insulating powers even when wet.

The Thinsulate™ brand is a trademark of the 3M Corporation for a type of synthetic fibre thermal insulation used in clothing. The word is a combination of "thin" and "insulate." Apparel made from this fabric is noted for being both light and warm. According to Crystal Dawley of the Textile Analysis Service at the University of Alberta, Thinsulate™ is a form of batting insulation. Its insulating ability depends on the amount of air trapped between its fibre surfaces. This so-called boundary air is a poor conductor of heat, which is held closely against the fibre surfaces, thereby slowing body heat loss and keeping the body parts warm. The greater the surface area of fibres in a given volume of material, the greater the volume of this boundary air will be. Because boundary air reduces heat loss, it has an insulating value. The product fact sheets supplied by 3M state that Thinsulate™ has about 20 percent greater surface area of fibres than other synthetic insulating products, which increases the volume of boundary air. This in turn improves the insulating qualities of Thinsulate™.

Thinsulate™ thermal insulation is up to two times warmer than down and other polyester insulation of equal thicknesses, according to the manufacturer. Finer fibres, especially when organized in several layers, capture air more efficiently than fibres with a larger diameter. The microfibres found in Thinsulate™ have more surface area to trap more dead air and therefore insulate better than the larger fibres in other kinds of insulation. The unique construction of Thinsulate™ arose from the need for an insulating material less bulky than down, but with adequate warmth. If you haven't tried Thinsulate™ products, maybe it's time to get some for cold-weather hunting.

Now, however, it appears as though a new generation of insulated down jackets that feature Omni-Heat® Thermal Reflective material is going to take outdoor apparel to yet another level. Manufacturers claim their jackets are at least 20 percent warmer because of this new technology. This thermal reflective technology helps regulate a person's temperature by reflecting and retaining the warmth the body generates while dissipating moisture and excess heat to keep the person comfortable. Field tests indicate that Omni-Heat® Thermal Reflective insulated hunting jackets and bibs are incredibly warm, quiet and breathable, which is more good news for outdoorsmen and women.

It's really important to have quality hunting gear during late-season hunts to handle the cold. A base layer of Merino wool thermal long underwear is hard to beat, particularly while on stand. Think polar fleece and Thinsulate™ for outer garments (i.e., gloves, vests, jackets and headwear). Insulated GORE-TEX® pants that are

Author wearing Predator brand winter jacket which is lined with Thinsulate making it light and warm.

waterproof and windproof will help you stay warm on the coldest of days. Don't forget a quality balaclava for those days when wind chill might be an issue.

Camouflage Clothing

When I bought my first camouflage clothing I opted for Predator Camo, Inc. because their product line featured Thinsulate™ brand apparel. This brand of clothing includes pants, jackets, lined or unlined wool pants, vests, bibs, lined mitts, face masks and hats. It is well suited for hunting in a wide range of terrain and features both windproof and water-repellent qualities. Good camouflage clothing is important (especially for bow hunters) and this brand, with its fall brown and fall grey patterns, works well under various field conditions. I've had elk, moose, coyotes, mule deer and white-tailed deer come with a few yards of me while on stands and not be able to discern my presence. Even if animals do happen to spot you, they don't seem to know what to make of you.

Shop around for clothing because many brands are available, and be careful which line you opt for because it's expensive, so you won't want to change brands unless absolutely necessary. Opt for camouflage clothing that's best for the range of hunting conditions you'll likely encounter.

Hunting Boots

I purchased a pair of Eddie Bauer boots with Thinsulate™ insulation many years ago when this insulation was still relatively new on the market. I eventually wore them out, but they convinced me of the value of Thinsulate™ during cold weather hunts. Eddie Bauer still manufactures boots with this form of insulation, although the style is different now. I can't say enough about the value of insulated boots during cold weather, particularly when stand hunting.

If you purchase boots with Thinsulate™ insulation make sure they have more than 600 grams for cold weather hunting, preferably 1000 grams. My newest lightweight boots are Columbia Titanium winter hiking boots with Thermolite insulation, rated down to −32°C. I can't overstate just how much difference insulated footwear makes on a hunt.

Buy the best winter boots you can afford. Back in the day when leather boots were the norm, so too were frozen toes. There's no need to risk this discomfort nowadays.

Cold Weather Hunting

"Where are you going?" I whispered to my hunting partner as he approached my stand. "That's it for me today," he replied. "I'm frozen, and there aren't any deer moving, so I'm going back to the truck."

―――――✕•◦●◦•✕―――――

My observation of hunting is that the focus of hunting has changed from interaction between hunters and animals and appreciation of the species and their environment to animals versus technology.

―Carol Kraft, Mel Kraft's wife and lifelong hunting partner, who also harvested a number of elk, regarding the proliferation of high tech hunting gadgets over the years

―――――✕•◦●◦•✕―――――

"Fine," I said, "I'll see you in a little while."

There were 25 minutes to go before the end of legal shooting time. I was going to tough it out, even though things didn't look promising. I scanned the feeding area to my right and the three willow clumps in the hayfield to my left. There were several white-tailed deer scrapes around each of the willow clumps. With any luck, a buck might still show up.

Actually, that late November day was warmer than some others I've experienced, with highs at –3°C and lows of –10°C. If the wind chill was factored in, however, it was quite a bit colder, ranging from –8° to –12°C. I didn't blame my partner for heading to the truck as the thought had also crossed my mind. With only two more days left in the season, I figured I'd better sit tight because we were running out of time. An early cold spell, drifted snow in the fields and ankle-deep snow in the bush all made for tough hunting conditions. Early, heavy snowfalls had already put deer on to haystacks, an ominous sign.

A local weather advisory was in effect, and I was hoping the flurries that were forecast would bring some deer out early. The odd flake had started to fall. There was already about 10 inches of snow on the ground, twice the normal amount for November. My thoughts went to the deer I had passed up earlier in the season—several white-tailed does and small to medium bucks. Was I going to regret being fussy this year when the deer seemed to be laying low?

Poor weather was also bringing out the worst in some hunters, who were sticking to their trucks with heaters going full blast. This was not good for hunters like me who prefer to hunt deer by lying in wait. Some hunters were also driving everywhere—right into prime feeding areas—which just made the deer even harder to hunt.

At least I was fairly warm, all things considered. I was pleased with my new gloves and hat, both lined with Thinsulate™. My hunting boots also had Thinsulate™ lining, with a soft rubber sole, keeping my feet warm. I'd had enough of cold feet the year before, and I'd broken down and bought some comfortable, lightweight, quiet winter boots. At the time, I didn't have a clue what Thinsulate™ was, except that it was some kind of insulation, and it was light. The new Thinsulate™ hat, gloves and boots definitely helped me stay warm, primarily because the extremities get cold first, particularly hands and feet. With my new hat, the old adage, "Put your hat on if your feet are cold," hit home, because much of a person's body heat is lost through the neck and head.

My partner was soon out of sight, and I was left to myself. Now there were only about 20 minutes to go until the end of legal shooting time and still no deer around. Judging by the lack of gunshots in the area, my guess was that the deer were not very active. With 15 minutes to go, I started to think about dinner and how good a warm meal would taste. Then I saw a white-tailed buck on the edge of the farthest of the three clumps of willows, about 300 yards away, in a rolling hay field. A quick look with my 10x50 binoculars told me it was a keeper and would be good enough for me, especially considering the late date in the season.

The buck moved to the edge of the willows, pawing one of the scrapes. Snow and dirt went flying for a few moments. Then it stopped pawing, raised its head, and took a look in all directions. Next, it thrashed its antlers against the willows several times and stopped, looking around once more. As if this wasn't enough, it raked the scrape with its antlers. Snow flew in all directions. Then it stopped, looking around again, surveying the countryside. After pausing for about a minute, the buck slowly moved off to the east and disappeared behind the middle clump of willows. Decision time…What should I do?

Should I wait or head for the middle clump of willows and try to intercept the buck. There was a lot of open ground in front of me, and if I didn't move quickly enough the buck might catch me out in the open and bolt for the nearest cover. Experience told me to sit tight. There is nothing worse than a running shot in fading light, particularly with snow starting to come down. I figured that the buck would go to each of the three clumps of willows and see whether a doe in heat had visited any of the scrapes.

Sure enough, a few minutes later he showed up beside the second clump of willows, standing broadside at a range of about 150 yards. By this time I was ready,

———— ‹•••› ————

A buck out at our favourite hunting spot might be that big in a few years; we nick-named him "Ferrari" 'cause every time we saw him he was running so damn fast you couldn't get your gun up on him.

–Curtiss McLeod, consulting biologist (retired) upon seeing a photo of a large, impressive white-tailed buck shot by a hunter from the Crowsnest Pass

———— ‹•••› ————

lying in the snow with my folding stool as a rifle rest. I put the crosshairs behind his shoulder and lined up for a lung shot. It took me a few moments to get my breathing under control before I slowly squeezed the trigger.

The .270 calibre, 130 grain handloaded Hornady bullet did its job well. The buck dropped in his tracks, then got up and staggered several yards before it collapsed in the willows. It was all over by the time I reached the fallen animal.

My watch showed that I had five minutes of legal shooting time left, and the snow was really coming down in earnest. The storm warning had been correct.

As it turned out, my partner had just reached the truck at the sound of the shot. With me being the only hunter left in the field, he figured I had something down and was soon on his way back to check things out. Snow was flying as the truck rolled up beside me. I was happy to see him, and before long we had the deer field dressed and loaded in the back of my truck. The "Thinsulate buck," I thought.

You need to be dressed properly to stay outdoors during cold-weather hunts. Try using insulating insoles to keep your feet warm and dry. When it's below –10˚C, I wear 100 percent wool underwear and socks, a long-sleeved, flannel shirt and a polar fleece shell underneath a hooded Thinsulate™ parka for extra warmth. The parka is a Predator brand camouflage and is designed with the cold-weather hunter in mind. I also use the Predator brand Thinsulate™ "Snow Masher" cap, great headgear for cold weather hunting. A lightweight athletic balaclava provides full face protection in extremely cold and windy conditions. On those cold November days when the east wind is blowing, a balaclava is a must to protect your face

*I'd rather be lucky
than good.*

Common hunting phrase that
illustrates the importance
of being in the right place at
the right time.

Additional Tips on Cold Weather Hunting

1. When the temperature drops below −12°C, there is an increased risk of frostbite, which occurs when exposure to cold temperature damages the skin or other tissue. Dress accordingly.

2. You'll burn a lot of calories in cold weather. Eat carbohydrates the day before, and have a hearty breakfast.

3. Drink plenty of fluids before venturing outdoors and during the day. Dehydration causes fatigue.

4. Ensure that your boots and garments are dry at the start of the day. Wet clothing will freeze and has no insulating value.

5. Allow for some wiggle room in your boots, or your toes will be cold.

6. Don't work up a sweat; perspiration causes heat loss. Try to pace yourself when walking.

7. Base layers (e.g., long underwear, either wool or polyester) worn next to your skin provide warmth and also wick away moisture. Cotton is not recommended as a base layer because it soaks up perspiration and dries slowly. Sweat-soaked cotton will conduct your body heat away to the cool outside air, which can lead to hypothermia.

from frostbite. I often wear Gore-Tex pants with polyester lining—rugged, wind-resistant and warm—in freezing temperatures. My gloves are Thinsulate™ mittens. I use gaiters that clip onto the front laces of my boots and lace up the back to keep the snow out and my ankles dry and warm.

With these garments I stay warm all day, even if the temperature is −20°C. Furthermore, as they are all lightweight products, so I don't feel overly tired and worn out at the end of the day after several miles of hard walking. I wore this same outfit in eastern Alberta during a late November deer hunt several years after taking the "Thinsulate buck," when the temperatures went down to −30°C with a wind chill of −40°C. I usually regard −20°C as the threshold for cold-weather hunting, and I think twice about hunting if the temperature drops below that point.

The secret to staying warm is air circulation and dressing in layers. Tight clothing causes people to sweat, which reduces body heat. Loose fitting apparel—polyester (or wool) undergarments if it's really cold, flannel shirts, pants lined with Gore-Tex, a polar fleece liner and vest, and Thinsulate™-lined boots, gloves, hat and jacket—have helped me meet the challenge of hunting in cold weather.

Essential Gear

Hunting just doesn't get any better than with today's new lightweight hunting accoutrements. There's a plethora of great products on the market for those who want to hunt light and go faster and farther in pursuit of game. Lightweight daypacks, micro-optics, compact hunting gear and new and improved lightweight rifles and shotguns take even more of a load off of your shoulders. I've assembled a number of light and compact must-have items for my pack that I find to be indispensable based on many years of hunting experience.

Backpacks/Fanny Packs

The Tarantula brand and Hidden Wolf Woollens brand backpacks and fanny packs feature the Predator Camo, Inc. pattern and are both durable and light. To keep things as light as possible, I'll use either the backpack or the fanny pack depending on where I'm hunting and what type of hunt I'm on. The backpack has padded shoulder straps with chest straps, as well as compression straps and a large main compartment plus a big back pocket and side pocket (or two, depending on the model). The fanny pack has several small compartments with enough capacity to hold all manner of hunting gear. I use it mainly when still hunting or during day hunts when I don't have to carry a lot of accessories. You don't even really notice the weight of this pack on your hips.

Communication

Communication is important during a hunting trip. Initially, I purchased Uniden hand-held, two-way radios several years ago to stay in touch with my hunting partners. This product is a lightweight, palm-sized radio. It has a clip-on design and features 14 channels, up to 2 miles of range, a backlit display, 50 hours of operation (typical), low battery alert, call tone transmission and channel scan features. If you're miles away from your hunting partners when afield or in separate vehicles, two-way radios provide reliable communications because cell phone coverage is not reliable in many areas in rural Alberta. I subsequently purchased two sets of Motorola Talkabout brand radios because they have many features that are ideal for

Compact fanny pack featuring Predator camo pattern

Motorola Talkabout 2-way radio is both light and compact.

hunters and have an even greater range than the Uniden brand. They have proven their worth on every hunt I've been on and are indispensable.

Optics

Good optics are vital on any big game hunt, and the smaller and lighter the better. You have to be able to spot game, see horns, count antler points and judge trophies under adverse conditions to be successful. The Bausch & Lomb Discoverer 10x42 power binoculars is one of the best sets on today's market. They are compact and waterproof/fog proof, and they feature a Rain Guard Coating, fully multi-coated lenses, cam-slotted twist-up eyecups and a rubberized protective coating. The eyecups are twisted down for people who wear glasses, up for those without glasses. There are other similar binoculars on the market, some of which come with image stabilizers, an excellent feature.

A good spotting scope is essential for bighorn sheep hunters, as well as hunters after trophy antelope, elk or mule deer. Usually, you can't judge horn quality properly without a spotting scope, particularly where there are legal requirements. The Bushnell Spacemaster Spotting Scope, with

Baush & Lomb binoculars are light and compact.

Spotting scope on a big game hunt

a 20-45X lens, has been around for a long time. It has proven itself to be one of the most reliable spotting scopes available. This spotting scope requires a "Shooters Stand" (tripod) for backpackers. A window mount can also be used with this and other scopes and is a good investment. As an added benefit, spotting scopes can also be used at a rifle range to check targets during range days.

I own a Leica Rangemaster CRF-1000 Rangefinder, which takes the guesswork out of estimating ranges and has greatly improved my hunting success. It's only natural that you'll have more confidence when you're shooting at known distances.

Range finders are indespensible.

Rangefinder binoculars are revolutionizing long-range shooting. Bushnell manufactures Fusion binoculars that have a built-in rangefinder and can provide a digital read-out that shows the line of sight, angle and bullet drop as well as information for hold-over. For instance, these binoculars tell you not only how far away the target is but also how far you need to hold over the desired point of impact for long-range shots.

But before you rush out and buy an expensive set of binos with rangefinder capability, remember that you'll have to pair them with a rifle and scope capable of long-range shooting, which don't come cheap. You'll be looking at a 3-12x 44mm to 4.5-18x 44mm riflescope to actually see the target clearly at a long range, and likely a magnum rifle with enough energy to kill an animal upwards of 300 yards and perhaps even 500+ yards. But it can be done.

Knives and Meat Saws

I've long had a Browning three-blade "Big Game" folding hunting knife, which has never let me down when field dressing all manner of big game. It comes with a saw blade that can be used to cut bone, a hide-cutter blade with a gut hook for making that first cut for skinning out the legs and a skinning blade. First, make a small cut in the hide on the legs with a skinning blade and then insert the hide-cutter blade and move it in a upward direction to open up the hide.

Don't forget an EZE-LAP pocket sharpener. Its shaft has a diamond surface that can sharpen knife blades in a few moments, which is very handy when field dressing a big game animal. It has a brass handle and comes with a leather belt-hanger case. A pocket sharpener is a must-have item to keep the blades sharp when field dressing and skinning large animals such as elk and moose, which have tough hides.

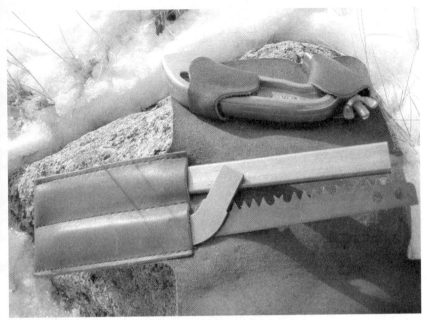
Wyoming (folding) saw with meat and wood cutting blades

To round off your field-dressing kit, a lightweight, folding Wyoming Saw fills the bill. It can be used to cut through bone in the pelvis, sternum, legs and spine. It features an 11-1/8 inch–long blade that permits cutting either on the push or pull, stainless steel meat saw blades and die-cast aluminum. It can be assembled in seconds. Wear it on a belt or carry it in a backpack. This saw also comes with a wood blade for chores around camp where cutting wood is necessary.

Firearms

I purchased a 270 Winchester and a 300 WSM Tikka T3 rifle for big game hunting as well as 204 Ruger calibre Tikka because I was so impressed with this brand's accuracy, durability and light weight. I opted for the high-grade stainless barrel and receiver with black synthetic stock. For the hunter who wants top performance and innovation in a bolt-action

rifle, the affordable Tikka T3 rifles really do set the standard in shooting value. Two of my Tikka T3 rifles are fitted with Leopold VX II 3-9X 40 mm riflescopes, which are compact and lightweight, great for all-purpose hunting. For upland bird hunting, where you'll cover a lot of miles in search of grouse and pheasants, look no further than the Browning BPS Upland Special 20-gauge shotgun. This light, rugged, fast-handling pump shotgun has proven reliable in the rain, snow, dust and mud.

Gun Cases

Kolpin makes a sturdy, weatherproof gun boot that fits most rifles with 50 mm scopes (with slings) and fits both right and left-handed bolt action rifles. It accepts a heavy-duty padlock and has a moulded handle and a foot for standing it upright. The heavy-duty polyethylene shell comes with a plush lining. You can put the gun boot in the back of your vehicle and rest

Light weight Tikka T3 270 rifle with Leopold 3x9 X VX II scope and Harris bipod.

assured that your firearm will not be damaged. In all the years that I've used this case there has been no change in the point of impact of my riflescopes, nor have there been any rub marks on the stock, scope or barrel of my rifles.

Lucid Snap Rack
A relatively new product on the market is the Snap Rack made by Lucid, which isn't on the shelf in Canada at press time and must be ordered online. It is used to safely store a firearm in a vehicle, so it's handy to use right behind your front seat. The Snap Rack is designed to work with the post(s) on the headrest of your vehicle; it takes up no room and holds your firearm safe and secure while on the road.

Ammo Pouches
I've used leather and synthetic ammo pouches for many years. They feature a two-level shell carrier and hold up to 10 rifle shells, up to and including .30-06 calibre. Always carry some extra shells; they could make the difference between life and death on some hunts. Ammo pouches are handy because you don't want your extra shells bouncing around in your pockets. The noise will scare game out of the country.

Shooting Aids
Although there are several brands of bipods on today's market, the Harris bipod I purchased years ago (when their patent cornered the market) has served me well. The Harris bipod has spring-loaded, adjustable legs that quickly fold down into a shooting position and are relatively light. They can be attached to the sling swivel on the forearm of a gunstock and folded in a forward position when the gun is slung on your shoulder. The rotating series permits levelling on uneven ground. These bipods have gun sling attachments, off centre on the forearm stud. A bipod is indispensable on many

hunts. To each his own, but I prefer a bipod over shooting sticks because they're more practical. Shooting sticks are portable lengths of aluminum that are similar in purpose to a bipod or tripod, usually featuring two attached, moveable legs.

Flashlights

I can't imagine going hunting without a Mini MAG-Lite flashlight; I don't know how many times it has enabled me to find a trail when it was pitch dark. Never mind those occasions when I've held one in my mouth while field dressing a big game animal in the dark or used it to signal my hunting partner(s). I now also pack a Byte mini headlamp to free my hands when necessary, along with spare batteries. The Princeton Tec® BYTE™ Headlamp is capable of packing a powerful punch thanks to a white Maxbright LED. The softer side of Byte comes in the form of a red Ultrabright LED to ensure your night vision is not compromised. Byte is equipped with an asymmetrical single arm bracket, easily accessible battery door enclosure and large push button switch, all at a mere 64 grams.

Accessories

I often pack a mini-thermos of black coffee or tea on my day hunts during cold weather to warm me up and give me a boost. Mountain Equipment Co-op makes a stainless steel vacuum bottle that rates up there with the best mini-vacuum bottles.

Fluorescent surveyors tape—used by surveyors to mark landmarks—is handy to mark the location where an animal has fallen so you can find it again. Strips of flagging can also be peeled off to mark your trail in unfamiliar territory or to mark blood trails of wounded animals. You'd be surprised at just how different things look in poor light or after a snowstorm when you're searching for landmarks.

I also pack tie-down ropes for field dressing big game animals and plastic bags for the liver and heart, along with a pocketknife for camp chores, in my hunting tool kit.

Safety Items

I've made a habit of carrying an ERMA SG67E pencil-type, hand-held flare gun with signal flares for safety reasons. I've used the flare gun on several occasions to signal my hunting partners as to my location.

I also pack some wind and waterproof matches and a signal whistle. A compact whistle is a must-have item; it makes an excellent signal for help, especially if you don't have a gun with you. Three blasts on a whistle are a universally recognized signal for help when in distress.

Harris bipod on Tikka T3 rifle

For added safety, I pack a small Space Brand Emergency Blanket and a small first aid kit, which has come in handy on more than one occasion. Likewise I'd never go on a hunt without a compass. A compass is key regardless of where you're hunting but particularly on the prairies in November when slate grey skies are the norm, and there's no discernable sun on the horizon.

There's no better time than the present to hunt light and go forward with a light-weight hunting kit. I wouldn't leave home without some of the items mentioned above because my life might depend on them. With my kit, I'm prepared to spend time in the bush overnight if I have too, under extreme conditions.

Big Game Carriers

A lot of hunters are interested in plans or specifications for a homemade "game cart" or "camp cart" as well as information about the various products on the market.

Back in the 1990s, I used game carriers purchased from Canadian retailer Whole-sale Sports Outdoor Outfitters. At the time they were the only commercial suppliers of game carts in Alberta, forerunners to Bass Pro Shops and Cabela's, the mega American outdoor retail outlets. The first model I purchased was "The Horse," which at the time of purchase was the top-of-the-line carrier available, with the greatest payload capacity.

Wholesale Sports Outdoor Outfitters had three models of game carriers at the time: "The Horse," "The Pony" and "The Mule." The maximum loads of these carriers are rated at 400, 250 and 300 pounds, respectively. I found "The Horse" model to be so useful that I subsequently purchased "The Pony" model, which is smaller and more compact, ideal for antelope and deer. Each model requires some assembly. The first two models are two-wheeled carriers,

Bull elk hind quarters on game carrier

whereas "The Mule" is a single-wheeled carrier. Both two-wheeled carriers use the same "zero weight on the handle" design, much like a rickshaw. "The Horse" was the largest carrier, approximately 86 inches long and 24 inches wide, with 20-inch tires. I wanted the stability of a two-wheeled carrier because of the type of terrain that I hunt in for elk and moose, where trails can be muddy or covered in deep snow. I also wanted a carrier that could handle at least half a moose or elk in one trip, with room left over to tie on some hunting gear.

I haven't built a game carrier. However, an old friend of mine, the late Chris Weintz, shared some information with me regarding his homemade version, which is quite similar to the commercial models I use.

Don't "scope" other hunters.

It's dangerous and a cardinal sin to glass another hunter with a rifle scope.

His carrier is made of a 1-inch aluminum tubing frame, which he purchased from Princess Auto. The dimensions of the carrier are 2 feet by 8 feet. The fender skirts are made of 1 inch x 1/8-inch aluminum angle iron; they are cut and bent, and bolted to the frame. There are five 1-inch aluminum tubing braces at intervals along the frame, with a large space near the front that is big enough for a man to slip into. T-shaped 3/16-inch aluminum brackets are bolted onto the bottom of each brace for extra support. Chris added two bed-spring slats lengthwise for stability. All screws are 1 1/2 inch x 1/4-inch long, National Fine thread, drilled and tapped by hand.

Chris's carrier operates like a rickshaw. He hand bent the aluminum tubing in front of the tires at an angle to suit his frame so that he could pull or push it forward. The front handle bar is covered in foam rubber to prevent it from rubbing in a vehicle and to provide a cushion when pulling or pushing the carrier. It has a joint mid-way down the handle with a 3/4-inch piece of aluminum tubing on each side that slides inside the 1-inch frame and is bolted in place for added strength. The carrier weighs 30 pounds and has a carrying capacity of 350 pounds. It's a two-wheeled version with 20-inch bicycle wheels and a single axle bolted to the frame and fender skirts. The axle is set 30 inches from the back of the carrier. Total cost of the carrier was $130 at the time of construction. Chris was an accomplished machinist, and I doubt that most sportsmen could build a carrier up to his standards, which was of factory-quality construction. That's one reason most outdoorsmen may want to buy a commercial model.

If you plan on hunting in places like Alberta's Kananaskis Country or on many large ranches in southern Alberta, you had better be prepared to pack an animal out, either on your back or with a game carrier. No vehicles or ATVs are allowed off road in Kananaskis Country, and many ranchers will not let you take a vehicle of any kind on their land in southern Alberta. You may be welcome to hunt but only on foot. This is another good reason to build or buy a game carrier. It sure beats trying to drag an animal out, which is a back-breaking experience. A carrier can also be used to pack your camp in. One man can easily manage loads of 200 pounds or more. You can walk a game carrier to a downed game animal over some fairly rough ground

Hold on hair.

Put the crosshairs on target when taking your first shot at a big game animal; don't hold over its back.

without much strain. The same goes for packing the game out, under most trail conditions.

I have dragged a lot of big game animals out of the field. I have packed out several as well in the mountains, foothills, aspen parklands and prairies of Alberta. I hate dragging an animal and would rather not drag one any farther than I have to. Packing is a lot easier on your back. But the game carrier is now my choice. I have used "The Horse" to take out several elk and deer and have not been disappointed. Likewise, "The Pony" model is ideal for deer. The carriers are easy to load and unload. They keep the meat off the ground and keep it clean.

You can haul a whole deer out on a game carrier.

Game carriers are actually fairly easy to move when loaded, provided that you handle them like a rickshaw. The trick is to balance the load on the axle. This takes some practice. Then all you have to do is push the cart forward and steer to keep it on a trail. One person can push and maintain the right balance while the other person can pull with the aid of a short, stout rope tied to the front. The rope comes in handy for pulling the carrier up any kind of grade. One person can easily handle a deer. You can load three-quarters of an elk, or the front shoulders and head of an elk, at one time on "The Horse." Snow is no problem, and I actually prefer to have some snow on the ground because it makes the ground smoother. Mud will slow you down, but if you are careful, it won't stop you. And, when you reach your vehicle you won't feel like you've been run over by a truck!

Quick Winch

The Quick Winch is advertised as the best portable hoist and winch assembly on the market. It's manufactured in Calgary, Alberta, by MCS Industrial Inc. It's the brainchild of a man named Dave Murray, who is a businessman by day and a hunter in his spare time. The company's ad says: "Field dressing your game is a snap, and you get a clean carcass as a result of using the Quick Winch." After field-testing this product over many years, I'd have to say right on! I've used it to skin out antelope, elk, moose, mule deer and white-tailed deer. Actually, as a utility hoist, the Quick Winch has multiple uses.

The Quick Winch is a collapsible metal hoist made from heavy gauge steel piping that is extendible—the extendible tube fits inside another tube with a greater diameter so it can slide in and out of the larger tube—with a built-in winch assembly that houses a 3000-pound capacity belt and a hinged boom on top. You simply lift an

White-tailed deer on Quick Winch covered with cheese cloth

to spare. This winch does not require any tools to set it up. It has a rated dead lift of 500 pounds and has been tested to 1000 pounds.

An optional bumper side mount receiver is available for the Quick Winch to allow off-centre mounting, which enables the tailgate of your truck to be opened. The hoist comes with a metal spreader bar that can be inserted into the hind legs (i.e., the hocks) of a big game animal and attached to a clip on the end of the belt for ease of lifting. Although Dave Murray recommends tying off the legs just to be safe, I didn't have any problems when I didn't tie them down.

It surprises me that nobody came up with this handy product until 2001. I wish I'd been able to purchase one many years ago. It would have given me so many more options during my long-range hunting expeditions and likely extended a good many hunts. The biggest issue hunters have to deal with when they are a long way from home is getting an animal off the ground to skin it out and then hang it somewhere where it's cool. There's nothing worse than trying to find a place to skin an antelope during a warm day on the Alberta prairies, for example, to cool the carcass off and prevent the meat from spoiling, likewise, for deer, elk and moose taken in the field away from home.

extension tube (a pipe inside a larger pipe) to sit "on top" of an insert pin, which can also be aligned with pre-set holes in both pipes, depending on the size of the carcass. If the inside tube (pipe) sits on top of the insert pin, the assembly is free to swivel.

A Quick Winch fits into a standard trailer hitch receiver. To be on the safe side, you should pin into your Reese receiver. While this isn't mandatory, you might accidentally pull the receiver out if you jump into the back of your truck while using the winch as leverage.

Easily stored and transported, the Quick Winch sets up in seconds, certainly in less than a minute. It is less than 48 inches long when collapsed, so it can fit in your car trunk or the back of your truck with room

CHAPTER FOUR

Your Rifle and Ammunition
Getting it Ready

>

The Basics

Handloading is to the rifle hunter what fly-tying is to the fly-fisherman. Your reward will be a tight group—tailored specifically for your rifle—and the pride of using ammunition you've loaded from scratch. Discounting the cost of reloading equipment, you'll realize an approximate 40 percent saving on the cost of ammunition—depending on the bullet specifications, powder type/charge and whether you're using new or spent brass—with even greater savings for magnum loads. Beginners can start handloading by purchasing a "starter kit." Major brands of U.S. handloading manufacturers are Bonanza, Lyman, RCBS and Sinclair. The equipment will last a lifetime.

A full-size reloading press accepts dies and shell holders for all the common rifle calibres on today's market. Dies are tools designed to size, or resize, new or spent shells while simultaneously removing spent primers and then subsequently

Handloading is to the hunter what fly-tying is to the fly fisherman.

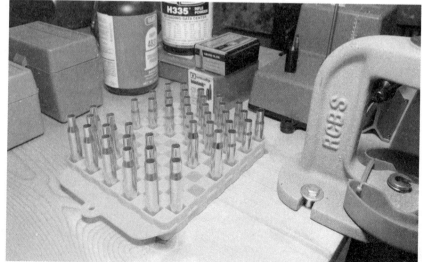

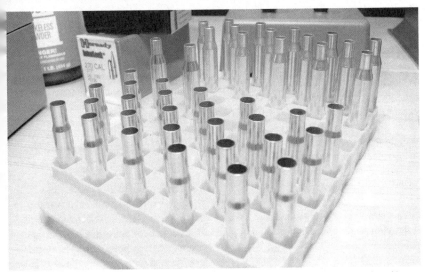

This brass has been polished, de-capped, trimmed with the necks canfured and deburred, and is ready to be primed.

seating bullets. The dies are screwed into the reloading press by hand; you must ensure that all the equipment is clean and free of contaminants. Mount the reloading press on a sturdy bench because of the pressure put on the cartridge cases during the reloading process, when the case/case neck are sized prior to being reloaded. In reloading terms, cartridge cases are called brass. "New" brass has never been fired, whereas "spent" or "old" brass has been fired one or more times.

You'll need three kinds of dies:

1. A "full-length" resizing die with a decapping stem,

2. A "neck-sizing or expanding" and "decapping" die, and

3. A "bullet-seating" die.

These dies are used to remove spent primers and expand the case/neck case to its proper size in one step (i.e., the primer is decapped in the process of sizing the brass cartridge case/neck).

Spent brass should be cleaned and polished to its original high gloss finish before reloading. While the most common cleaning method (of large batches) is by "tumbling", brass can also be chemically cleaned with solvents and polishers, hand cleaned using steel wool or ultrasonically cleaned. Tumbling brass is done in an electric drum which contains a special grit to polish the brass casings, a process that takes several hours, at least, depending on how much grime is on the cases. If it's a spent case, rather than new brass, you should ream out burnt powder residue in the primer pocket and chamfer the neck, deburring the flash hole at the same time. "To chamfer" is simply a process of symmetrically shaping the mouth of the brass casing so a bullet will slide into it without catching on a rough surface on the edge of the mouth by "deburring" it of any sharp or uneven features. There are various tools that can be used to chamfer and debur the neck of cases, so bullets don't catch while being seated. Use an air compressor or canned air to blow out any traces of powder residue inside the case and primer pocket. Special manufacturer polishing equipment should be used to clean inside the neck of the cartridge case

When I first started reloading, I used a simple, multipurpose primer pocket cleaner—an inside-outside deburring tool called a "cricket." It's a hand-held device used to ream out burnt powder in the primer pocket and debur the flash hole. I've subsequently purchased an RCBS Trim Mate "Case Prep Center" power tool used for case chamfering and deburring, primer pocket cleaning, crimp removal and flash hole deburring to speed up the reloading process.

Wear safety glasses when seating primers to protect your eyes in case of an accidental primer explosion

Next, prime the case by carefully seating the primer in the primer pocket then fill the case with the correct powder charge. The "correct powder charge" is the amount of powder recommended by a manufacturer in their reloading books. Avoid using online sources because these are not always reliable. The bullet can then be seated in the primed and loaded case. Bullets are seated using a "bullet seating" die that must be adjusted so that the bullet is placed at the proper depth in the shell casing. Follow the instructions included with sets of dies or in reloading manuals regarding "bullet seating." Primers are seated with a tool on the reloading press, one at a time.

If you do decide to do some handloading, it's a good idea to purchase a reloading manual that provides an introduction on reloading and information about cases, primers, bullets and powder for the calibre of your rifle. Manuals provide step-by-step instructions for handloading, as well as troubleshooting and special reloading techniques. They contain information on how to use reloading tables, as well as safety tips. Don't take any shortcuts or deviate from the recommended procedures. Keep to a routine when handloading and always keep things simple. Minimize distractions. Never use more powder than the maximum loads in the reloading tables.

Reloading manuals give suggestions on the types and weights of bullets for various game animals. There are many different kinds of bullets on the market (e.g., Spitzer boat tail, hollow point, flat nose, round nose, jacked soft point, full metal jacket, and so on), and they usually come in packages of 100 to a carton.

Tips and Tricks for Handloading

Generally, a handloader performs one operation at a time on a lot of cases: sizes and decaps the cases, primes and fills them with powder and finally, seats the bullets. "Priming" a case means seating a primer. The primer ignites the powder charge when stuck by the firing pin in the bolt of a rifle. There are small rifle, large rifle and magnum primers, so be sure you purchase the right kind for your calibre of rifle. Powder is measured with either a beam, digital or auto-dispenser scale. Add the powder measure to each case once they're primed using a powder funnel. I use a loading block that can seat 50 shells at a time.

It's also a good to buy a bullet puller in case you have to take a bullet out of a shell because it isn't seated properly. Sooner or later you'll make a mistake, regardless of how careful you might be, and it will be necessary to re-seat a bullet.

Brass expands after being shot, so cases should be trimmed with a case trimmer to their proper length. Use callipers to check brass casings for their proper length; trim an excess if necessary so they're not longer than they should be. Brass can be reused many times before being discarded. After each firing, check the case for cracks, especially in the neck, or for signs of stress near the base of the shell (e.g., a bulge or a hairline crack) the two areas brass tends to weaken after repeated use. During time spent on the rifle range, I make it a practice to buff the neck and base of each spent case with steel wool as an aid to spot any fissures. The "hotter" the loads, the greater the stress on the cartridge case! In between shots at the range I check each case for any cracks or signs of stress near the base of a shell.

Be resourceful! Look for spent casings at rifle ranges. I've found hundreds of rounds of perfectly good used brass at ranges that were put back inside factory ammunition boxes after only one firing, and subsequently discarded. It is not uncommon for some shooters to put their spent casings

Discard used brass that shows hairline cracks.

> *Assume that a gun is loaded.*
>
> Always open the breach of a firearm to ensure there are no shells in the chamber to be on the safe side.

back in a manufacturer's box after shooting them only once and then throw the box in the trash.

Use resizing lubricant to lubricate shells, so they'll fit into dies without jamming. Although you can put this lubricant onto pads—lubricating several shells at the same time—I generally apply it with a rag so I don't get any on the shoulder of a shell, which will cause the shoulder to crimp. While crimped shells can still be fired (and the firing will reshape the shell) it's best to avoid crimped necks for safety reasons. Remove the lubricant from the brass casing with a solvent before it is primed and loaded with powder.

Use a primer tray to align the primers right side up, making it easier to pick them up and seat them with a seating die. Keep lubricant off primers because it's corrosive and can cause a misfire. Clean your hands to make sure they are free of any contaminants that might corrode the primers.

Bullets; powder; primers and bulk, centre-fire unprimed brass round off your shopping list (bulk, centre-fire unprimed brass comes in plastic bags in variable amounts, usually 100 cases per lot). Brass can be reloaded several times until it shows signs of damage. However, don't take any chances with a hard extraction when hunting; use only new brass for hunting. Keep brass polished so that it chambers easily, especially on cold days. Manuals have explanations of the types of powder loads and the weight in grains that can be safely used with different bullets, as well as bullet weights and projected trajectories. You can customize your handloads to match your rifle, optimizing accuracy by working up loads, which will be described later in this chapter. You should get tighter groups compared with factory loads. I routinely shoot one-inch groups at 100 yards with handloads, occasionally with all bullet holes touching each other, when shooting from a bench rest. I could never match this level of accuracy when I used to shoot factory loads, though they've seen great improvements in accuracy over the past few years.

You'll enjoy shooting hand loads at the range and will become a better marksman in the process.

Remember, accuracy can be the difference between a hit and a miss. If your sights are on a trophy of a lifetime, you want to have confidence in the consistency of your cartridges. Once you get into handloading, there's no turning back. You'll spend more time at the range, shooting various calibres and becoming a better marksman in the process because you'll realize the financial savings and be able to afford spending more time at the range.

On the Production Side

The previous section describes the fundamentals of reloading rifle shells and how to get started. Let's assume that you've purchased a starter kit, which has all the basic tools needed for reloading.

A reloading manual provides an introduction to reloading and the range of cases, primers, bullets and powder selections for your rifle. For example, for Sierra bullets there are at least nine different weights and types of bullets for the .270 calibre; 13 varieties for the popular 7 mm calibre and 27 choices for .30 calibre bullets. There's plenty of variety, which makes reloading exciting since it allows you to pick and choose different types and weights of bullets and a range of powder loads to fit your particular rifle and match your quarry. Try different types of bullets and powders to see which ones work best in your rifle; these should be superior to factory-loaded ammo.

There are many different kinds of bullets in the marketplace, so do some research to determine what brand should perform best in your rifle(s) relative to your quarry. Let's say you have a .270 calibre rifle, which is one of the most popular cartridges among big game hunters, probably matched only by the .30-06. The ongoing debate is whether the 130- or 150-grain bullet is best in the .270. Some hunters believe the

You should be able to save more than 40 percent of the cost of factory loads by hand loading.

130-grain bullet does too much tissue damage because of its higher velocity compared with the heavier, slower 150-grain bullet. This belief is based partly on theory because I've had 150-grain Hornady Spire Point bullets go right through several elk, which are large animals, while the 130-grain bullets have performed the same way on many deer and pronghorn antelope I've shot.

I prefer the 130-grain bullet for deer and pronghorn antelope and the 150 bullet for elk. I've found that each bullet weight has done its job with one-shot kills many times, so the velocity theory is rather academic. The perceived issue of "tissue damage" is likely related to shot placement, not bullet weight. Years ago, some American outdoor writers popularized shoulder shots, instead of lung shots. Quite naturally, animals shot in the shoulder suffer major tissue damage, which is why I prefer lung shots. If you target the area just behind the shoulder for a lung shot, the bullet may or may not hit a rib. Regardless, it will still be a killing shot, and the animal will quickly die from a loss of blood. If the bullet hits a rib, it should expand and cause more damage than if it missed a rib. There are many other bullet weights available for the .270 depending on what kind of game you're after: 100 grain, 110 grain, 120 grain, 140 grain, 160 grain and 180 grain.

Earlier in this chapter I made reference to "working up a load." This entails test firing the same brand of bullets, of the same weight, with incrementally different amounts of the same type of powder (e.g. 55 grains, 57 grains, 59 grains) at a gun range and assessing which load shoots the tightest pattern. Using the .270 as an example, with 130-grain Speer 1459 Spitzer Soft Point bullets and Hodgdon 4831 powder, a load with 59 grains of powder performed best in my Tikka T3 Lite rifle, as compared with 55 and 57 grains.

Both Speer bullets and Hodgdon powder are popular among hunters, but many other brands of bullets and powder are available. Experiment with different brands to see what works best for your rifle.

By way of comparison, when shooting 180-grain Nosler Partition bullets and IMR 4831 powder in my .300 WSM Tikka T3 Lite, the best load featured 63.5 grains, as compared with 64.5 and 65.5 grains of powder. Interestingly, in my .270 a hot load worked best, while in the .300 WSM the light load performed better.

Most of my hunting is done on the open range where shots are generally 200 to 300+ yards, so I use relatively light bullets that are designed for ease of flight (e.g., a boat tail) and have little drag. If your intended quarry is an animal in heavy bush or timber, a slower, heavier bullet with a flat base would be better because they lose velocity faster than one with a boat tail and carry more energy at shorter ranges. There is no such thing as a "brush busting" cartridge or bullet. These are myths; they don't exist. Any object that gets in the way of a bullet will deflect it.

Always resize your brass, even new brass, to make sure that it chambers properly. Trim spent cases to ensure they are the correct length, or you will jam the shell in the chamber and have a hard extraction. It's possible that this could happen with a reload, although it has never happened to me. I have fired thousands of rounds of reloads, but I don't take any chances on missing the trophy of a lifetime on a missed opportunity for a shot because of a hard extraction.

There are many kinds of powder on the market, from fast- to slow-burning varieties. Reloading tables stipulate the weight in grains of different kinds of powder that can

> ### I "ranged" it.
>
> The hunter used a range finder to determine how far away his quarry was located.

be used safely for the variety of bullets on the market. Always follow safe storage instructions for powder; it is combustible, therefore highly dangerous. It should be stored in a dark, dry location. One of my hunting partners shot some 25-year-old shells I reloaded for him, which held a group less than an inch in diameter. Powder is stable, probably indefinitely, and once shells have been reloaded, they will last a lifetime.

Once you really get into the production side—if you do your homework properly—don't be surprised if your groups can be covered with a loonie the next time you visit the rifle range.

Sighting in your Rifle: Bullseye!

Accurate shots don't just happen; they're the result of a lot of practice on the range. However, unless your rifle is properly sighted in, you'll be lucky to hit the target, regardless of how often you practice. This chapter provides some basic sighting-in procedures and target practice suggestions to help you become a competent shooter under field conditions, plus some tips on shooting at running game.

Virtually every time I visit a gun range, I witness shooters making some fundamental mistakes when they sight in their high-powered rifles. It's absolutely essential that rifles be properly sighted in, preferably at an official rifle range under controlled conditions. If you ingrain known distances in your mind by shooting at approved ranges, this knowledge will be indispensable under field conditions. While I have a laser rangefinder, I find that my estimates are usually quite accurate up to 300 yards based on mental extrapolations founded at the various rifle ranges I've frequented over the years.

Following are my suggestions on how to get it right:

1. Use a bench rest at a gun range with known distances at intervals of 25, 100 and at least 200 yards but preferably 300 yards. Sight in your rifle at an approved range, primarily for reasons of safety but also because you'll be shooting at standard, known distances.

2. Adjust the seat at the bench rest so that your eyes are on the same plane as the rifle scope; not above or below the plane of the scope. Get comfortable. Relax. Never rush the sighting in process. Get your breathing and heart rate under control. It's important to be calm.

3. Always ensure you have a backstop to prevent unwanted ricochets and adhere to established range rules.

4. Use sandbags or a commercial shooting stand to steady the rifle. Unless the rifle is on a solid rest, you're wasting your time because the point of impact will vary from shot to shot. There are many commercial shooting stands on the market. They'll pay for themselves after just a few trips to the range. However, if you're on a budget, pick up some used shot shell cloth containers, fill them with

Close-up of rifle resting on a bench rest at a gun range

sand and sew them tight. You'll need three bags for the forearm and two for the rifle stock for a solid rest. Some shooters use all manner of rests from sleeping bags to pillows, which obviously don't cut it as solid rests. You can shoot all day with these types of rests, and you'll never zero in your rifle. A good example of the need for a solid rest occurred when I checked out my rifle along with one of my hunting buddies. He initially took several shots using a commercial, plastic rest at 100 yards. He shot a 2x3 inch group which seemed odd because we knew his rifle could shoot tighter groups. I suggested he fire some more rounds, using my solid rest. Subsequently, he shot a group that was less than a ½ inch! Are you a believer now?

5. If your rifle has not been previously sighted in, have it bore sighted and start by shooting one shot at 25 yards then another at a 100-yard sighting-in target.

Aim dead centre at the target. If the bullet hits dead centre, your rifle should shoot between 2 and 3 inches high at 100 yards. Sporting goods store staff normally bore sight a riflescope when it's purchased. If your rifle isn't dead centre at a range of 25 yards, adjust the Minute of Angle (MOA) clicks for windage and elevation so that it's dead centre.

6. Next, take three shots at 100 yards—adjust the scope so that the rifle is sighted in to be either (a) dead centre, or (b) 2 to 3 inches high at this distance depending on your personal preference. You'll have to move the windage and elevation dials by four clicks (i.e., minutes of angle) to move the point of impact one inch at this range. The "windage" dial aligns the sights from left to right; the "elevation" dial aligns the sights up or down. Triangulate the approximate centre of impact by connecting the bullet holes. I suggest

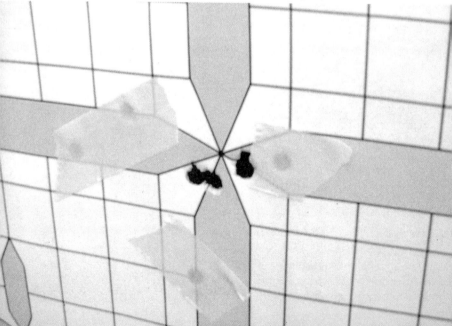

The first group (taped) was fired without a solid rest; the second group was fired from a solid rest.

Official 100-yard sighting in target—note group of shots approximately 3 inches high.

sighting in your rifle 2 to 3 inches high at 100 yards based on my personal hunting experience. Shots will then be on target at a distance of about 225 yards for most calibres. You can, however, sight your rifle in for 100 yards so that the point of impact is centred in the bullseye at this distance. A word of caution: All calibres have different trajectories; consequently, it is essential that you calibrate your firearm accordingly. I recommend zeroing your rifle for 100 yards if you're a bush hunter or 225 yards if you're hunting where long-range shots are more common, which is the case throughout much of western Canada. I've paced off the distances of my killing shots for all manner of big game, and they average 225 yards.

7. Always space your shots so that you're shooting from a relatively cool barrel. As the barrel warms, the spacing between the shots will increase. Allow time for the gun barrel to cool between shots. Don't be surprised if your first shot is a flyer, a bit higher than you'd expect. This is normal when shooting from a clean barrel, especially if there's oil residue from when it was last cleaned. If all goes well, you should be able to get a one-inch group of shots at 100 yards, even with factory ammunition.

8. When you're confident that your rifle is zeroed in after having sighted it in at either 100 or 225 yards, you're set for some target practice.

To ensure consistency of shots, make sure to check that your rifle is properly sighted in each year before going hunting. With modern rifles and scopes, it's rare for the line of sight to change from year to year, but don't take any chances. Personally, I never rely on my first four shots to be accurate. The first shot will always be high coming from a clean barrel and the next three farther apart than normal. Once I settle down, I'll take another three shots. At least a couple of bullet holes will usually be touching each other, and the remaining hole within a one-inch radius.

Safety While Shooting

Hearing protection is a must while sighting in your rifle to protect against hearing loss. It's also a good idea to wear shooting glasses for eye protection, and amber-tinged glasses will improve down-range visibility. It's always a good idea to wear suitable field clothes at the range, preferably those you'll be hunting in to make certain that your rifle feels comfortable under field conditions.

It's perfectly normal for shooters to flinch, but you want to avoid flinching so you're on target, otherwise you'll be a lousy shot. The crack of a rifle is enough to make almost anyone flinch, and the jar of a rifle makes matters worse. Modern rifles are much less prone to cause flinching than older models because they generally have a shock-absorbing recoil pad instead of an unforgiving solid butt plate. They also usually have little trigger creep, which lessens flinching.

Flinching is a hunter's worst nemesis. It usually requires a conscious avoidance reaction because it's not always just the result of being gun shy. It's normal among most shooters and is a form of overreaction to anticipated noise or recoil. Wearing ear protection at the range will minimize flinching associated with noise. When firing at game most hunters don't notice the noise of a gunshot or a gun's recoil.

Many hunters will still tend to get excited and jerk the trigger prematurely or perhaps flinch in anticipation of recoil, especially if they hurry a shot. Try to control your excitement and keep your heart rate

---

The secret to being a good shot is to squeeze the trigger, not pull it, or you'll miss your target.

–Bill White, author's second cousin from Bellevue, who at age 90, tagged a mule deer and white-tailed deer in 2017. In an interview, Bill said "I'm a meat hunter, not a trophy hunter, always have been." He added, "On November 9, 74 years ago [1943] when I had just turned 16, I shot my first bull elk, the biggest I ever shot. Four guys could stand inside the antlers!" Up until a few years ago Bill carried a Husqvarna .30-06 Springfield calibre rifle he bought in 1949 but now hunts with a .25-06 Remington calibre rifle which he claims is "deadly."

---

and breathing normal. Focus on the fundamental principles of good marksmanship to improve your accuracy and avoid problems associated with jerking the trigger or flinching. Most new rifles have an adjustable trigger pull from 2 to 4 pounds, which has largely eliminated trigger creep issues. But total concentration is necessary to shoot accurately at ranges over 100 yards.

If you're sighting in a new rifle, follow recommended break-in procedures even though most manufacturers claim these are no longer really required. First, clean the bore with a gun solvent. Next, make two sweeps of the barrel using a gun cleaning rod with a dry cloth, and one oiled patch every second shot, for the first 10 rounds fired from a new rifle to burnish the bore (i.e., closing the pores of the barrel metal which have been opened and exposed through the rifle boring process.

There's no substitute for practice at a range or under field conditions to get used to the feel and action of your firearm. Shoot from a variety of positions because you'll never know what may happen when a shot opportunity presents itself. Start by shooting from a standing position, putting your left foot forward if you're a right-handed shot. Next, switch to a sitting position, probably the most common of all shooting stances. Finally, take some shots from a prone

position, the most reliable field position favoured by experienced hunters. When you can consistently place three shots in a 6-inch bullseye at 100 yards (from a sitting position), you're ready to go hunting.

Missed Shots!

In this section I'll explain how to think and act strategically when out hunting in order to hit a big game animal in a vital area. It's not just long shots that are missed; sometimes those close shots are problematic, too. Furthermore, you have to know what leads are required on running shots or you may as well save your ammo by not taking such difficult shots.

Leads are a big issue; improper leads result in many missed shots at running game. You will not have time to think about proper leads when a big buck bolts into an

Practice shooting from a standing position at the range so your prepared for these shot opportunities in the field.

opening in front of you and heads for the nearest cover. You must remember to lead it one body length at a range of 100 yards and two body lengths at a range of 200 yards. Adjust your lead at other intervals, for example half a body length at 50 yards, one-and-a-half body lengths at 150 yards. The same applies to elk and moose. I'm not going to address leads for pronghorn antelope because they are simply too long for most hunters. I do not recommend shots at running animals at distances greater than 100 yards because most hunters simply don't have the skill to connect and should not risk wounding an animal under these circumstances. In most cases you'll only have time for one shot at a running big game animal, so make it count!

> *Dr. H.M. Smith of Napanee, Ontario, provided a formula to calculate the correct amount of lead in the Outdoor Canada 2001 Fishing magazine. The equation you should use is as follows:*
>
> *Lead (feet) = Distance (yards) x Animal Speed (mph) x 4.4 ÷ Projectile Velocity (fps).*
>
> *This works out to be 3.8 feet at a range of 100 yards with the .270 calibre 130-grain loads I use most often for deer.*

It's a rare hunter who hasn't missed shots at big game. I've blown shots at antelope, bighorn sheep, elk, moose, mule deer and white-tailed deer. On the other hand, I once had a streak of 11 consecutive killing shots back in the day. In retrospect, I've learned something from every shot that I've missed, not just the killing shots. Why? Because few shot opportunities are the same, and it takes years of shooting experience to build a skill set to connect when you do get a chance for a shot at a big game animal.

There are many reasons why hunters miss shots:

- Certain species, such as antelope because of their small size, and their light colour, tend to make hunters perceive them as being farther away than they actually are.

- Having trouble shooting on inclines either uphill or downhill

- Incorrect leads on running shots

- Not using proper rests while hunting or an attachable bipod or shooting sticks

- Problems with wind, causing bullet drift

- Flinching and improper breathing prior to pulling the trigger

- Trigger creep in older firearms, in particular

- Simply not being aware of personal shooting tendencies.

I've changed hunting rifles several times over the years. Each time I've faced challenges in getting used to new actions, different safeties, differences in recoil and the overall feel of the new rifle. Make sure your rifle is a good fit and has a natural point of aim, or you'll never shoot well.

The best way to speed up the learning curve is to practice shooting at the range until you achieve a desirable comfort level with a new rifle. Don't go hunting with a new rifle until it feels like an old companion, and its workings become second nature.

Today's hunters are blessed with better products than ever before: excellent rifles, scopes, better quality factory ammunition and laser binoculars and scopes to accurately measure distances in the field in either Imperial or metric. Don't laugh. For different age groups, the difference between Imperial and metric units can be confusing, and laser binoculars and scopes come in both units! I purchased a laser scope several years ago and use it routinely to take the guesswork out of estimating ranges, which can be difficult and exasperating at times. Under poor light, especially at dawn and dusk, big game animals will appear to be farther away than they actually are, causing many hunters to aim high and shoot over their backs.

Another problem that hunters have to contend with is shooting at an angle (i.e., incline) either uphill or downhill at various distances. Regardless of whether you're shooting uphill or downhill, a bullet will rise, and the path of the bullet will vary depending on its ballistic coefficient (or

Author spotting on Alberta's prairies

configuration), which is affected by air drag, among other things. The path of the bullet can change by several inches at ranges between 200 and 300 yards at various angles because the force of gravity is different than on the level. Hold low when firing uphill or downhill and check out the parameters for your calibre online or in handloading books to estimate the path of particular bullets under field conditions at different inclines.

If at all possible, use a rest when shooting at big game animals, regardless of the range. Your primary goal is to make a clean, one-shot kill and not miss or wound an animal. While any rest is a good rest, I've gone to a Harris bipod, which rotates to either side for quick leveling on uneven ground. You can't always count on finding a natural rest. You can use an attached bipod when shooting prone, sitting and/or in a kneeling position. The one I use has folding, spring-loaded extendable legs that can be set up quickly when necessary.

Another option is to use shooting sticks which are gaining in popularity among hunters. They come in many designs and are also popular. The only drawback to a detached bi-pod is that it's a bit awkward to carry in the field. You can use all manner of objects in the field for a rest, such as boulders and trees, but where possible, use a glove to cushion the forearm of your rifle stock on such rests. Once, during a pronghorn antelope hunt on the Alberta prairies, I used Pentax 10x50 power binoculars for a rest and took a non-typical buck at a range of ~300+ yards. I put the binoculars on top of my hat with the eyepieces facing up and rested the gunstock between them, which did the job.

Every hunter must contend with some personal tendencies that can only be identified by shooting under controlled conditions at a gun range. For example, if you've got

Get all your practice shots in the bullseye at 100 yards.

a good group but with some erratic shots, you're likely flinching or guilty of trigger pull. If your group is strung up and down the target, you're probably breathing when you're shooting. If you've got a tight group but it's out of the point of aim, wind may be a factor, or your scope may have an incorrect zero. Once you've identified the cause of these tendencies you can work on corrective action.

Factors associated with missed shots are best dealt with at the gun range by adhering to the basic principles of marksmanship training so that when you're shooting under field conditions your training kicks in and firing at big game becomes second nature. You don't want to start second guessing yourself when the opportunity to bag a trophy arises!

CHAPTER FIVE

Hunting the Elusive Bighorn

Trophy Sheep

Bighorn sheep are the largest of all North American sheep species and are an iconic symbol of Alberta's stunning Rocky Mountain region. Sheep range throughout our mountains, spending summers in high alpine zones before migrating to lower altitudes in fall and winter. If you are a seasoned sheep hunter, you already know about Alberta's reputation for outstanding sheep quality and quantity.

- Hunting seasons for bighorn sheep typically start on September 6 and close November 30 in Mountain WMUs. WMU 400 is open only for full-curl rams; other WMUs are open for trophy sheep.

- Hunting of sheep is prohibited in several areas specified in the "Alberta Guide to Hunting Regulations."

- A trophy sheep licence can be purchased across the counter for rams. Non-trophy sheep are subject to a draw. A resident who kills a sheep, except a legal non-trophy sheep, in one year cannot purchase a trophy sheep licence in the following year.

- The rut occurs in November and December.

Trophy Sheep: A male bighorn sheep with horns, one of which is of sufficient size that a straight line drawn from the most anterior point of the base of the horn to the tip of the horn extends beyond the anterior edge of the eye when viewed in profile.

Full-Curl Trophy Sheep: A male bighorn sheep with horns, one of which is of sufficient size that when viewed in profile, its tip extends upward beyond a straight line drawn from the rear-most point of the base of the horn to the centre of the nostril.

- Bighorn trophy sheep are often difficult to judge at a distance in the field, so quality spotting scopes and binoculars are a must.

- Mountain terrain can test the conditioning of any hunter and demands a rifle that is easy to pack. Opt for a lightweight rifle in a calibre that you shoot effectively, from the .270s up to the .300 magnums. Although shots less than 200 yards (180 metres) are the norm, you may have no option other than to shoot at longer distances, so practice at extended ranges before your sheep hunt.

The Ultimate Challenge

Alberta is world-renowned as the top producing area for record-class rams, but that doesn't make it any easier to tag one. Bighorn sheep can be elusive and difficult to hunt, so it's not uncommon for hunters to go an entire season without seeing a legal ram. They live in remote areas, are difficult to spot and are few in numbers.

I've taken a ewe on the Livingstone Range and a ram west of Pincher Creek, which doesn't sound like much, but experienced sheep hunters will understand that it is

a real challenge to shoot any legal ram. Most hunters simply will not make the effort required to shoot a ewe. Getting the meat back to the trailhead usually involves a lot of hard work. More telling, perhaps, is that I have missed good opportunities to shoot a couple of other rams, which I'll probably never get over.

On one hunt, I was so close to a legal ram in the headwaters of the South Castle River that I could see its nostrils move. It bolted, and I never did get a decent shot opportunity, though I took a fleeting running shot

Alberta boasts the top bighorn sheep rams in the world.

Bighorn sheep have a distinctive white rump patch.

and missed. My partner and I spotted the ram the day before the season opened, and we watched it bed down on a cliff as the sun set. We scaled a mountain in the dark on opening day only to find that another ram had joined it during the night, and both were bedded down on the cliff within range. A light rain was falling. Mist hung on the mountain slope. Trouble was I wasn't expecting two rams, so I didn't bring my spotting scope. Consequently, I couldn't be certain which one was legal in the poor light of dawn with the mist and falling rain. The rams got up from their beds and moved off the cliff, feeding briskly along a grassy slope, coming toward me. My partner had stationed himself lower down on the mountain out of sight of the sheep. Because the rams were headed in my direction, I got in a prone position with my head down as there was scant cover nearby. Before long, one of the rams was right in front of me. I could have hit him with a rock. As I mentioned earlier, he was so close that I could see his nostrils

flaring. It turned out this was the legal ram we'd spotted the day before. Unfortunately, he was facing me, and I couldn't accurately judge whether the ram was legal until he turned his head. The ram eventually spotted me lying right in front of him. He twitched, side-stepped, then bolted, heading into some trees and ran over the crest of a saddle into another valley. I could have cried as I watched him disappear.

Yet another time, after hunting hard for several days, my hunting partner and I came across a band of eight rams during a late October hunt in the Crowsnest Pass area. The small herd had at least three legal rams. As we flipped a coin to decide who would shoot which of the legal rams, we were dismayed to see another hunter sneak in right in front of us. He shot one of the legal rams under our noses, which was hardly sporting on his part. It was unethical to spoil our hunt because we were there first.

Granted, sheep hunting is competitive, but hunters should follow the cardinal rules of sportsmanship: ethical, appropriate, polite and fair behaviour. It's heartbreaking for a sheep hunter to miss an opportunity to shoot a ram—they are difficult to hunt, and shot opportunities are so rare.

If my family savoured the taste of bighorn sheep meat more, I might have tried to shoot more of them. However, quite frankly, sheep were never a culinary hit, which tended to dampen my enthusiasm. Under Alberta law, it is illegal to waste the meat of a big game animal. What you shoot, you must eat.

Back in the day, my prime sheep hunting territory was south of Highway Number 3. Unfortunately, there was a huge die-off of bighorn sheep in this area from tuberculosis, beginning in 1982. Actually, Lorne Fitch, one of my old sheep-hunting partners, and I spotted the first infected bighorn ram in Ptolemy Creek south of the Crowsnest Lake that year. We were dismayed as we watched the ram in the throes of a coughing fit. By 1984 about 65 percent of the population was gone. Quite naturally, hunting success really tapered off following the major die-off.

I have a lot of respect for successful bighorn sheep hunters, especially those who have bagged several rams. I know how hard it is to even locate a legal ram, never mind kill several during a lifetime. Successful sheep hunters put in a lot of time and effort to study the distribution and habits of their quarry. They go to a great deal of expense to scout sheep before the season even opens. They are true students of bighorns and have worked hard to understand where to locate legal rams throughout the season, from opening to closing day.

Bighorns are creatures of habit and can often be found in certain areas year after year. The trick is to locate these areas, keep the information quiet and hope nobody

Bob Scammell understood in his blood that to keep our wild places and creatures, we first need to take care of the land and water they need to survive. He was a great conservationist, a champion of public access and a spokesman for those creatures that do not have a voice.

—Trout Unlimited Canada tribute on Bob's passing

else discovers your secret. However, as veteran bighorn guide Bill Michalsky of Lundbreck, Alberta, was fond of saying, "It's hard to keep a good thing secret." Go-to spots often eventually leak out, which undermines their value in the long run. Bill was a founding member of the Alberta Wilderness Association and a respected mountain guide who guided famed Jack O'Connor, *Outdoor Life* gun editor, in the Elbow drainage on a successful sheep hunt where he took "Krag" of the Alberta Rockies. "Krag" was a fictional trophy ram that O'Connor dreamed about. There was no ground shrink in O'Connor's trophy ram.

It may be a sorry reflection on the part of sheep hunters, but very few will divulge any useful information or tips when it comes to sheep hunting. The standard reply when asked where they shot a ram is "through the lungs," if that.

There are some things a neophyte can do; however, to get started in the right direction.

Scouting trips play a key role in finding bighorn sheep.

Scouting

For the most part, bighorns are found in the most isolated and remote alpine areas of Alberta's Rockies, generally above timberline. They will, however, move into the trees for shelter to escape storms and bed where they have good sight lines to spot any danger, which usually comes from below. Consequently, most successful stalks are from above because sheep tend to look downward for danger. They also tend to use well-travelled game trails as they move about alpine areas. If there is snow on the ground, look for tracks, which will usually lead to sheep. If there's no snow and you're on foot, look for their wafer-like droppings, which, when fresh, indicate they're nearby.

Behaviour

Sheep are grazers and can be spotted shortly after daybreak on alpine pastures when they start their daily feed, often for an hour or longer. During midday, they'll usually be bedded down on talus slopes or high-elevation saddles, where they blend in well with the slate grey rock. At night, they tend to bed on cliffs to avoid predators. High-powered binoculars are necessary to spot sheep, and a spotting scope is useful to better judge the size of rams. "Let your glasses do the walking," is an old saying that is good advice because it takes hours to carefully glass suitable sheep habitat.

Bighorns will often get up from their beds during the noon hour to stretch and move about, probably to get their circulation going. So pass on that nap after lunch, and keep looking.

Rams also like to have a drink of water in the evening before they bed down, and they will travel well over a kilometre to water, if necessary. Watch for rams moving during the evening. It's far easier to spot a sheep when it's feeding, standing up and stretching or moving to and from a watering hole than when it's bedded down.

It was a real wall hanger.

The game animal was of trophy status.

as Waterton Lakes, Banff and Jasper, as well as near the Cadomin Mines and other game sanctuaries.

You'll need to be in good physical shape to hunt bighorns. It's usually a test of stamina and endurance. Hunting conditions in the Rockies can often be brutal, with gruelling climbs, treacherous slopes where a misstep can be fatal, and hurricane-force winds, driving rain and snow. Each day starts long before daybreak and ends after the sun goes down.

Sadly, hunting bighorns has degenerated into a foot race in the more accessible parts of Alberta, which has brought out the worst in some irresponsible hunters. For hunters with scruples, however, a bighorn hunt is the standard that sets the bar for all other big game hunts in Alberta.

Sheep are also gregarious by nature and are usually found in herds. However, it's not unusual to find solitary rams in late October, travelling about their ranges prior to the November rut, when the season is generally closed.

Many of the top rams are taken near the borders of national parks in Alberta such

Mature bighorn rams head butting to establish dominance for breeding ewes.

Mature male mountain goats, called billies, are solitary animals found in remote alpine areas of Alberta's Rockies.

Mountain Goats

A full chapter on mountain goats isn't warranted. They are found in the alpine zones of Alberta's Rocky Mountains and often share the same range as bighorn sheep. They're subject to a limited entry draw with few permits issued annually. Because of the limited number of licences, a draw priority does not apply, and the draw is strictly random. This resident-only draw is heavily subscribed, and the annual success rate of being drawn is less than 0.10 percent. In 2016 only 7 tags were available, one each for 7 different WMUs in Alberta's Rockies, southern Alberta and the Willmore Wilderness Park area. Resident hunters successful in drawing a Goat Special Licence may designate a resident youth partner to hunt with them and share the special licence tag. The season runs from either September 10 or 17 to October 31.

CHAPTER SIX

ELK HUNTS

Elk

Elk are truly majestic big game animals, every bit as wily as a mature white-tailed buck, if not more so. They are challenging to hunt and test a hunter's skill and knowledge to the limit. Veteran elk hunters will attest that a record-book elk is harder to take than a record-book bighorn ram. Elk are expanding their range into Alberta's prairies, parklands and boreal forest from the traditional hotspots in the mountains and foothills.

Typical Hunting Season Starts (always check dates in case of changes)

- Most archery seasons start September 1.

- Most rifle seasons run until the end of November, with some extending into mid-December.

- Prairie WMUs start September 1 and extend until the end of the first week in February in CFB Suffield.

- Parkland WMUs seasons begin September 1, with some lasting until late January.

- Foothills WMUs seasons start August 25 and run until January 20.

- Mountain WMUs seasons run from August 25 to November 30.

- Boreal WMUs seasons start September 1 and end October 31.

Licenses

Antlered and antlerless types of licences are available with antlered licences subject to 3-point and 6-point or larger males.

- Antlered elk: an elk having an antler exceeding 4 inches long

- Antlerless: an elk that is not "antlered" (as defined above)

- While bulls can be taken with .270, .308 and 30-06 calibre rifles, most elk hunters prefer magnum rifles—.300 H&H, .300 Weatherby, .300 Winchester, .300 Winchester Short and 7mm magnums, preferably with 180 grain loads. Big bulls can tip the scales at 800+ pounds and can be hard to put down, so make your first shot count. Shots are generally in the 200- to 300-yard range, so a bipod is an asset.

Bull elk profile

The Strategic Approach

My hunting partner and I could never figure out how some guys from Medicine Hat consistently scored on elk. They shared the same campground with us in the Castle River area, usually arriving late at night and setting up camp in the dark. By the next afternoon, they often had an elk. Although we never did find their honey hole, we were pretty sure where it was located by using a process of deduction. They never divulged any secrets and always said they were just lucky. Lucky, my foot! They knew how to hunt elk!

We would hunt all week and maybe get one shot off, sometimes connecting, sometimes not. After a few years, however, we started to tag elk regularly after we'd put the pieces of the puzzle together. I've subsequently followed a lot of the same basic elk hunting steps over the years and have enjoyed much more consistent success.

Elk hunting can be exhilarating at its best, exasperating at its worst. An elk hunt has many twists and turns. It's seldom dull. A lot of planning and preparation go into an elk hunt, long before you actually get in a position to pull the trigger. Although there are no sure-fire strategies to ensure success on any given hunt, a hunter can do a lot of little things that can make a big difference. Mess up on any one of them, and you'll likely get skunked. Granted, there are some hunts where shooting an elk can be a bit like a crap shoot, but by taking the following strategic approach you can greatly increase your chances of success.

Understanding Elk Behaviour

Like all animals, elk are creatures of habit, so one of the keys to success is having a good understanding of their behaviour during the hunting season.

Elk feed for a couple of hours in the early morning and evening regardless of the weather; foul weather does not interfere with their feeding patterns. If you hunt in prime elk habitat, you'll be able to spot elk accordingly. After elk have fed, they'll bed

Non-typical elk in Alberta's Rockies

down where they feel secure. Daytime bedding spots may be in heavy timber or secluded stands of aspen during September and October or on sunny, south-facing slopes in November. In areas of heavy hunting pressure, feeding elk will never be far from escape cover and can disappear in a heartbeat once alarmed.

Elk are social creatures and tend to travel in herds, often in a dozen or more animals during all times of the year. Mature bulls will form bachelor groups in remote areas post-rut but are generally solitary creatures during the peak of the rut. One of the largest bulls I've taken was herd master of 14 to 15 cows. I shot him at 9:30 AM on a mid-September morning bedded down smack in the middle of his harem. He must have thought he was on the top of the world.

Try to take different scenarios into account when strategizing your elk hunting plans with regard to seasonal differences in elk ecology and behaviour.

The peak of the elk rut is in mid-September. Elk will almost always be found in clusters just prior to and during the rut. A herd bull will gather a couple dozen or more cows while subordinate satellite bulls will stage themselves on the perimeter of the harem until the rut is over. It can be exasperating to hunt herd bulls under these circumstances. Many eyes are watching, and cows are ever alert for foreign sounds. The satellite bulls surrounding the harem might be alerted during a stalk because elk have excellent vision and a keen sense of smell. To make matters worse, the herd bull often positions itself in the middle of its harem, which can make it challenging to get off a shot. Sometimes, it's easier to pick off a satellite bull than a herd bull.

The rut ends by October, and mature bulls will go off to join bachelor groups and seek out the most remote areas in their home range as winter approaches. Look for groups of bulls, not solitary animals, which are more commonly seen during

September and October. Most of the cows in a harem disband and form herds of two dozen or so animals. It's not unusual for cow herds to contain spike or raghorn bulls (spike bulls have at least one antler beam without any branch; raghorns are young bulls with small branched antlers).

One paramount rule of elk hunting, though, is to get away from the crowds, and hunt areas away from travelled roads. Elk are shy by nature. Studies have shown they do not tolerate human activity. Consequently, it's rare to find elk near areas of human activity, such as well sites, active logging operations, gravel pits and the like. Granted, you may occasionally find them travelling near such areas, but these are exceptions to the rule. Elk generally frequent inaccessible areas that are a ridge top or two away from the nearest travelled road or are separated by a wide valley or lot of bush. Gone are the days when you can shoot elk from a travelled road. Almost all of my successful elk hunts took place some distance from the nearest road. Wild elk don't like being around humans. It's as simple as that!

Scouting

Advance scouting before the seasoning opens is job one before going on an elk hunt. Even if you think you've got an area nailed down, scouting is crucial to success because conditions and land-use activities can change and impact elk behaviour.

I stand by what I've said many times: one of the best ways to find elk is to go grouse hunting. Don't laugh! Elk and grouse have overlapping ranges, so once you've decided where you're going to hunt elk, spend some time in the area hunting grouse to locate elk sign before the season opens. It matters not whether you're hunting blue grouse in the mountains, ruffed grouse in the foothills or aspen parklands, sharp-tailed grouse in the prairies or spruce grouse in the boreal forest; you'll be walking the hallowed ground that elk call home during your grouse hunt. You'll also be toughening up the soles of your feet and improving your cardiovascular system for what will no doubt be a rigorous elk hunt down the road. It's surprising how often you'll find elk sign during a grouse hunt; you'll even bump into the odd elk.

Look for several bull elk in bachelor herds in November.

Elk will bed where they feel secure.

Scout remote areas when you begin searching for elk sign; don't waste your time scouting near roads or areas where human activity is taking place.

During your scouting forays check for elk tracks, droppings and wallows, rubs, feeding and bedding areas. Because elk are herd animals, it usually isn't hard to find their sign, which is often quite plentiful and fairly obvious.

- *Elk beds are usually found in the open near escape cover and sheltered from the wind, often in clusters. Distinguish these beds from those of other ungulates by checking for droppings. Once you find several fresh bedding areas, you can bet elk have been using the area on a consistent basis.*

- *Feeding areas are fairly easy to spot. Although elk are browsers, their preferred forage is grass. They are also suckers for oats and second-cut alfalfa, if you're hunting in agricultural areas. Look for small craters in grassy areas in fields and forest openings where elk have fed; they tend to focus on relatively small areas when feeding on grass and chomp it down unevenly.*

- *Fresh droppings will likewise indicate that elk are in the area.*

- *Tracks and the number and size of beds will give you an idea of the number of elk nearby and whether any large animals are in the vicinity. Keep an eye open for tracks around springs and waterholes.*

- *Look for elk hair on bushes and any barbed wire fences in the area to better understand where they're travelling and to pin down crossing points.*

- *Check for rubs on trees where bulls polished their antlers.*

- *Listen for the sounds of elk; they are the most vocal of all ungulates.*

- *Once you've analyzed the sign, you can estimate how many elk are in the area, where they are bedding and feeding, and their preferred travel routes to and from day cover. With this information, you can plan the best place to position yourself when the season opens.*

Because I've spent a lot of time scouting my current WMU hunting area, I know some out-of-the-way places where elk will likely be present year after year. I can connect the dots (so to speak) based on where I find the most sign in any given year, without actually seeing any elk.

On one hunt a few years ago, foul weather prevented me from getting out on opening day, which can be a real blow in zones where hunting pressure is high. I figured

Check for fresh elk tracks on game trails.

I had little chance of getting an elk because of blizzard-like conditions, and I reasoned that because other hunters would probably stay home, it was worth the risk to wait until the weather improved. It turned out to be a good decision. As dawn broke on the day I was finally able to get out, two raghorn bulls (i.e., young bulls with small branched antlers) crossed an opening within range, but they presented a tough shot, so I passed. Shortly afterwards, I spotted the antler tips of a mature bull as it walked through a swale. Almost at the same time, three other bulls appeared a couple of hundred yards distant. I pondered what I should do and decided to take one of the three bulls. Two shots through the lungs of the trailing bull, and it was all over.

So what's the moral of this story? I had a chance at six different bulls within an hour of the start of my elk hunt because

I positioned myself where I thought I'd find elk based on advance scouting and despite not being able to get out opening day. A word of caution, though: It's best

Look for fresh elk droppings when you're on a scouting trip.

Position yourself for a shot prior to first light.

not to be overly active while scouting just prior to the opening date because you could put local elk on their guard, to your disadvantage.

Putting Yourself into Position

Next comes positioning in anticipation of getting a shot. Where possible, I like to engage elk rather than stand hunt, though both approaches work. Here are some basic recommendations for getting ready:

• Try to get into position before first light.

• Wear camouflage clothing.

• Slowly work your way into position with the sun at your back and the wind in your face, if possible.

• Move slowly along the edges of clearings or trails so as not to spook any elk that may be feeding in the vicinity.

• Don't make any noise. Elk can hear, see and smell humans from great distances. Making noise, exposing yourself or getting caught upwind of elk will cause

them to quietly fade into the bush. You may never see them again.

Your main job is to position yourself where you're most likely to run into elk during a hunt. While this is easier said than done, it is one of the cardinal rules of elk hunting. Take the hunt to the elk, and you'll get chances for a shot. If you've done your scouting, you should have a good idea where elk are holed up, where they're feeding and where their travel lanes are situated.

Before first light, you should be in position where you expect to find elk feeding. As you work your way into the area, periodically search out the area in front of you with your binoculars and try to spot elk, either bedded down or feeding. Look for their light rump patch. Once you've arrived at your "stand" be prepared to sit tight and wait. Stay concealed and don't move.

It's surprising how often elk will materialize out of nowhere if you're in the right place. Just like real estate maxim: Location, location, location is everything in an elk hunt!

Listening for Elk

Elk are vocal animals and communicate with a variety of calls. You'll often hear elk before you see them:

- the soft mewling and squeals of animals in a herd as they travel in the early morning hours;

- the clashing antlers of young bulls as they jostle amongst themselves;

- cows chirping to attract attention;

- the grunts and bugles of mature bulls at virtually any hour of the day during the prime rut;

- the sound of branches being broken as a herd goes for water, especially in the quiet of the evening;

- the bark of a startled cow that you might frighten unexpectedly.

I've listened to elk in herds call back and forth many times as they approached feeding areas at dawn, and they make quite a racket as they travel through the bush, whether you're hunting in the mountains or aspen parkland, especially if conditions

Bull elk (bugling) and cow

are dry. Until recently, most bulls stopped bugling by the end of October, but now it is not uncommon to hear some bulls grunt and bugle right up until the end of November—perhaps a sign of global warming or climate change. Young bulls will spar with each other until mid-November, so don't be surprised to hear the clash of horns well past the rut.

Listen up when in the field. On a November 2 hunt, on my second day out, I heard a bull bugle. A second bull called, followed by a third bull. I had my cow call, even though the rut was long over. I headed toward the third bull, set up my rifle for a shot and called twice. A 6-pointer stepped out of a stand of aspen followed by several cows. He started to move his harem into an adjacent stand of aspen but made the mistake of hesitating, then stopping before a fallen tree on the trail. It was all the time I needed. One shot through the chest, and he was down.

Equipment

My checklist for elk hunting has been pared down to the bare essentials with the goal of travelling light because elk hunts can be gruelling affairs. The following equipment list is customized for the September to November elk hunts when the weather can be variable:

- ☐ *full camouflage clothing—fall brown or fall grey depending on whether snow is absent or present, respectively—and light, sturdy, insulated hiking boots. Warm gloves are essential.*
- ☐ *fanny pack or daypack depending on location to carry lunch, water and hunting accessories*
- ☐ *extra ammunition*
- ☐ *first aid kit*

- ☐ lightweight 10x42 power binoculars; make it a habit to check the focus when in the field. I don't use a spotting scope when elk hunting in aspen parkland, which have been my usual haunts over the past several years. I also pack a rangefinder.
- ☐ three-bladed Browning knife and a sharpening stone
- ☐ some rope
- ☐ Wyoming knife to quarter or half a carcass
- ☐ two-way radio to stay in touch with my hunting companion(s)
- ☐ cow call
- ☐ matches and survival gear in case of emergencies. Prepare to stay in the bush overnight if necessary.

Gun and Ammunition

Although I've taken most of my elk with a .270 Winchester calibre rifle (using 150-grain bullets), a few years ago I switched to a .300 Winchester Short Magnum (also known as .300 WSM) shooting 180-grain bullets for added knock-down power. It's a decision I don't regret. Although there's nothing wrong with a .270 Winchester calibre, it doesn't match the .300 WSM for taking down big animals such as elk and moose, and it has additional range. My rifle is fitted with a 3x9 variable scope and a bipod, which has saved the day on more than one occasion.

Elk Hunting Savvy

Expect surprises during an elk hunt—they're all part of the elk hunting scenario—but anticipate success if you do your homework.

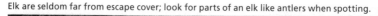

Elk are seldom far from escape cover; look for parts of an elk like antlers when spotting.

Take the Hunt to the Elk

While you can fall back on "spot, stalk and shoot" tactics on occasion, this is generally the exception to the rule because your window of opportunity tends to be short once you spot a bull. Keep your eyes peeled for parts of elk and elk movement when out hunting. Sometimes you'll only see part of an elk, such as the tips of a bull's antlers.

Hunt all Day

Another elk hunting lesson is to hunt all day. You just never know when you're going to locate elk. I've taken them from sunrise to sundown. There is no best time of day to shoot elk, although my preference is in the morning.

Be Prepared for Running Shots

It's not uncommon for elk to spot you at the same time as you see them. They'll head for cover, and a running shot may be your only option. Seconds really count under these circumstances. The saving grace is they are big targets; if you've been practicing at the range, running shots are doable.

Seize the Moment

Things often happen quickly when the moment of truth arrives during an elk hunt. Split-second decisions will affect the outcome. Once I missed a chance—in a matter of a heartbeat—at an awesome bedded bull I had stalked on a wind-swept mountain. It was a near-perfect stalk; however, I wasn't able to get a bead quickly enough on the big bull as he rose from his bed, turned and vanished into the trees in a split second. He was only 50 yards distant.

Another time I was guiding a hunting partner who had a bull tag. I spotted a herd of six bulls at sunrise. What a sight! Five large bulls stood sentinel, less than 150 yards distant. I watched as steam rose from their breath. A sixth bull fed nearby.

Note the herd bull (background) with a harem of cow elk.

I motioned my partner to move forward and get ready for a shot. Unfortunately, he was too slow, and the bachelor herd quickly vaporized into a stand of aspen.

You have to be pro-active when hunting elk. When an opportunity arises, be decisive and seize the moment! It may well be the only chance you'll get.

Armed with the foregoing knowledge, you should be better prepared for your elk hunt. Just remember: Get up early, hunt all day until the end of legal shooting time and don't quit!

Elk Hunting Success: Just Luck or Good Management?

In 2012, I tagged a 6-point bull elk on the second day of the hunting season, after having been weathered out on opening day. Some folks said I was just lucky. Was I lucky? ABSOLUTELY! But I wasn't "just lucky." It was the fourth time (in a row) that I had shot a bull elk in different locations in this particular WMU on either the first or the second day of the season. So, although luck played a part, something else was at play. That "something else" is a good tactical approach.

The following is a description of what I did to be in the right place at the right time during this elk hunt, and how you could do likewise during your elk hunting forays if you follow this advice. I've been hunting elk in the aspen parkland for many years, but the same principles apply to other areas, such as the boreal forest, foothills, mountains or prairies.

An elk's biggest weakness is its appetite. During my last elk hunt, I scouted an area I was already quite familiar with to make sure the local herds were still active and to

determine where they were feeding. It's not hard to find their feeding areas because they eat grass, being primarily grazing animals. They usually chomp off clumps of grasses, which creates the appearance of craters. A large herd will make a lot of feeding craters over a period of a few days. If you find fresh droppings in feeding areas, you know you're in the game.

Next, I searched out elk tracks to figure out their travel routes to preferred bedding areas. You can't get up too early when elk hunting, so I made it a point to be in position for a shot opportunity well before daylight. I chose a stand just inside an aspen grove within shooting range of a travel lane I thought the local herd would follow to their bedding area after they'd fed. As things turned out, a 6-point bull and three cows were feeding in the area.

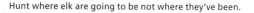

Hunt where elk are going to be not where they've been.

Time spent feeding is the Achille's heel of elk.

I watched them slowly work their way across a field before they disappeared in a draw. When they reappeared, they weren't in the open very long before sauntering into the bush. There just wasn't enough time for a shot. Rats! It's key to be patient at times like this and not give up the chase. So I knew a small herd was nearby, and I decided to stay in the area to see what would happen next.

I moved along the edge of the field in a northerly direction because this is the direction I thought the elk would take if they left the cover of the bush. Nothing happened until about 10:30 AM when, sure enough, first one cow and eventually two others came into a clearing, slowly making their way toward another patch of aspen, chirping and mewling as they travelled. Before long, the herd bull stepped out of the aspen on the trail of the cows. He hesitated just for a moment as he listened for their calls. It was all the time I needed. I extended the legs on my Harris bipod, got into a shooting position, lining up the crosshairs behind his shoulder. At the crack of my rifle he dropped in his tracks, only to get back on his feet and walk a short distance before I hit him a second time, a killing shot. None of this was rocket science, just a matter of connecting the dots and being patient when my initial plan didn't work.

There's a saying: "Luck comes when preparation meets opportunity." Hunting is no different. If you study your quarry, thoroughly scout your hunting area and use the right tools, luck will more than likely come your way.

CHAPTER SEVEN

MAD ABOUT MOOSE

Moose

In Alberta, moose can be found in almost every ecological region. Most are classed as Canada moose, although the smaller but equally impressive Shiras moose inhabit southern Alberta's foothills and mountains.

Alberta moose can reach weights of more than 1000 pounds and can stand taller than 7 feet (2 metres) at the shoulder. Antler spreads can reach 6 feet (1.8 metres) tip to tip, with 60-inch (150-cm) plus bulls taken every year.

- Moose tags (antlered or antlerless) are issued by a draw in Alberta.

- Archery moose seasons typically start in late August or the beginning of September and end at the end of October or November depending on the WMU.

- Antlered and antlerless seasons in the Prairie WMUs run from September 1 to November 30.

- Antlered and antlerless seasons in the Parkland WMUs run from September 1 to November 30, with some minor exceptions in season dates for WMU 936, CFB Wainwright and MWU 248.

- Antlered and antlerless seasons in the Foothills WMUs run from either August 25 or September 1 to November 30.

- Antlered and antlerless seasons in the Mountain WMUs run from either August 25 or September 6 to November 30.

- Antlered and antlerless seasons in the Boreal WMUs run from either August 25 or September 1 to November 30.

- Popular calibres for moose start at 7 mm magnums and range to .338 Win Mag.

Think BIG

Moose hunting has not been my forte. The last time I had a bull moose tag, I spent nine days in the bush without even seeing one,

though I did spot a dozen cows. I guess that's why it's called "hunting" not shooting!

I'll be the first to admit that I'm still a moose-hunting student and have yet to

Moose are often found near lakes and marshlands.

bag one. Mind you, I've only hunted them a few times in recent years because, back in the day when I lived in southern Alberta, it was such a long shot to get drawn that I had little interest in hunting moose, e.g. it would take about 15 years to get drawn for a tag. Moose aren't as glamorous as elk or bighorn sheep, but I have a lot of respect for moose. More recently, I have been on hunts where my son tagged a bull and a cow. So I'm not a total greenhorn when it comes to hunting moose.

The closest I came to taking down a moose was a few years ago when I had a tag for a bull moose in WMU 937, which encompasses the Blackfoot Recreation Area. On a cold November day following a snowfall I cut a track of a wounded moose and took up its trail. Numerous blood splatters made me wonder why the person who shot

Moose often believe their ears before they believe their eyes.

–Don Meredith, writer and biologist on moose reacting to a hunter's moose call grunt

Lanny Amos with a hard-earned bull moose

it wasn't following it. I actually thought I might find it dead but didn't know whether it was a bull or a cow. The trail led me across some clearings into an aspen stand where I thought it would likely be bedded down. Most wounded animals will head for cover; if they're not disturbed, they'll lay down in a state of shock, often bleeding to death. Chase them; however, and they'll get an adrenalin rush, bolt and may never be seen again, even when badly wounded. It was late in the season, November 20, and I didn't want to mess up this chance. I was very careful as I took up the chase, stopping frequently to see if I could spot the wounded animal. After following the trail for about half a mile, I finally spotted what turned out to be a wounded bull about 50 yards ahead of me, standing, watching his back trail and fully alert. Trouble was there were lots of branches and bush between him and me, and only a narrow shot opportunity, off hand, which

is never a good option. I'd have to hit him in the neck to finish him off, and he was facing me, so I didn't have much of a target. I'll never forget this particular moose because it had non-typical antlers and would have been a great trophy with its misshapen beams. Just as I squeezed the trigger the moose turned, and I missed! He bolted and ran away, in high gear. Although I followed his trail for the rest of the afternoon, I never saw him again, which made me think the wound was only superficial.

Most moose hunting in Alberta is now on a draw, and the tags are highly coveted because moose are prime meat animals—great eating. As a bonus, large bulls are spectacular trophies. Because moose hunting is so popular, it can take more than a decade to draw a tag in heavily subscribed zones, especially for antlered (bull) moose. Despite their enormous size,

The moose-calling season in Alberta is in late September to early October.

moose are surprisingly agile animals and can move very quietly through the bush. They have good hearing and a keen sense of smell, but their vision is poor. Their key habitat is boreal forest, but they're not uncommon in Alberta's foothills and mountains and are expanding their range in the aspen parklands and prairies.

Strategy

The mating season is late September to early October, which is the calling season when bulls will respond to calls. It is one of the most popular times to hunt bull moose because they are more mobile than at any other time during the hunting season and are therefore easier to spot. Following the rut, bulls tend to band together in bachelor groups (much like bull elk) in remote areas and can be hard to locate because they're seemingly all in one spot. It's not unusual to find groups of four or five bulls in a herd in late October and November. This makes them hard to hunt because they're not spread throughout their usual range. However, there are exceptions. For example, in mid-November 2016, I spotted a massive solitary bull bedded in the shelter of an aspen stand. This bull had already shed its right antler, which was odd.

For November seasons, it may be more expedient to apply for an antlerless tag instead of an antlered tag if you're after moose meat because cows are often easier to locate. On the other hand, you'll also run into solitary moose during November, so you should look for both bachelor groups and single animals. Odds-wise, the success rate for drawing an antlered moose tag in some areas might only be 10 percent, whereas it might be 25 percent for antlerless moose in the same area. Consequently, the chances of being drawn for a cow moose tag are more than 2.5 times greater. Keep this in mind when strategizing your chances of being drawn successfully.

Because of their enormous size, it's important to hunt moose with a group of hunters, and even then it can be a back-breaking job to field dress such large animals and get the meat back to camp.

Moose can weigh over 1000 pounds and are too large for one man to move by himself.

CHAPTER EIGHT

White-tailed Deer and Mule Deer Hunts

White-tailed Deer

White-tails are the most abundant deer species in Alberta and the most popular to hunt. Although Alberta's white-tail bucks average about 200 pounds, mature bucks can be very large with some exceeding 300 pounds. They're found in virtually every region of the province but are particularly abundant in the prairie, parkland and southern boreal zones.

- Archery seasons generally start in late August, running until the end of October or November.

- Rifle seasons start in late October or November 1 and close on November 30. The rut typically occurs in mid-November.

- Huge-antlered whitetails are taken every year in Alberta, making the province a premier destination for those seeking that once-in-a-lifetime buck.

- Calibres for white-tailed deer are similar to those used for mule deer: the .25-06, .270, 7 mm and on up to the .30 caliber magnums are all good choices.

Scoring on White-tails: Make Your Own Luck!

Just when you think you've seen it all, a white-tailed buck will do something completely unexpected. I've spotted them bedded down sunning themselves beside busy highways in broad daylight. I saw a buck in pursuit of a doe dart among several hunters stationed along a country road at high noon without a shot being fired. Once I watched a record-book buck amble along in a ditch beside a road in a no-shooting zone, not 50 yards away, in midday. I've had lovestruck bucks practically run into my truck several times during the rut. I've watched does in heat being followed by mindless bucks at all hours of the day. I saw a near-record-book buck stand motionless, at sunrise, at the edge of an aspen stand not 200 yards distant for more than a minute—with its breath clearly visible in my binoculars—on the last day of the season. Too bad my tag was already filled.

What does this tell you? For one thing, anything is possible when you are hunting

White-tailed deer buck

white-tailed deer. So expect the unexpected or be doomed to miss out on some great opportunities. All bets are off during the rut, in particular!

Despite the aforementioned events, which were largely fortuitous, you're better off making your own luck when pursuing white-tailed bucks. Such events do happen, but if you think you're going to consistently fill your tag by playing hunting roulette, you'll be disappointed.

There are several ways to hunt white-tailed deer: pushing bush, spot and stalk, stand hunting and using calls (i.e., doe bleats and rattling antlers) from stands. Bow hunters recommend stand hunting as being the most reliable of all your options.

So, how do you make your own luck and get into a shooting position to take advantage of shot opportunities.

For starters, when out hunting, stay positive and try to create opportunities by carrying the play to the deer. You will be rewarded with opportunities to take a good buck if you hunt smart, but you need to be in the right place at the right time.

Most hunters who are fortunate to tag a white-tailed buck hunt strategically to maximize their shot opportunities. It all starts with scouting. Successful hunters begin getting to know their hunting area before the hunting season. They have a good idea where both the prime feeding areas and key game trails are located by scouting for deer sign. Many keen hunters use trail cameras to get forensic evidence that bucks are in the area.

Second, strategize by capitalizing on deer behaviour during key phases of the rut: the pre-rut, the rut proper and the post-rut.

Pre-rut
During the pre-rut, successful deer hunters generally use blinds in sight of scrape lines and game trails and use their stealth to outsmart deer. They are on stand before sunrise and hunt throughout the day, not just at dawn and dusk, because they know

Familiarize yourself with your hunting area before opening date and look for rubs to narrow down where bucks range.

The rut is a great time to use deer calls, especially a doe bleat, which will draw bucks in from considerable distances under ideal conditions. A grunt tube will also bring in eager bucks during the rut. Have confidence in doe bleats and grunt tubes; they do work, as does deer rattling, especially during the peak of the rut.

There's also a good chance of catching a buck bird-dogging during the rut. Keep your eyes peeled for bucks in the open following the trail of a doe, especially in the morning.

Post-rut

During the post-rut, successful hunters remain on a good stand as long as necessary for a good shot opportunity. They are prepared to sit and wait all week long, not freezing to death because they are properly clothed. They know it's necessary to be persistent to enjoy success.

Depending on the amount of hunting pressure, it's possible to catch a buck out in the open at any time of the day checking his scrapes and looking for late-season receptive does. Chances are usually better at daybreak and dusk, the best times to watch a scrape line, when bucks visit their scrapes for signs of does still in estrus. Take a stand a ways back from a scrape line and pay attention. Bucks often appear seemingly out of nowhere. They're on full alert. When they reach a scrape, they'll check for scent. Next, they'll paw the scrape to clear it of snow. Sometimes, they'll rake nearby shrubs and trees with their antlers to leave their own scent. All of these things happen rather quickly, so be prepared for a shot opportunity before they move on to another scrape.

With this information in mind, you'll be well positioned to tag a trophy buck during the next hunting season.

that bucks will often travel all day long. Granted, they also hunt feeding areas, which are prime spots, but they play the odds that the chances of shooting a decent buck are better by hunting specific locations between feeding and bedding areas, particularly near pinch points.

One of the best ways to tag a buck during the pre-rut is to set up a ground blind near a travel lane between feeding and bedding areas, especially during the morning, and then watch for deer activity and ambush bucks.

The Rut Proper

The rut can be one of the most difficult times to shoot white-tailed bucks because they will spend about 48 hours with a doe in heat before the love affair ends. They can be very secretive and elusive during this time. It's usually easier to tag a buck during the pre-rut and post-rut periods.

Mule Deer

Mule deer are one of the West's quintessential game species. They are big-bodied and wily, and they sport impressive racks, so it's no wonder people travel from all over North America to hunt Alberta's "mulies."

Mule deer are found throughout much of the province, but most commonly in the western foothills and southern prairies. They are much more likely to be found in the mountains than their white-tailed cousins. In Alberta, mule deer bucks average about 250 pounds, but mature animals in excess of 300 pounds are not uncommon. And for those seeking record book–qualifying deer, mule bucks exceeding 190 points are taken practically every year across their range.

• The archery season for mule deer typically starts in late August and runs until the end of October or November depending on the WMU.

• Rifle seasons vary (some of which are split seasons in prairies WMUs), depending on the zone and WMU, generally starting November 1 and closing on November 30. The rut generally occurs in late November.

• Because the terrain can vary greatly, from dense woods to open alpine meadows, calibre options range from the .25-06, through the .270s to 7mms, .280 Remington, .308 Winchester, .30-06 and the .300 magnums.

Myles Radford with a late-season white-tailed buck

There are some huge mule deer in Alberta's Rockies.

The Skinny on Alberta's Mule Deer

I doubt that most Albertans have seen mule deer hunting as good as it was around 2005 and 2006, certainly not during my lifetime, in terms of their overall abundance, distribution and especially the number of outstanding trophies that were taken. Actually, it was almost too good to be true, and deer numbers subsequently crashed after a series of tough winters beginning in 2010. The years following the period from 2005 to 2010 marked a turning point in the abundance of deer in Alberta and serve as a lesson regarding how things can change for the worse.

For the statistics buffs, in 2006, the number of mule deer hunters in Alberta was 33,638, with an estimated harvest of 18,286 animals and a whopping 54 percent success rate—the highest overall for elk, mule deer, moose and white-tailed deer that year.

Since 1997, Sports Scene Publications Inc. has presented the Annual Hunters of the Year award for elk, mule deer and white-tailed deer with the following winners in the mule deer category:

Year	Winner	Score	WMU	Location
1997	Peter Egge	178 $^5/_8$	204	Galahad
1998*	Andy Charchun	192 $^2/_8$	238	Vermillion
1999	Hal Czeck	180 $^5/_8$	158	Drumheller
2000*	Roy Jr. LeBlanc	196 $^3/_8$	160	Hussar
2001*	Karey Seward	181 $^5/_8$	104	Foremost
2002	Jerry Ewasiuk	170 $^7/_8$	unknown	Veteran
2003	Sheldon Coderre	201 $^2/_8$	124	Medicine Hat
2004*	Cyril Paquin	198 $^6/_8$	527	Peace River
2005	Brady McLachlan	187 $^5/_8$	305	Pincher
2006*	Randy Repas	200 $^4/_8$	151	Jenner
2007*	Colin Campbell	196 $^4/_8$	208	Big Valley
2008*	Jan Allen	196 $^7/_8$	110	Pincher Creek
2009*	Ryan Hickle	200 $^2/_8$	160	Hanna
2010*	Kevin Gustafson	198 $^3/_8$	521	Debolt
2011	Simone Dold	176 $^7/_8$	158	Three Hills
2012*	Chase Heck	195 $^3/_8$	200	Czar
2013*	Michelle Kuny	187 $^4/_8$	246	Leduc
2014*	Taylor Johnson	200 $^5/_8$	234	Chauvin
2015*	Joshua Stewart	187 $^5/_8$	158	Three Hills
2016*	John W. Adkins	203 $^2/_8$	212	Okotoks

* Alberta Hunter of the Year award winner

One can't help but notice that mule deer won the prestigious Alberta Hunter of the Year award in 14 of the 19 years on record, in a province that's world renowned for monster white-tailed deer. Well, the secret is finally out. Alberta is also renowned for some terrific mule deer, and the above records illustrate just how large some of the trophies actually are. I'd be remiss if I did not mention that women took Alberta top mule deer four times during this period!

Also of note is the fact that these record deer are coming from all over the province: the prairies, foothills and boreal forest. I know from personal experience there are some outstanding bucks for the taking in Alberta's Rockies. The best-eating mule deer I've feasted on was a giant taken in September by my hunting partner in the Carbondale drainage in 1969, which weighed in at the local butcher shop at 169 pounds, dressed.

Trophy mule deer are one of Alberta's most challenging big game animals to hunt.

Jack Graham, Past President of the AFGA and dean of Alberta Boone and Crockett official scorers, told me in an interview that perhaps as many as six mule deer might make the book annually, with most coming from the Mighty Peace River country. Graham said that the Peace-country bucks usually have massive-beamed antlers that tend to score better than their prairie cousins, which have relatively light beams by comparison.

Alberta's historical mule deer population hit a plateau in the 1950s with numbers estimated at more than 150,000. Populations then declined in the 1960s and early 1970s—estimated at fewer than 60,000 animals—as a result of some tough winters and a rather liberal harvest regime, according to government records. The population increased to an estimated 86,000 deer in 1985 just prior to the publication of the Management Plan for Mule Deer in Alberta (1989) under a more conservative harvest regime following some successive mild winters. This somewhat

dated management plan is posted online on the then Sustainable Resource Development (SRD) website (Note: SRD subsequently became Environment and Sustainable Resources Development (ESRD) and then Environment and Parks (AEP) in 2015.

One of the goals of the management plan was to increase the provincial mule deer herd to 97,000 from the 1985 estimate while providing a variety of hunting opportunities (e.g., any buck, trophy bucks, antlerless deer and archery only areas).

Up until around 2010, Alberta's mule deer provincial population estimate was about 185,000. This is one of the main reasons why the then SRD adopted a liberal set of hunting regulations to try to curb its skyrocketing growth. During the 1970s and '80s, government officials tried various hunting regulations for mule deer, finally deciding that to produce some quality bucks it would be necessary to factor in better escapement into the management regime. Previous to this era, regulations such as the old 4-point rule had been tried with limited success. Under this system hunters could shoot any 4-point buck. Biologists determined that the best way to achieve better carryover of mature bucks was to use a special licence draw for both antlered and antlerless mule deer, with the caveat that hunters may not possess both an antlered mule deer special licence and a (general) mule deer licence. In 2007, most of Alberta's WMUs were being managed under this system, which received widespread support among most hunters because it created relatively large populations throughout the province with some dandy bucks.

While the bighorn sheep is widely viewed as Alberta's most renowned trophy animal, and rightly so, mule deer are beginning to finally get some of the recognition they deserve. In the 2007 edition of Alberta's Professional Outfitter—the official magazine of the Alberta Professional Outfitters Society—the editor wrote: "...one of the best-kept secrets in the mule deer hunting world is the province of Alberta. Most hunters are surprised to find that Alberta holds the World Record for Non-Typical Mule Deer at 355 2/8 Boone and Crockett points. A record that has stood for over 80 years and may never be broken." This phenomenal record deer is the famous "Broder Buck," taken by Ed Broder in 1926 near Chip Lake west of Edmonton. It is one of the most outstanding of all big game trophies ever taken in North America.

Alberta's mule deer populations are still in pretty good shape despite a few tough winters in the past several years. More and more big bucks are being taken each year, as the limited-entry draw allows for added escapement of bucks, which continue to grow larger and larger antlers up to a point. Milder winters, when they do occur, also promote better survival.

Mule deer that the author tagged after seeing only its ears while it was bedded down.

Mad About Mule Deer!

I've taken mule deer in the mountains, foothills and prairies, and each area has to be hunted a bit differently. If I've learned anything about hunting these deer, it's that they're pretty sneaky, regardless of where you're hunting—maybe even more so than white-tailed deer. Why? It's all a matter of deer behaviour. Mule deer evolved in the open spaces of western North America and use this space to their advantage. Hunting them can be like playing a game of hide-and-seek. They stick to places where they have good sight lines, can spot trouble coming a long way off and they'll use whatever cover is around to hide, virtually in plain sight by staying still and blending in with the local terrain.

So where are you going to find mule deer? Think browse! Mulies are mainly browsers—they like to eat the tips of willows, prickly rose, Saskatoons, chokecherry and red osier, for example, during the hunting season. Where are you going to find browse? Well, for the most part you'll find these bushes in riparian areas in the bottoms of coulees or draws, or on north-facing slopes where moisture levels should be higher than elsewhere. Mulies also have a taste for cereal crops and alfalfa in farming country, and any source of water, such as a spring or artificial watering trough, will attract deer.

Where will the deer be bedded down? Try looking along the edges of river breaks, coulees, timberline and in stands of trees—again, places with good sight lines. Mulies like to see what's going on. They will travel a fair distance, more than a mile from bedding areas to feeding areas on the prairies and in the foothills. The trick is to watch the feeding areas in the morning and evening. Don't forget open spaces, though. I've seen many mulies out in the open during the day.

Mule deer buck and harem of does

Hunters should continue to be patient during hunting trips and wait for whatever happens next; being observant is paramount.

–Duane Radford, writer and biologist

A big buck usually sticks to cover when on the move, much like a white-tailed deer. That cover might be a creek bottom or a line of trees, even a draw, anything to break its outline. If pushed, it may bed down in the smallest patch of bush and sit still just like a jackrabbit. The trick is to get behind it, and downwind, so that you can make a stalk.

If a deer is spooked and on the move, do not attempt a running shot. Mule deer can be tough to hit when they start to bound, and they can hit speeds of over 30 miles per hour. Stay cool, and wait for it to stop. If mulies have a weakness, it's their tendency to stop, turn broadside and take a look back when they think they're out of the danger zone. Be ready for this moment, and make your shot count. You may not get another. Remember, they like to have some space between themselves and potential danger.

Where the season opens early, in late summer or early autumn, mule deer bucks will often still be in bachelor herds. I've seen mule deer bucks in bachelor herds of two to five animals, and up to over two dozen at a time. All those eyes make for good watchdogs, so be careful during your stalk.

Don't think that shooting rutting mule deer is a pushover; it isn't. Quite often the harem is on red alert all day long, and with a dozen or more skittish does on the lookout, a herd can be hard to approach. I've seen some herds bolt when they see a hunter more than a mile away and clear the horizon as they make for parts unknown. A careful stalk will put you in shooting range, though. Keep out of sight and don't move if the herd can see you.

A buck on its own during the rut is another matter. I've seen some that are as dumb as a sack of hammers; they are no different than rutting white-tailed bucks, which might try to run over you if they are on the trail of a doe in heat.

Mule Deer: Walk or Wait?

"I can't believe how many deer we're seeing!" exclaimed my hunting partner as we enjoyed our midday lunch. He was right; we had seen more than a dozen bucks—at all hours of the day—during the past two days, and I had passed up several shooters in the hopes of finding an exceptional trophy. What were we doing right to be seeing so many deer, all day long, from sunrise to sundown?

For starters, mule deer behaviour can be exasperating, depending on the time of the year that you're hunting, for example pre-rut, during the rut or post rut. Consequently, you should vary your hunting tactics depending on the time of the year, regardless of whether you are hunting in the mountains, foothills, parklands or open prairies in Alberta.

Male mule deer form bachelor groups in March, stay together until late October then disperse before the November rut. Although most of these bachelor groups are relatively small, with several males being most common, I have seen herds of more than two dozen bucks on some occasions, and groups of a dozen are not rare. Don't necessarily be looking for solitary animals prior to November; rather, as a rule, look for a herd of bucks.

By the second week in November, dominant bucks will gather a harem of does, and this group will stay together, more or less, until the end of the month. By the last week of November, most of does have been bred, so you may run into solitary bucks and does, or groups of does, often with bucks nearby. You are likely to see solitary bucks in pursuit of does in heat at any time of the day during the last three weeks of November. After the peak of the rut, bucks tend to gravitate to winter ranges, where they may form bachelor groups again or remain alone. Some bucks may appear to be dumbstruck during the rut and will hang out in the general area of does all day long. I've seen other bucks that are as cagey as ever, only travelling at dawn and dusk, always beside escape cover and usually out of range.

On a recent hunt on the Alberta prairies, I recall watching a mature mule deer buck bed down after its morning feed. The buck made its bed high on the slope of a rugged coulee and reminded me of a bighorn ram as it pawed the ground and

> ### It would have made the "book."
>
> The trophy would have qualified for entry in the legendary Boone and Crockett Club record book.

settled in for the day. There was no way to approach it without being seen. No wonder it had a rack to die for.

Regardless of where you are hunting, look for mule deer in or near open spaces and along the edge of open spaces, whether it is an alpine meadow in the Rocky Mountains, beside a stand of aspens in the foothills or parklands, or along the breaks of rivers and coulees in the prairies. The best locations are generally those near rugged terrain where mule deer will take cover if trouble materializes.

If anything alarms mule deer, they'll bolt from their beds or feeding areas and put some space between themselves and whatever frightened them. They can cover a lot of terrain in a hurry with their bounding gait. This calls for a lot of spotting and strategic thinking before deciding on a stalk. They are creatures of habit; however, and tend to favour their home range. Consequently, if you do inadvertently send them running, all is not lost. Often, they will return to the neighbourhood later in the day or the next day.

What sort of tactics should you use to capitalize on their tendencies, at various times? For example, should you try to walk them down or wait them out? Walking them down entails either tracking them if there is snow on the ground or trying to still hunt them, as best possible, in the open terrain they inhabit.

Waiting them out involves sitting tight at various strategic stands and then waiting for them to make the first move before you decide on a course of action: shoot or execute a stalk. I tend to use both tactics on any given mule deer hunt, depending on the weather. If the winds are calm and the skies clear, I prefer to walk and look for mule deer in areas they're likely to be found. I'll walk until I find a good area

It's a good idea to take to the chase during late season hunts for prairie mule deer.

where I can see a lot of country and just watch to see what happens.

During a recent mule deer hunt, I positioned myself on a finger of high ground near the edge of a prairie coulee where it fanned out into the uplands. I kept my back to some aspens to break my silhouette. In less than half an hour, I spotted four separate trophy mule deer from this one vantage point. Some were alone, and some were in pursuit of does. Just sitting tight, waiting and watching often pays dividends.

If the weather is poor (e.g., cold, windy or overcast), I may stick close to a vehicle and see what happens because mule deer tend not to be active on blustery days. I've found that when it gets −20°C, mule deer don't move around much at all, regardless of the stage of the rut. They prefer to stay

put in a sheltered area and wait for the weather to improve. Also, whether you're hunting in the mountains, foothills or prairies, deep snow will drive the deer from their summer and fall range to wintering grounds regardless of when it falls.

I have seen as many mule deer during midday in November, in particular, as at dawn or dusk, especially bucks. You have to be patient and watch openings between likely feeding and bedding areas to spot them. Also be alert and don't daydream. Mule deer can cross an opening at any moment, and you may only have a few seconds to pick them up in your binoculars, make a judgment call regarding their size and decide if they're worth a stalk. The key is to be in a spot where you can see a lot of ground in front of you and to keep your eyes open.

Don Meridith with a mule buck taken by waiting it out

I have taken mule deer throughout Alberta, in the mountains, foothills, prairies and parklands, and I've learned that you have to keep your options open if you expect to connect on mule deer on any given hunt. Some days it pays to start walking, while at other times you may just as well sit tight and wait for a deer to materialize. Should you walk or wait? It depends on the weather, the time of year, hunting pressure and a lot of other factors.

The Land of the Deer Hunter

Albertans are blessed with a wealth of mule deer and white-tailed deer hunting opportunities. Both species are found in every wildlife management unit (WMU). Deer numbers remain relatively high provincially, with literally hundreds of thousands of animals in Alberta. If it's November, the deer season is top of mind for most hunters. Who knows what next year will bring because Mother Nature can be cruel; periodically, a severe winter causes a major crash in deer numbers. Hunters must adapt with different hunting techniques for the various regions in Alberta and consider variability in the quality of deer in each region when deciding where to hunt.

This section contains information on deer hunting in Alberta's five major hunting zones (mountains, foothills, prairie, parkland and boreal) to help hunters strategize approaches that will pay off in the field. I've hunted deer in all the zones in Alberta, some more than others. While numbers of deer may be high provincially, they do vary considerably among the various regions and over time; consequently, you have to use a different hunting approach for each region to be successful.

Mountains

The mountains zone is probably the most difficult of all regions to hunt both mule deer and white-tailed deer because of the rugged terrain and uncertain weather. The mountains often produce some huge mule deer bucks but are not known to be great producers of trophy white-tailed bucks.

Typically, if the weather holds, mule deer bucks are found in the same terrain as bighorn sheep and elk from late August until the end of October—high alpine country—and can often be spotted in bachelor herds until just prior to the rut. Does can be found in valley bottoms. During the rut, mule deer bucks are notorious for their mobility, so be on the look-out for deer on the move, not unlike bighorn sheep rams in late October. Once it starts to snow, mule deer will migrate to lower elevations. A heavy snowfall will trigger a mass migration of mule deer toward their winter range in valley bottoms and the adjacent eastern foothills. You'll have to take the chase to be successful hunting mule deer in Alberta's mountains by covering a lot of ground and by extensive spotting with scopes and binoculars.

White-tailed deer are generally found in the valley bottoms and riparian areas but have expanded their range during the past few decades well into the headwaters of many drainages. It's really quite surprising where they can be found these days. Most white-tailed deer hunting will be a matter of low-percentage chance opportunities in valley bottoms.

Foothills

Conditions in Alberta's foothills are almost always better for hunting both mule deer and white-tailed deer than in the adjacent mountains. Over the past couple of decades, the foothills have produced some excellent mule deer because the draw system has greatly reduced hunting pressure and allowed bucks to become mature and realize their trophy potential. Large white-tails are less common.

Deer distribution is more widespread and predictable in Alberta's foothills. They're

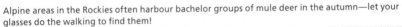
Alpine areas in the Rockies often harbour bachelor groups of mule deer in the autumn—let your glasses do the walking to find them!

After antlers are fully grown, the velvet is shed, usually by later summer.

often found in agricultural areas, particularly white-tailed deer. Alfalfa fields act like magnets, and deer will be nearby. Pre-season scouting trips will help you determine where concentrations of both species are located. Because much of the land is privately owned, it's essential to obtain permission prior to going hunting. Don't wait for opening day to get permission to hunt. Get out early and approach landowners before there's a lineup. Look for mule deer on south-facing slopes, especially on the leeward side of ridgelines. Drive backcountry roads in search of white-tails and set up stands in strategic locations once you've located prime areas. White-tailed deer will often bed down amid shrubs in coulees to get out of the wind.

Prairie

The prairie zone is a Mecca for deer hunters. The Milk River and Milk River Ridge, Cypress Hills and Red Deer River are all famed deer hunting spots. Although it takes a nearly perfectly symmetrical white-tailed deer in this region to make the record book, the prairies regularly produce some of Alberta's top mule deer. Also, it's not unusual to see high ratios of bucks to does in many WMUs, so your chances of success are excellent. I'd rate the prairies very high for the serious mule deer hunter. Because of the extensive agriculture in this area, it's only natural that deer will be associated with alfalfa crops, while sources of water on native prairie are important to mule deer.

Successful hunters do extensive pre-season scouting to search out deer in creek bottoms and coulees. While in the field, they'll hunt the entire day, from sunrise to sundown. Spot-and-stalk hunting works best.

Successful hunters generally take to the chase when hunting mule deer. However, to be successful hunting white-tails, hunters focus on specific areas known to hold white-tailed deer and stand hunt. Most

Prairie deer hunts require plenty of walking.

trophy white-tailed bucks are ambushed. I found one such area where I shot large white-tailed bucks four out of five years from exactly the same stand on one particular ranch. Successful hunters will glass extensively for mule deer and use stealth to bag a white-tailed deer. Good binoculars are essential in either case.

Flat-shooting rifles are a must when hunting both species, and hunters should expect shots in the 200- to 300-yard range. My advice is to sight in your rifle for 225 yards to make it shoot even flatter.

Parkland

Most of Alberta's top white-tailed deer are taken in the parkland zone. This zone also produces many outstanding mule deer, whose distribution is a bit spottier (except in the far eastern WMUs, where both species abound). In some of these particular WMU's there were upwards of 10,000 deer during years of peak numbers, but no longer. The number of deer have probably been cut in half or more.

The Battle River Breaks are renowned for producing some of Alberta's best deer. In most parkland areas, it's important to be mobile and search out mule deer, whereas stand hunting is tops in my books for hunting white-tails.

Boreal

Although some hunters may consider the boreal zone fringe deer range, many outdoorsmen and women in the know claim that record white-tailed deer are there for

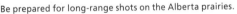

Be prepared for long-range shots on the Alberta prairies.

The parklands produce some of Alberta's top white-tailed deer.

the taking. The Peace River Breaks are well known for some of Alberta's top mule deer. Although hunting conditions can often be tough in the boreal region, the persistent hunter can score with exceptional deer, if he is prepared to hunt hard under rigorous conditions. Still hunting, stand hunting and spot-and-stalk hunting are all productive. Most of the top white-tailed deer are taken during the rut by stand hunting, especially in agricultural areas. Patience is essential. A hunter may have to sit on a stand for an entire week for one good shot opportunity.

As a result of relatively low hunting pressure, both species of deer are much more active during the day than in the prairie and parkland zones, whereas they can be almost nocturnal where hunting pressure is high. Hunters should capitalize on the opportunities that result from low hunting pressure as well as the greater percentage of older-aged bucks.

Early vs. Late Season Deer Hunts

Whether you choose to hunt deer during the early season or late season is largely a matter of personal choice. However, consider many factors when you're planning your deer hunt, and the following information should help you make a decision that suits your situation.

For most Alberta hunters, the deer-hunting season is synonymous with the month of November, at least for rifle hunters. They are then faced with the question of whether to opt for an early-season trip (often tied in with opening day) or perhaps a late-season trip (to close out the season). Some places have special late season hunts (such as CFB Wainwright, better known as Camp Wainwright), which feature only late-season deer hunting.

I've hunted both early and late in November as well as during the December hunts that were suspended in 2010, during the general season and in Camp Wainwright. I have also hunted in the non-resident season in Saskatchewan. The pros and cons of early- and late-season hunts should be taken into consideration when trip planning. For example, should trophy hunters opt for opening day before the animals are spooked to bag that big buck? Or should they wait until later in the season in the hopes that they'll see more animals, one of which might be the buck of their dreams?

Familiarity of the Terrain

If you are hunting new grounds, I'd opt for an early-season hunt. However, if you are familiar with an area, you can go either way, or you might want to hunt both early and late in the season.

Size of the Deer Population

Although it should be obvious, it bears repeating that the annual deer population will be at its highest level during the early season, so hunters will have all options open if they start hunting on opening day. Many of the largest deer are also taken on opening day, especially by local hunters who have done their homework and have patterned the quality bucks. Bow hunters who didn't tag out during the bow season often switch to rifle hunting and close their tags on bucks that eluded them during the bow season.

Pre-season scouting and spotting are of fundamental importance for the early-season hunter when it comes to bagging a big buck. It's not just hunting mortality that decreases the number of bucks after opening day; many bucks are also killed by vehicles. I've seen all manner of both white-tail and mule deer bucks killed

The weather can often be brutal during late season hunts.

during the rut by vehicles and have had several close calls myself. There's no question that late-season hunters have slimmer pickings some years if hunting conditions are favourable for early-season hunters. The pool of deer and big bucks diminishes with each passing day, and for this reason, many hunters try to get in some hunting early in the season if at all possible. If you can't get out until later on, you could try focusing on more remote and inaccessible hunting territory, where hunting pressure would likely have been relatively low.

Deer Behaviour

During the early season, deer are relatively undisturbed and less wary of hunters, except where bow-hunting pressure is high. By the time the late season rolls around, deer have usually been disturbed by both bow and rifle hunters and are often wary. There's likely no place in Alberta where this is more obvious than in Camp Wainwright, where the deer are also affected by military operations. I'd rate these deer as the some of the most high-strung big game animals I've ever hunted. In some years, particularly if access has been favourable, deer are really skittish near the end of the season and will bolt if they see a vehicle or hunter. More stealth is essential to hunt deer during the late season, especially on the prairies.

During the early season deer tend to be spread out throughout deer country because food and water are generally in abundance. Look for deer just about everywhere because they will occupy their entire available habitat. However, during the late season, deer tend to be more concentrated around food sources and water, so they are usually much easier to locate. They are also much more predictable to pattern when the weather turns cold.

It can be hard to pattern deer during early season hunts because it's more difficult to find sign.

It's easier to find deer sign during the late season.

Visibility of Deer

It's rare to have snow during the first part of the deer hunting season in November, and this makes it hard to spot deer, find travel lanes, beds, droppings and other sign, but easier to find shed antlers, which stand out on dry ground. Keep your eyes peeled for sheds; they define the home range of bucks, which can live to a ripe age where hunting pressure is relatively low. The big buck that dropped its sheds might be just around the corner in such areas.

There's no question that it's much easier to spot deer and to judge antler size when there is snow cover. Dark antlers, in particular, stand out like a beacon and are much easier to size up. It's also easier to locate bedding areas and other sign, which will help you determine the most productive spots to set up your stands.

Deer Activity Levels

The activity level of deer tends to be more confined to prime feeding times in the morning and evening during the early season, so it can be harder to locate bucks, in particular. However, the rut will be on during the late season for both mule deer and white-tailed deer. Bucks are highly mobile during the rut, so expect to see them on the move throughout the entire day from sunrise until sunset during the late season. This is quite an advantage over early season hunts, so many more deer will be sighted. The rut is one of the few times when larger bucks drop their guard and move about during the day. However, expect both bucks and does to bed down in shelter during storms and on windy days.

Vehicle Access

Roads and trails are often hard and dry and generally present few driving challenges during the early season. During the late season, however, you'll probably need a four-wheel drive vehicle to get around in deer country, and even then you might get stuck. Late season hunts often present all sorts of logistical issues if the weather is cold:

- Plug in your block heater.

- Winter tires are a must, and you might even need tire chains.

- Pack a shovel in case you get stuck.

- Don't leave water in your vehicle overnight; it will freeze.

During some years, I've had to reschedule the timing of late season hunts many times because of inclement weather, and I have also been stuck in camp because of blizzards on more than one occasion. If you're hunting late season, ensure that you have suitable clothing and footwear to hunt in cold weather. Where permitted by law, also have suitable camouflage clothing of appropriate

Be prepared to hunt under brutal conditions in late November.

colours for both autumn and winter conditions. I'll pack camouflage outfits that can be used for conditions with and without snow on the ground regardless of when I'm hunting in November because conditions can and do change.

They grew out of the ground.

–Jack Graham, Past-President and Boone and Crockett Club Official Measurer (retired) of the Alberta Fish and Game Association referencing how game animals often seemingly appear out of nowhere.

Hunting Mobility

During the early season, you can dress light, be more mobile, often cover more ground and usually hunt all day compared to many late season hunts when the weather can be brutal. It's also usually easier to be quiet in the field during the early season, which makes it easier to approach deer. In the late season, there can be issues with freezing temperatures, and deep snow can hinder your mobility. Furthermore, if there's been a heavy snowfall followed by a warm spell, watch out for crusted snow, which makes it next to impossible to be quiet when hunting.

Field Dressing Deer

Field dressing deer can be a bit messy at times without snow cover during the early season. However, there are usually few issues related to field dressing deer or cleaning up and handling carcasses during late season hunts unless temperatures are well below freezing. (For more detailed information on field dressing, see Chapter 15, page 209.)

During warm weather, deer may have to be taken to the nearest meat locker or butchered quickly before spoilage sets in. I've been on some hunts in mid- to late-November in Alberta when temperatures have hit 20˚C to 25˚C for example, far too warm to hang a carcass. It's essential to skin a deer as soon as practical after it's been shot during warm weather to cool the carcass, otherwise the meat will spoil quickly. Ditto for some late season hunts because a thick hide can retain heat, which can also lead to spoilage.

Get the hide off deer even during late season hunts to cool the carcass.

It is usually much easier to get a deer into a butcher shop in the early part of the season; there won't be a long lineup at sausage shops. If it's not cool enough to hang a deer at your residence in the early season, you may have to take it to a meat locker. During the late part of the season, it's often much more difficult to get a deer into a butcher shop, which can be stacked with carcasses, and there will already be a long lineup at sausage shops. In my home town of Edmonton it's not unusual to have queues at the more popular sausage shops with a waiting list in the order of a couple of months or more during and after the hunting season. However, late in the season it's often cool enough to hang a deer at your residence to let it age for several days and tenderize the meat.

Tracking Wounded Game

During the early season, it can be difficult to find wounded game if there is no snow on the ground. Actually, blood trails can be difficult to follow at the best of times, but it's much easier when there is snow on the ground. (For more detailed information on tracking wounded game, see Chapter 13, page 195.)

Deer Calls

If you use bleat calls and grunt tubes, I'd go for a late-season hunt. For white-tailed deer rattling enthusiasts, mid-November during the rut is probably the best time.

Busting BIG Bucks!

It's not getting any easier to bust a big buck; consequently, hunters in search of trophy deer are always looking for an edge. This section contains tips on taking trophy deer, starting with the old adage: "If you're after big bucks, don't shoot the small ones!" There will be seasons where you won't fill your tag, but that's the price you'll have to be willing to pay if you're holding

I always pack a grunt tube and a deer bleat to attract bucks.

out for a trophy buck. For example, I passed on several great mule deer bucks the last two times I had a tag because I have high standards and am prepared to go home skunked if I don't see an outstanding shooter.

Locate Top-producing WMUs

One key to success is your choice of hunting territory. If you're after big bucks, hunt areas that produce big bucks. Go to the top-producing WMUs and determine the prime locations in these areas. The following tips will help you find out where the top-producing areas are located in Alberta:

- Search the local record books and make a list of the locations where the largest animals have been taken historically.

- Check out the annual provincial records because conditions change.

- Get in touch with provincial and local Boone and Crockett Club Official Measurers to ask them where the largest deer are being taken.

None of these sources can tell you the exact location where the largest trophies come from, but they will point you in the right direction. My old friend, Jim Wiebe, official scorer with the Saskatchewan Wildlife Federation, fondly refers to an area in Saskatchewan as the "golden triangle" because of its reputation for producing the world's largest white-tailed bucks. If you do some detective work, you'll find there are similar areas in Alberta that typically yield the largest deer.

Narrow Down Your Prime Hunting Territory

Once you've decided which WMU you're going to hunt, narrow down your prime hunting territory by doing some surveillance of the general area. Although I've hunted many different places in search of big bucks, over the past several years I've focused on one particular WMU. I chose this area over several others through a process of elimination based on first-hand knowledge and deer sightings. About 10,000 deer had been counted in aerial surveys in the area when the population peaked, so the odds of seeing many deer are high, although numbers have been down in the past several years because of a couple of tough winters and slow population re-bound.

Scouting

How should you actually hunt your chosen WMU, and what can you expect during your first time out and thereafter? You'll have to do some scouting to get the lay of the land and obtain permission to hunt on private land. Before the hunting season begins, drive around the WMU and determine which areas look promising, then ask the landowners for permission to hunt on their property.

Timing

When I first started hunting, I was under the impression that if you wanted to shoot a big buck, it was important to go hunting on opening day. I've subsequently found that opening day might be one of the worst times to hunt for big deer. Actually, I don't even get excited about hunting deer until after the opening week of the season. Why? For one thing, unless you've got a big buck nailed down, hunting pressure alone on opening day can make deer skittish and hard to hunt. If the countryside is swarming with hunters, deer tend to lay low.

These days, I focus on hunting when the rut picks up for both white-tailed deer in mid-November and for mule deer in late November. Bucks drop their guard during the rut and are also more visible as they move about their home range in search of receptive does. Mule deer bucks are notorious for prowling over great distances during the rut and could show up almost

AFGA Scorer Dean Bromberger with a mule deer rack that grossed 205+ taken by Myles Radford.

anywhere. White-tailed bucks don't move over such large areas but will bird-dog in search of does during the day throughout their home range. Almost any taxidermist will tell you that the most and biggest bucks are shot during the last week of the season in November.

The Best Time of Day

It's a myth that the best times of day to bag a big buck are daybreak and just before sundown. Although these are prime feeding times and good times to go hunting, bucks don't feed much during the rut. Consequently, you should expect to see big bucks at any time of the day during the rut. So hunt the whole day, from sunrise until sunset! I've taken both mule deer and white-tailed bucks at all hours of the day during the rut, including at high noon on more than one occasion. If you see a doe or a group of does, look

Duane Radford took this white-tailed buck in an area he'd scouted previously.

Scout for white-tailed deer rubs in the area you plan to hunt.

for a buck. They're seldom far away when the rut is in full swing. In fact, you should expect a shot opportunity, so get your gun ready in case a big buck materializes in the vicinity of does.

Hunters who consistently tag big deer are not just lucky. They earn their trophies by doing their homework and putting in the time. To bag that buck of your dreams, make sure you hunt where the odds are the greatest of busting a big buck and follow my advice during your hunt.

Doe Bleats and Grunt Tubes

A large white-tailed buck bounded toward me like he was on a string!

Two bleats from the Primos doe bleat can brought him charging upslope from more than 100 yards away. He didn't stop running until he was about 10 yards distant, when he suddenly halted, snorted, did a 180-degree turn, jumped and darted backwards, only to stop again a short distance away.

Because I was dressed in full camouflage clothing, sitting on my haunches amid some shrubs, he couldn't make me out. A grunt from my Carlton's Call grunt tube stopped him in his tracks. He stood broadside for a couple of minutes and then casually walked into an aspen stand, seemingly unalarmed. I could have shot him a dozen times, but he wasn't quite what I had my sights set on.

This wasn't the first time I'd called in a white-tailed buck with a doe bleat or stopped one in his tracks with a grunt tube. I actually called one buck in so close that I could see his nostrils twitching as he tried to scent what he thought was a doe in heat. On another occasion, a bird-dogging buck came in from over half a mile distant.

Deer bleat calls and grunt tubes have been on the market for years, and they work, but not all hunters carry them in their arsenal of deer hunting equipment. Go figure! In my mind, no hunter should leave home without them. The calls work for both mule deer and white-tailed deer, although I've found they're probably best for hunting white-tailed deer. How do these calls work? Where and when should you use them? Where can you purchase them?

For years I've been using a quiet carry Primos long-range estrus bleat call that imitates the call of a doe in heat. The manufacturer makes the canned call in two sizes: one for short ranges and the other for long-distance calling. These pocket-sized calls come in the shape of a can. They're silent until they're tipped upside down, when they emit a doe bleat. The manufacturer claims they're perfect for white-tailed deer and mule deer. I've had far better luck with white-tails than mule deer, but they'll attract both species of deer. You can also purchase a compact Primos Trophy Grunter Deer Call in the shape of a tube that can be adjusted for

Primos deer bleat call works particularly well on white-tail bucks.

estrus and doe bleats, as well as several variations of grunts. I've had mule deer within a stone's throw and white-tails come within spitting distance on several occasions by using the canned calls. A word of caution, however, always take a couple of these calls with you when hunting away from home because they can fail to work on occasion.

Some of my hunting buddies question whether these calls are effective, but I can say without hesitation that the calls work. I've been hunting for many years and have to admit that I've only heard bleating does a few times when out hunting, but does do make calls, particularly during the rut. It's the bleat that catches the attention of bucks. I make it a practice to use doe bleats throughout the day when I'm hunting during the rut for both mule deer and white-tailed deer.

During the pre-rut, white-tailed bucks are more likely to respond to deer calls than later on during the rut (as well as the sound of antler rattling, which also becomes less effective as the rut advances). The peak of the rut is one of the most difficult times to pattern bucks that are distracted by receptive does. The late November post-rut can be one of the more productive times to take a trophy white-tailed buck. Try to catch them bird-dogging and check their scrape lines to see if any does that didn't mate earlier have come into heat again. At this time, the bucks will readily respond to doe bleats.

Usually, I'll make two or three doe bleats when I'm on a stand, and then I'll sit tight for 15 to 20 minutes. Bleats should last for only one or two seconds. You can vary the sound and volume of the bleats by cupping your hand over the top of the call if

Mule deer does—note their large ears.

Carelton Calls grunt tube will bring in bucks and stop them in their tracks.

you're using a can. I'll repeat the bleats followed up by a couple of grunts from one of my grunt tubes before moving on to another stand.

A grunt gets the attention of a buck that probably thinks an intruder is trying to horn in on the action on its home range. The sound of a doe bleat from a can carries for at least half a mile if there's little or no wind and the ambient temperature is around 0°C. Give bucks a chance to respond to doe bleats. It may take them several minutes, or more, to close the distance if they're not in your immediate vicinity. Also, stay hidden as much as possible and watch in all directions for an approaching buck. Bucks will usually make a beeline toward the call. When they think they're close to the origin of the call, they'll try to get downwind before coming right in.

There's quite a difference between the sound of a buck "snorting" when it's startled and "grunting" when it's on the trail of a doe, the latter sound being guttural and repetitive. It's not unheard of for a rutting buck to respond to the grunt tube call without any doe bleats if it thinks another buck is intruding on its home territory. A grunt tube is a great way to stop a buck in its tracks, regardless of whether it is a white-tail or a mulie.

Bucks of both species are active throughout the day during the rut, so continue to use a doe bleat and grunt tube all day long. If you're still hunting, use a grunt tube from time to time to imitate a buck, which will not only catch the attention of nearby deer but will also make them think there is no cause for alarm should they hear you moving about in the bush.

Several varieties of grunt tubes are available on the market. I've used a Carlton's Call brand of grunt tube for many years because I know from experience that it works, but I have every confidence in the Primos Trophy Grunt Deer Call, which is much more compact.

You can purchase deer bleats and grunt tubes in most big box sporting stores and many mom-and-pop outlets or online. Ask around to see which brands work best in your area before you decide, but don't wait until hunting season rolls around because inventories are often depleted by then.

Deer Hunting Success: A Summary

With hunting, you can't just show up and expect to be successful. Your reward will be commensurate with the amount of time and effort you put into preparing for the hunt as well as the hunt proper. I don't shoot a deer every year, partly because I'm fussy about what I'm after, but also because the stars don't always line up. I may blow

an opportunity. It doesn't hurt to have a bit of karma in your favour, but you'll never tag a nice buck if you stay at home and just grouse about issues related to deer hunting. Act strategically to build success.

The Gun Range

Start by ensuring that your hunting rifle is properly sighted in for the weight of bullets you intend to use while deer hunting. I don't know how many times I've been to a local gun range and witnessed shooters improperly sighting in their rifles before going hunting. No wonder they miss shot opportunities.

Before you leave the range, ensure that you can put your shots in a 6-inch bullseye at 100 yards from a sitting position, one of the most common field positions. Once your rifle is sighted in and you're able to consistently place your shots in the bullseye, you will have confidence in your ability to hit a target at least up to 100 yards distant. Confidence is the key to success when hunting.

Sight your rifle in for the distance you'll likely be shooting at in the field.

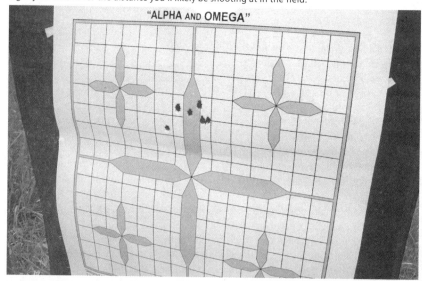

It's essential to use a solid rest when sighting in your rifle or checking to make sure that it's properly sighted in.

To take the guesswork out of sighting in distances, I went through my hunting journal and tallied the average range of the last 30 mule deer and white-tailed deer that either I or someone else in my hunting party shot. The average range of killing shots was as follows: 122 yards for white-tailed deer (20 deer), 167 yards for mule deer (10 deer).

Statistics don't lie. Be prepared for close-in shots on white-tailed deer and mid-range shots on mule deer. You'll likely be fine if your rifle is zeroed in at 225 yards for either species under most circumstances.

Use a bipod whenever possible or shooting sticks if that's your preference. It's much easier to score on deer that are more than 100 yards distant if you have a decent rest.

In many cases you'll have ample time to set up a bipod or get shooting sticks in position for a well-placed shot.

Scouting

Do not expect to be consistently successful hunting deer if you don't scout your hunting territory. Conditions change, and the distribution and number of deer can be highly variable from year to year.

In one of my favourite spots, the number of white-tailed deer has plummeted over the past several years, likely as a result of winterkill and coyote predation. In another spot, numbers are down at least 50 percent because of a severe winter in 2010–11.

It's a good idea to also spend time becoming familiar with your hunting territory to make sure you know where and when you're most likely to find deer and what sort of tactics you should employ to get in position or be ready for a shot. During your scouting, acquire local knowledge of where deer feed, water and travel to be successful.

Understand Deer Biology and Behaviour

Be familiar with the habits of deer before, during and after the rut, which should influence your hunting strategy. Your strategy should also vary depending on whether you are hunting mule deer or white-tailed deer.

Although their ranges may overlap, mule deer are creatures of open country, whereas white-tailed deer tend to be more secretive. White-tails are found most often in or near cover, unless they're feeding, or in the case of bucks, bird-dogging in the open searching out does in estrus.

Mule deer seldom respond in earnest to deer calls whereas white-tailed bucks can be suckers for doe bleats, calls from grunt tubes and antler rattling. I've attracted white-tailed bucks with doe bleats from more than half a mile distant and have had bucks come to within spitting distance. Not so for mule deer bucks.

Mule deer bucks are mobile before and after the rut, and can be spotted at any time of the day, whereas white-tailed bucks are more often spotted in the early morning hours or just before it gets dark. Mule deer are also difficult to pattern, but white-tailed deer are much more creatures of habit and, although they are almost always wary, are easier to hunt strategically from ground and tree blinds. Study the habits of both species so you're on top of your game during your deer hunt.

It's easier to pattern deer when there's snow on the ground.

A couple of juvenile white-tailed bucks sparring during the rut

Timing

When you choose to hunt is a personal choice; however, timing is often an important factor in a deer hunt. Generally, I opt to hunt late in the season when there is snow on the ground. It's easier to find bedding spots, feeding areas and travel lanes. It's also much easier to spot deer and judge antler size after a snowfall because the deer stand out more than when the ground is dry. Snow also makes for better field dressing conditions. Lastly, it's much easier to follow up on shot deer that don't drop in their tracks if there's snow on the ground. I've taken a lot of deer, and while many have fallen dead almost immediately, some have travelled a fair distance after being fatally shot through the lungs. It's a challenge to find wounded deer when there's no snow on the ground.

Optics

It is vital that you have good optics to locate deer, especially when engaged in spot-and-stalk hunts. I recommend 10x42 or 10x50-power binoculars for deer hunts that have high enough magnification to judge antler size at distances up to half a mile away. If you're a trophy hunter, a spotting scope is essential to judge quality bucks at a distance.

Rangefinders can be game changers; I wouldn't leave home without one, particularly for spot-and-stalk hunting. Binoculars with a built in rangefinder and/or image stabilizers are a bonus. Rangefinders also play a key role if you're stand hunting. They can take the guesswork out of estimating ranges when I first take a stand, not when I spot a deer while on stand. Time is precious when hunting deer. You'll have more success when you check the range in your field of view before a deer shows up, and you'll know in advance what you're up against.

The Day of the Hunt

You really should be in a position for a shot before legal shooting time if you want to be successful. Both mule deer and white-tailed deer can be out in the open at any time of the day during and following the rut, but to improve your chances, be on stand before daylight to take advantage of deer being on the move at first light. This is especially true for white-tailed deer.

I'm usually more inclined to take the chase to the deer in the early morning when there's the advantage of poor light, which makes it harder for them to make you out. However, I'll generally do more sitting and watching during the rest of the day and let deer make the first move. Standard hunting procedures apply when you're taking the chase during a deer hunting trip:

- Hunt with the wind in your face and the sun at your back.

- Stay along the edge of escape cover to break your outline where possible.

- Go forward in draws to avoid being sky-lined.

I researched my hunting journal to see what time of day most mule deer and white-tailed deer were shot. For mule deer, out of a sample size of 10 deer, 40 percent were taken before noon and 60 percent were taken after. For white-tailed deer, out of a sample size of 20 deer, 80 percent were taken before noon and 20 percent were taken

Be ready for a shot opportunity on white-tailed bucks any time before or after the rut.

Mule deer bucks will gather a harem of does by late November and can often be seen out in the open.

after. Further, more than 80 percent of the white-tailed deer were shot before 9:00 AM, whereas 90 percent of the mule deer were shot after 9:00 AM. Shocking isn't it? The journals offer proof that early white-tailed deer hunters will get their deer, while sleepyheads will do okay on mulies!

Be Patient

The importance of patience and perseverance cannot be overstated. All good things come with a price tag, and hunting deer is no exception. If you do see a deer and it gives you the slip, don't despair. Unless it's been alarmed, it won't leave the area. Wait a while and go to the chase again later on in the day, or the next day. With a bit of luck, you just might find it again.

Physical Fitness

Another important factor is what happens before the hunt in terms of conditioning. The actual hunt is often similar to the playoffs; you really have to be ready to hunt from dawn until dusk over the course of at least a week to have any hope of success. Are you in the best possible physical shape to compete at this level, and if not, what should you do to get in shape? There's no substitute for a physical fitness program that includes frequent walks or jogging, where you build up a sweat. Such a program will toughen your leg muscles, strengthen your heart and build up your wind so that you won't tire quickly.

When Seconds Count

I had time for maybe one shot as a 4-point mule deer buck bolted from a stand of aspen and streaked across an opening in the prairie. At the crack of my .270 calibre rifle, the big buck folded and skidded to a sudden stop in the tall, dry grass.

What did I do correctly to be in the right position at the right time? How did I manage to make a tough shot and cap off a successful hunt?

My hunting partner and I had spotted the buck with a small harem of does late in the afternoon as they fed into an aspen stand on a nearby hillside. There was rolling prairie to the north and a large, open hay field to the south.

We decided that I would take the north flank along the edge of the aspen stand, and my partner would skirt the southern edge of the stand. We would stalk the deer along the edge of the aspen copse as they worked their way eastward—the old squeeze play. I made haste to get on top of the hillside, and it wasn't long before I caught sight of them as they worked their way through the aspen. My partner was out of sight, presumably to the south, working his way eastward, parallel to me.

As the deer approached the far end of the aspen stand, I could see they were getting nervous and figured that it was just a matter of time until they spooked. I turned the power on my variable scope down to 2X. I knew that if I did get a shot, it would be at a running deer. I wanted to be able to pick it up as quickly as possible in the scope. I also reminded myself of proper leads on running deer—one body length at 100 yards, two body lengths at 200 yards and so on. My Husqvarna rifle had a Mauser action, and all I had to do was work the bolt to cock it as a round was already in the chamber. I held it in the ready position, anticipating an offhand shot.

I was as prepared as I was ever going to be when the deer started to leave the stand of aspen and headed north, less than 100 yards from where I was stationed. I could see the buck was a dandy as it bounded from the security of the poplars and headed for another nearby stand. I picked up the deer in the scope, followed through with a body length lead and slowly squeezed the trigger. The bullet did its job, and the hunt was over. I had connected on a witching hour buck

I can't believe how much it shrank when it hit the ground.

–Jack Graham, Past-President and Boone and Crocket Club Official Measurer (retired) of the Alberta Fish and Game Association remarking how lots of hunters felt when they saw close up that the antlers or horns were smaller than they originally thought

just minutes before the end of legal shooting time by hunting strategically. I had only seconds to make the shot.

It wasn't dumb luck that I connected on this buck. I knew there were mule deer in the area, and my partner and I had worked hard to spot the herd with the trophy buck. After that it was a matter of developing a plan, executing a stalk, harrying our quarry just enough to get them to leave the security of their cover and then making a difficult shot count. When the time came to shoot, I had only a matter of seconds to pick up the buck as it bounded away, but I was ready. Being ready for the shot is often a crucial factor on many big game hunts.

There were many white-tailed deer in the same general area where I took the eleventh-hour trophy mule deer, but it took me a while to figure out their movement patterns. When it finally dawned on me

Don't be surprised to have shot opportunities on mule deer any time of the day during the rut.

how they travelled between their feeding and bedding areas, I connected on four nice bucks sitting in exactly the same stand four out of five years. All good things must come to an end, though. The end to hunting at this deer factory came when the land changed owners, and developments precluded hunting. It was sure good while it lasted.

What I did was stake out a stand on the edge of a large field where I had seen bucks crossing at various times of the day and took my chances. I knew that it was just a matter of time until I got a shot. Beforehand, however, I paced off distances from this stand to all quarters of the field so that I knew how far away a deer would be depending on where it appeared. This was back in the day before rangefinders were on the market. This step is essential when you're shooting at moving targets, and I knew from experience that most white-tailed bucks that crossed this field would be on the move. I might have to lead them by one or two body lengths, for example. I rarely shoot at a moving target beyond 200 yards because these are really tough shots.

To spot a buck in time for a shot, I glassed the far edge of the field every few minutes to pick them up while they were still standing securely checking things out before deciding to cross.

Don Meredith geared up for a prairie deer hunt

It worked every time. Sure enough, when they built up enough courage to leave the aspen stand on the far side of the field and trotted across the field, I was ready and waiting. I knew precisely how much of a lead was required, and I waited until they were no more than 200 yards distant before I fired. I also made a couple of standing shots at ranges from 100 to 300 yards when the bucks stopped to feed in the early morning.

Only once did I have much time to think about the shots; in other cases it was ready, aim and fire. It was all over in a matter of seconds.

How do you make sure you get off your best shot? By knowing how your rifle works and by being prepared to make a shot under less-than-ideal conditions.

Be prepared to make the best of your opportunities when time is short. Generally, a hunter will have only a few seconds to make a shot when the chips are down. Always hold on hair on your first shot (on standing shots) and position yourself so that you can get off a good shot, if only one shot, and try to make it count

CHAPTER NINE

Hunting the Prairie Speed Demon: Pronghorn Antelope

Pronghorn Antelope

Pronghorn antelope are highly sought-after trophies. They have incredible speed and vision, and will bolt for the next township if alarmed, leaving in a cloud of dust. They are creatures of wide-open prairies and are mainly found in southern Alberta, though some herds live year round farther north near Provost.

- Archery seasons run from early September to near the end of the month.

- There are two split rifle seasons north and south of the South Saskatchewan River in early/late October, respectively. The split rifle season is structured to address different agricultural practices and the timing of cattle roundups from pastures on the north and south side of the river. Calendar dates vary slightly annually around the start of October and third week of October.

- Because of the open terrain, it can be difficult to get within shooting range. Consequently, shots up to 300+ yards may be your only option. Flat shooting rifles such as the .25-06 and .270 Winchester are ideal, the latter loaded with 130-grain bullets.

- Because of their relatively small size and light colour, pronghorns are often perceived to be farther away than they actually are, causing some hunters to shoot over their backs. A rangefinder and 10x42 or 10x50 binoculars are must-have items, and image stabilizers are a bonus. Binoculars with built in rangefinders are ideal.

- Always remember the cardinal rule to "hold on hair" for your first shot, especially when hunting antelope!

One of Alberta's Premier Big Game Trophies

I've taken seven pronghorn in southern Alberta and have been fortunate to hunt them in several different hunting zones.

These experiences have provided me with a better appreciation of how to hunt pronghorn antelope in varied terrain. One of the seven antelope I shot made the AFGA official records book, just missing

Without doubt, pronghorn antelope are one of Alberta's most sought after big game trophies.

the Boone and Crockett Club record book. Another buck just missed the Boone and Crockett Club record book when the minimum score was at 80 points, lower than the present 82 points. I've passed up many decent bucks on my past few antelope hunts, holding out for an exceptional buck and not pulling the trigger. Don't let my standards put you off shooting a less-than-record-book-quality pronghorn. Every antelope is a real trophy, just like a Canada goose or a cock pheasant!

What should you focus on when judging whether your target is an outstanding pronghorn or just a respectable buck? How do you judge horn size, and what should you look for in prongs (paddles) and horn mass to get the best possible score if you're looking for a buck that might make the record book? If you'll settle for less than a buck that might make the book but is still an outstanding trophy, where do you draw the line?

A trophy buck will stand out from lesser animals in several ways. It will have long, curved horns—with massive bases that carry their weight toward the tips of the horns—with exceptionally long prongs. The Boone and Crockett Club scores antelope on the length of each horn, the circumference of the base and the first, second and third quarters, as well as the length of the prong. Horns in the shape of a heart with tips that curve inwards tend to score high because of their sweep, compared with horns that are straight. It's necessary to view a buck head on to appreciate the tell-tale heart-shaped appearance. Bucks with horns less than 15 inches long normally do not make the record book, so it's important to scout for one with horns in the 16-inch-plus range, and those are rare indeed. As a yardstick for hunters to judge horn length, keep in mind that the length of the ears on a mature buck is about 6 inches. Viewed in profile, horns with bases 3 inches wide (or greater) will score well, and the paddle should be at least this long to add points to the total score. In other words, the paddle should be as long as the base is wide, or greater. A buck with good bases and decent paddles with 14 to 15 inch horns will make a fine mount, and on many hunts you will be hard pressed to find anything better.

Unless the buck has it all—long horns, heavy bases (with mass that carries toward the tip of the horns) and big prongs—it won't score well. A shortfall in any of these key factors will subtract from the overall score necessary to make the record book. The horns are also scored on the basis of their symmetry, and any differences in the various measurements will be deducted from the total score.

As an aside, non-typical pronghorn antelope are extremely rare; I've only seen a couple out of literally thousands of bucks, one of which I took with a near impossible shot at a range of 300+ yards in 1976. My son, Myles, shot another rare non-typical antelope buck in 2014. Authorities believe there are several factors that can cause non-typical or deformed antlers or horns. One of the most common causes of non-typical antlers or horns happens when the male damages the pedicle or base where the antlers or horns grow.

Although these speedsters are creatures of native prairies and are heavily dependent on sagebrush as a staple in their diet, agricultural crops can act like a magnet, and water holes are of paramount importance to them.

Myles with his non-typical antelope, taken by being persistent after first spotting it during a scouting trip.

Pronghorn are most active while feeding in the morning and evening but can be spotted throughout the day. Once you've located a herd, it's time to set up a spotting scope and do the math on the horn size of any bucks present. One of the worst things you can do if you decide on a stalk is to try to get too close in a vehicle. If pronghorn antelope feel the least bit concerned, they will disappear in an instant. They've been clocked at speeds of more than 60 kilometres per hour when trying to outpace vehicles and will be out of sight in a heartbeat. Pronghorns are more comfortable with a lot of distance between themselves and vehicles, or a hunter on the ground.

It is often necessary to make long stalks, which should always be downwind, to get within range. Crawling on your belly is frequently the only way to get close enough to get off a shot—amid prickly pear cactus and all manner of rocks. Leather gloves,

heavy denim pants and jackets are essential when stalking pronghorn antelope because of the abundance of cactus on the range. I've seen hunting partners develop serious infections within minutes of being pierced by cactus thorns, so be wary of the plants. Contrary to popular belief, the prairies are not flat. You can use coulees, gullies, hills and depressions to stay out of sight before making your final approach. The prairie landscape is beautiful and is one of the main reasons I keep going back on antelope hunts again and again!

The best gun for the job is a flat shooting rifle zeroed in for 225 yards, but be prepared to shoot 300 yards or more. In all my hunting experiences, I've never seen an animal that can frustrate hunters more than the pronghorn. I've watched many good hunters miss shots at them by shooting over their backs.

Pronghorns with heart-shaped horns and wide bases typically score better than those with straight, narrow horns.

Long-range shots are often necessary during an antelope hunt which is why magnum rifles are becoming more popular.

Should you have a successful hunt, after field dressing your carcass I strongly suggest skinning it (and cape it out) before returning home. Skinning can be done while the animal is lying on the ground (or by using a commercial portable winch). This will cool the meat. "Caping" means cutting the skin away from the neck and head of the animal before either chilling the "cape" for the trip home or adding salt to dry it out so it doesn't spoil. Pronghorn antelope have hollow hair, which is a great insulator, and their body will not cool well unless they are skinned fairly soon after being shot. Pronghorn meat is very good eating if properly cared for but can be awful if it isn't handled properly. Hang the head and cape to cool, and place the carcass in a commercial game bag after it has cooled to ambient air temperature. Then keep it shaded and pack some ice in the body cavity to keep it cool for the trip home. The carcass should be butchered within three days, otherwise unsightly mucilage will form on its skin.

Ensure that the hair is cleaned of any blood immediately as it is hard to wash out of a cape once it sets. Protect the horns from rubbing on the body of your truck because they are soft and will wear. Getting a trophy antelope mounted at a taxidermist isn't cheap, and you may want to mount the horns yourself. If you choose to go this route, it's absolutely essential that the horn sheaths be removed from the skull plate and cleaned of gelatinous matter before they're set in a filler resin, otherwise they'll stink the house up as they rot.

Skinned and hung antelope cooling off before being butchered

Of all the big game animals I've hunted, the pronghorn antelope (aka the prairie speedster) stands out as one of the most challenging. It offers hunters a unique opportunity to put all their hunting skills to the test.

Alberta's Antelope-Hunting ABCs

This section about Alberta's "New Antelope Hunting ABCs" is a primer for antelope-hunting neophytes to get them started on the right foot. It's also a refresher of sorts for those folks who haven't hunted antelope in a while. Pronghorn hunting has changed greatly since my first pronghorn hunt back in the heydays of the '70s. These changes have inspired me to put together the modern-day ABCs of hunting pronghorns in Alberta.

"A" is for Access

Access has had a major impact on antelope hunting, especially in areas where grazing leases, grazing associations and grazing reserves are common (i.e., on public lands). It's a different ball game now that most of these areas have been declared off limits for vehicles as a result of changes in government policy.

What should hunters do now that most hunting is on foot only on Alberta's public lands?

For starters, you're going to have to figure out a way to get your game back to your vehicle without killing yourself. If you don't have a game carrier, you'll be rather limited in your hunting territory. Antelope are not too heavy, so you could pack out your game on a pack frame. If you are not too far from a road, you could even cloak it in a plastic tarp and haul it out over the prairie. Don't laugh; I've seen it done!

Respect local hunting signs that indicate foot access only.

Typical antelope range on the prairies of southern Alberta where flat shooting rifles are a must.

"B" is for Binoculars

Binoculars are essential because you'll really have to search for antelope to spot them, particularly following a killing winter. You'll also have to look much farther afield because vehicular access is now so restricted. The pronghorns are not going to be just off the road, like they might have been 10 or 20 years ago. Also you'll be up against an animal with excellent vision, rated at 8-power, and hearing as sharp as an owl's! They'll usually see you long before you see them and will be on guard if they feel the least bit threatened. I once made the mistake of having some loose shells in my pant pocket when stalking some antelope. They picked up the sound several hundred yards distant and bolted.

Instead of 35X field glasses, I'd opt for 10X binoculars. And don't leave home without a 20–60X spotting scope if you're going after a trophy buck, and consider bringing a window mount and a tripod as well. It's often possible to glass antelope from trails and roads, which is where a window mount is useful. Surprisingly, these colorful animals blend in well with their native habitat and can be hard to spot without good optics. If you get a good vantage point and spend some time scanning the prairies, you'll be surprised at how many pronghorn antelope you'll spot, if you're patient.

"B" is Also for Bipod

A bipod a must-have shooting aid for antelope hunting; there's no excuse for not having one. I'd pick a bipod over shooting sticks because it's often necessary to lay prone to stay out of sight. If you have to crouch in a sitting position to use shooting sticks, there's a much greater chance you'll be spotted at a crucial moment. This is a radical change for me. I'd never found it necessary to use a bipod when I first started hunting antelope, but it's a different ball game these days.

Bow Hunting

I say this without prejudice, but "B" is also for the impact that bow hunters have on

Pronghorn antelope bucks sparring during the September rut

antelope during the pre-rifle hunt. The first separate antelope archery draw started in 1988. Prior to that, there was an archery season before the trophy and non-trophy seasons. Now that the archery season takes place before the rifle season, the influences on pronghorn hunting are two-fold. For starters, advances in antelope bow hunting techniques are allowing bow hunters to take some fine bucks, which are then removed from the trophy pool for rifle hunters. Secondly, interest has grown since the first archery antelope season, and the added hunting pressure makes the animals warier by the time the rifle season starts.

"C" is for Communication

Communications between hunters and between hunting parties is crucial if you are in different vehicles hunting in a group. Walkie-talkies or two-way radios with ranges up to 25+ kilometres (15 miles) are now the ticket for the modern-day antelope hunter. Unfortunately, cell phone reception is spotty in much of the country where antelope are found resulting in too many blind spots, so they're not reliable. During a recent hunt, I heard of one particular hunter who walked more than 10 kilometres (6 miles) in search of a buck, during which communications with his hunting partner would have been absolutely vital.

"C" is also for Camouflage

Camouflage clothing is almost another must-have item. I would not leave home without camouflage clothing. It is one of the few items in your arsenal that can give you a leg up on antelope because of their excellent vision.

"C" is for Calibres

Calibres are important because more and more hunters are opting for magnum guns, which have extended ranges. Although I'm not a subscriber of long-range shots, you must be able to shoot at greater than average distances when hunting antelope. You should have a flat shooting rifle zeroed in for 225 yards and be prepared to shoot at 300+ yards.

"C" is for Conditioning

Conditioning has taken on a new dimension now that "foot access only" is the norm on so many ranches. You'll also need to stay hydrated during what may turn into a marathon hunt if you're after a trophy buck. Granted, if you and your buddies are hunting on private land, know the lay of the land and where the bucks are located, it's still possible for two or three hunters to limit out (fill your tags) in a single day, if you're not particular about what you shoot. However, if you're after a trophy buck with heavy horns in the 15-inch+ range, with large paddles, and you aren't prepared to relax your standards, you could be doing a lot of walking during the course of

a week-long antelope hunt. In other words, get in shape and be prepared to do some walking.

"C" is also for Carrier

Although I certainly didn't need a game carrier when I started hunting antelope, they're almost a requirement nowadays because many ranchers will not allow any vehicles to drive off-road on their property. Several models of game carriers on the market fit the bill. Check them out and decide what kind will meet your needs. Because Alberta's prairies have cactus, I'd opt for a carrier with solid rubber wheels rather than one with tube tires that could be punctured.

Other Items of Note

Although they don't fit in with the "ABCs," there are other items that are worthy of mention and will make your hunting experience easier:

- A laser rangefinder or binoculars with a built in rangefinder is an essential

Tough winters can wreak havoc on Alberta's pronghorn antelope causing populations to crash.

The Tipi Ring near where the buck fell—note the circular pattern of stones.

gadget. It's difficult even for experienced hunters to judge shooting distances when hunting antelope. A laser range-finder compensates for people's failings.

• A portable hoist assists in lifting the carcass off the ground to skin them out as soon as possible. Antelope carcasses should be cut and wrapped for the freezer within three days after the kill to prevent a liver-like or mushy texture forming on the surface of the carcass.

That's a summary of the modern "ABC's" of hunting antelope in Alberta for those hunters who were fortunate enough to have been drawn to hunt one of the most challenging and exciting big game animals in Canada. On that note, the new norm is a 10-year or longer wait to be drawn for a trophy antelope tag in Alberta.

The Tipi Ring Antelope Hunt

Sometimes, strange things happen during a hunting trip. During my last antelope hunt, for example, I tagged a buck within a stone's throw of an ancient tipi ring on Alberta's sweeping prairies south of the legendary Cypress Hills. Was this just a coincidence? Or was it perhaps a testament to the fact that antelope often travel in a circuitous route around their home range?

An antelope's home range affinity is actually what sealed the deal for me on this particular hunt. It could be a key factor during your next antelope hunt, too.

Over the years, I've hunted antelope eight times, tagging seven and passing over several decent bucks on the one hunt where I didn't shoot even one. I think this may be some sort of record for an Albertan,

Man's lack of respect for his environment has got us into a fine mess, and there is no excuse for it.

—Andy Russell, renowned Canadian conservationist who lived at the Hawks Nest, near Twin Butte

My tag was for WMU 102 and 118 where a six-day season is open in late October. I enjoy hunting antelope in WMU 118 more than in WMU 102 because WMU 118 is characterized by rolling prairie with majestic coulees, meandering creek bottoms and deep draws. The varied relief oftentimes lends itself to classic spot and stalk hunting opportunities. In WMU 102 the terrain is rather flat, so getting within shooting range can be more of a challenge.

Prior to the season opener, I located a small herd of three bucks south of the Cypress Hills in WMU 118 while I was scouting the area. One of the bucks that caught my eye had heart-shaped horns with decent paddles and good bases, even though it didn't have exceptional length.

because nowadays it often takes a decade (or more) to get a coveted tag. It's getting harder by the year to be successful at the draw because applicants rise, and herds diminish. I waited seven years between my last two antelope hunts.

My standards rose after shooting a couple of trophy bucks that just missed the Boone and Crocket Club record book minimum score of the day, which is why I passed up several shot opportunities the only year I didn't tag out. Because I enjoy eating antelope, however, I vowed I wouldn't go home empty-handed the last time I had a tag.

I used a number of lessons learned during previous antelope hunts to take this particular buck, with a strong focus on antelope behaviour and habits as well as advance scouting. My last hunt also involved a textbook spot and stalk approach, often a key requirement to close the range. This buck was actually one of the smaller ones I've shot.

Hunters should expect to wait about 10 years or more to be drawn for a trophy antelope in Alberta.

Despite a lot of scouting I didn't see many other bucks, so I decided to hunt this herd on opening morning, only to find another party had the same idea. The other two hunters just beat me to the punch at dawn. Unfortunately, they spooked the herd, which bolted to the north, without getting off a shot. The two hunters took off in pursuit as the herd headed north. I decided to swing east to see if I might cut the antelope herd off, so I had a ringside view of the shenanigans. I try not to let this sort of event get under my skin because the other hunters were no different than me; they just happened to be a minute or two ahead. Although they followed the herd for about an hour, they eventually gave up. I took up the chase, finally spotting the three bucks later in the day when they joined another small herd of antelope.

The herd bedded down in an open field in a creek bottom about a mile distant, where a stalk was next to impossible.

I watched them for a couple of hours, and then a coyote showed up and spooked the herd. They headed east in a cloud of dust into an area where I didn't have permission to hunt. By this time it was late in the afternoon, so I headed back to my truck, disappointed but not heartbroken.

One thing I couldn't help but notice was the low numbers of antelope on the ranch where I was hunting as compared with other trips.

I've learned over the years that if you have several days to hunt and you're persistent, you should get more than one chance to tag an antelope. On this trip, however, the antelope just weren't there, and despite searching high and low in both WMU 118 and WMU 102, I couldn't find a decent shooter over the next couple of days. I talked to some Alberta Conservation Association biologists stationed along Highway 41, also known as the Buffalo

Running pronghorn antelope—it's a good idea to pass on shots at running antelope as leads are just too great to connect in most cases.

At times, pronghorn bedded down can be difficult to spot on Alberta's prairies.

Trail, late in the afternoon on Day Three. They were wrapping up a survey of antelope hunting success in the area. Their results corroborated what I'd noticed. Numbers of antelope were way down, and success was poor with only one larger-than-average buck taken on the opening day, which scored in the low seventies.

When a hunt turns south, it's often a good idea to go back to where you started, so that's what I did on Day Four, searching high and low for a shooter. Sure enough, at about 10:00 AM I spotted the same herd of three bucks I'd seen the weekend before the season opened. You guessed it; they were in the same place I'd seen them originally! They were bedded down just below the crest of a hill that sheltered them from a strong westerly wind. It had rained the previous day and there was a chill in the air, so they were soaking up some sun out of the wind. They had a panoramic view of the lonely prairies from their lofty vantage point and could see danger coming from miles away, except from the north.

It was out of range.

The quarry was too far away to shoot at.

Author with the Tipi Ring buck, taken during a classic "spot and stalk" hunt.

There was a ridge to the west of where they were bedded down, on the edge of a coulee, that would shield me during a stalk, at least until I could get within shooting range. If I could get behind the ridge, there was no way they'd spot me. With any luck they wouldn't hear me either with the wind blowing, nor would they pick up my scent because of the direction it was blowing. So, out of sight, I slowly worked my way toward the top of the coulee behind the ridge to get in a shooting position. The stalk took the better part of an hour.

I crawled on my stomach the last several yards before I peeked over the crest of the ridge, trying to spot the herd. Sure enough, the three bucks were bedded down about 125 yards away. I had judged the elevation correctly. They were at the same elevation as I was.

The tall prairie grass swayed in the wind like ocean waves.

The buck with the heart-shaped horns was bedded down quartering away from me, looking toward the east. I could see his mane rippling in the wind. ("Quartering away" means an animal is looking away from a hunter.)

There was only one shot opportunity, at the base of his neck, just above his shoulder. I positioned my bipod and settled the crosshairs in the target area low on the back of his neck, confident in my shot.

At the crack of my .270 calibre Tikka T3 Lite rifle, the buck folded, its neck broken by a 130-grain bullet.

By the time I reached his side, at 11:15 AM, it was all over. It was then that I noticed the tipi ring nearby. The buck had travelled full circle over a period of four days, as had I during my quest to fill my tag.

Antelope are no different than other big game animals, all of which have a home range. Unless they're harassed, they'll stay within their home range. So, don't despair if they give you the slip early in the hunt. There's a good chance you might catch up with them later on. Maybe even close to where you first spotted them!

Third Time Lucky on Pronghorn

The old saying, "third time lucky" came true for my son, Myles, during an antelope hunt in southern Alberta in 2014.

There's nothing quite like an antelope hunt. The pronghorn is a favourite big game animal of mine, one of the key reasons being that you usually get a second (or even third) chance if you mess up on your earlier opportunities.

If the argument against hunting is an argument against death, then it is essentially an argument against life. Things die so that other things might live.

–Kevin Van Tighem, Alberta naturalist, author and outdoorsman, in *Alberta Views*

Antelope are creatures of Alberta's wide open prairies where long shots are often necessary.

Prairie where Myles took his pronghorn antelope

You can't do too much scouting prior to any hunt. But if you're in search of a trophy antelope, advance scouting is even more important because competition for them is keen.

It's common knowledge that some hunters stake out a trophy pronghorn buck in the days leading up to the start of the season, put it to bed the night before and get in a shooting position before first light on opening day. As soon as legal shooting time begins, they take their best shot. I, too, believe in this philosophy, if not to the same degree, at least in principle.

In our case, we were hunting a new zone near Oyen where I had no previous hunting experience. We were in new territory because of a conversation I'd had with an old friend of mine who was familiar with the area. He'd seen some decent bucks there while hunting waterfowl and said that hunting pressure wasn't as high as in my usual haunts south of the Cypress Hills.

Myles and I covered a lot of ground during the two days before the season opener and saw quite a few antelope, with three bucks that were shooters. As we got more and more familiar with the terrain, it became clear that one buck, a non-typical antelope, stood out from the rest. During our scouting forays, we contacted key landowners where we'd spotted decent numbers of antelope and the best bucks to obtain permission to hunt on their land.

On opening day, long before legal shooting time, we were beside a fence line not far from where we'd seen the non-typical buck with his harem the night before. As it began to get light, we searched the prairie or signs of the herd. As luck would have it, they weren't far off. Myles took to the chase and headed off toward the herd, which was slowly feeding in a northerly direction. He'd covered several hundred yards and was just about in a shooting position when I heard the sound of an ATV side-by-side coming toward me.

I knew we were in for a confrontation as the side-by-side sped along a trail heading in my direction. It turned out to be the lessee's father, who was rounding up some stray cattle. Sadly, the son hadn't mentioned to his dad that we had already asked for his permission to hunt on their lease. Unfortunately, the damage was done. The sound of the ATV spooked the antelope, which bolted for far-off places. Quite understandably, Myles had a long face when he returned to the truck. I couldn't blame him. You wait a long time to get drawn. We'd done everything right, but the confrontation had blown what was likely

the best chance he'd get to tag the trophy he had his heart set on.

We spent the rest of the day in search of the two other decent bucks we'd spotted earlier to no avail, so toward evening we went back to where we'd seen the non-typical buck earlier in the day. Low and behold, we located him with his harem of does a few miles from where they'd bolted in the morning. Myles took off on another stalk. The herd was really skittish and wouldn't stay put for long in any one spot. When Myles closed the distance and got within range he decided to take a shot. Unfortunately, he missed. The herd took off west where we'd seen them earlier that day. Needless to say, Myles was disappointed as we headed back to a local bed and breakfast where we were staying.

During the night, I listened with dread to the pitter-patter of rain on the roof of our cabin. There's nothing worse than rain on the Alberta prairies, which can make the

ATVs on the prairie can spook the wildlife.

Trails like this can become impassible following rain on the prairies.

trails impassable. Sure enough, when we headed out the next morning, the roads were really muddy; we needed to engage 4-wheel drive even on the main roads.

When we got to the pasture where we'd lost sight of the non-typical buck the evening before, I told Myles it was foolhardy for me to drive too far because we might get stuck far from help. He'd have to hoof it until the sun came up and dried the trail. But a bit of bad weather doesn't discourage Myles. Off he went with his rifle slung over his shoulder. We had two-way radios, so staying in touch wouldn't be an issue, if he needed help.

Myles hiked several miles in a light drizzle. The rain finally stopped when he spotted the buck he was after, bedded down with his harem of does, about a mile away. He

was in plain sight of the antelope, out in the open with nowhere to hide. With no obvious solution, he sat down, despondent. The antelope began to rise from their beds, some milling about as if getting ready to bolt. Suddenly, the herd buck got to its feet.

Ground shrinkage

Phrase used by hunters who realize, upon close inspection, the size of the antlers or horns of a big game animal are not as large as they thought before they pulled the trigger.

A rare non-typical pronghorn antelope

The buck must have thought that Myles was another antelope and decided to run him off. It literally streaked toward Myles.

At top speed a pronghorn can cover a mile in one minute. Within a short time, the buck had closed the distance to about 200 yards. It stopped in its tracks, quartering to its side. Everything happened so quickly that Myles barely had time to extend the legs on his bipod and settle in for a shot. He had just enough time to find the buck in his crosshairs and drop him with one shot from his 7 mm magnum.

What a relief it was when Myles connected with the buck after two failed tries on Day One, validating the "third time lucky" saying and perhaps proving the point that persistence does (eventually) pay off. Even more rewarding was that he tagged the particular buck both of us deemed the best trophy we'd seen while scouting.

If there's a lesson I've learned during a lifetime of hunting pronghorn, it's that you make the best of your opportunities, as imperfect as they may be. If you stay positive, you'll likely be rewarded.

The ears on a mature buck are about 6 inches long. The horns on a trophy buck would be at least 12 to 14 inches long.

CHAPTER TEN

Upland Game Birds

Alberta has several species of upland birds, three of which are not native to the province but have become naturalized since being introduced many years ago, for example, the Chinese ring-necked pheasant, gray (Hungarian) partridge and Merriam's (wild) turkey. The dusky (blue), ruffed, sharp-tailed and spruce grouse and ptarmigan are native to Alberta.

The season on sage grouse is closed because they have been declared an endangered species in Alberta. This chapter contains information about the more popular introduced and native upland birds.

Pheasants have long been one of the most prized game birds, going back to when they were first introduced in Alberta. The actual date that pheasants were introduced is disputed, cited as 1908, 1909 and 1928.

Merriam's turkeys, however, are a more recent arrival. They were first introduced into Alberta's Cypress Hills in 1962 and later into the Porcupine Hills, Lees Lake and other areas. Hungarian partridge were introduced in 1908 (Meredith and Radford, 2008). Ruffed grouse are the most popular native game bird in the aspen parkland and boreal forest, whereas sharp-tailed grouse tops the charts in the foothills and prairies, though it is found throughout the province.

Ring-necked Pheasant

- Alberta has a liberal season on pheasants that extends from September 1 to January 15 in some WMUs, while the season runs from October 15 to November 30 or September 8 to January 15 in other WMUs.

- The daily limit at the time of publication was 2 birds with a possession limit of 6.

- There are no pheasant tags, but hunters must purchase a Pheasant Licence as they cannot be taken with only an Upland Game Bird licence.

- Either a 20-Gauge or 12-Gauge shotgun is recommended, preferably with an improved cylinder choke.

- Any game loads between #4 and #6 shot size would be acceptable as pheasant loads, but #7½ is considered too light except for early season birds.

A ring-necked pheasant in the grass doesn't need much cover to hide out of sight.

Hunting Ring-necked Pheasants

Have you ever encountered a bird more than 30 inches long and 16 inches high, weighing about 3 pounds, that could hide so well in a summer-fallow field that you couldn't spot it even if you were within spitting distance? Or, have you ever stood right beside this upland game bird and then walked right on by, not even knowing it was there because it held so still, only to have it flush behind you as you walked ahead, cackling so loudly that you almost dropped your shotgun? Did this majestic bird have more colours than a rainbow, with a white ring around its neck and a bright red eye patch on an iridescent head? Were you so rattled that when you managed to turn around, find the safety and put a bead on the quickly disappearing target, you missed three shots in a row? Never mind the volley that your hunting partner(s) also fired off without so much as touching a feather. If not, then you haven't hunted ring-necked pheasants.

I've hunted blue grouse, ruffed grouse, sharp-tailed grouse, sage grouse and spruce grouse, all native birds, and I have a great deal of respect for each of these species, but none of them tend to unnerve me, time after time, the way a cock pheasant can and invariably does. That damn cackle is what rattles my nerves, and the sheer magnificence of the fleeting target just makes matters worse. My heart rate hits the roof when they burst from cover, and my adrenaline level goes off the scale!

Pheasants are the most colourful of Alberta's upland game birds.

The gray partridge, a European import, is another fine game bird, and one of the tastiest, but it is a fairly predictable bird so there is no danger of it causing a heart attack. The distribution of the gray partridge is usually spotty throughout their range, and for this reason, most birds are taken incidentally while hunting either pheasants or sharp-tail grouse. They are often found on abandoned farmsteads usually associated with shelterbelts.

So, how do you improve your chances and take the odd brace or two of pheasant? For starters, the best pheasant habitat is in southern Alberta, particularly in the County of Newell surrounding Brooks. This is farm country, and much of it is irrigated land interspersed with native prairie and tame pasture. Where there are seepage areas, there will be cattails—the prime winter cover of pheasants throughout their range. If there are cattail stands, there will be pheasants nearby, especially after the first snowfall. Willows stands are a close second, and cornfields are not far behind. If you are hunting in ranching country near Medicine Hat or in the Lethbridge area, brushy draws with rose and Saskatoon bushes, tall grasses and willows, and the riparian zone beside prairie streams are always a good bet.

Pheasants are most abundant in the "Chinook belt" in southern Alberta, where warm Chinook winds keep the snow off grain fields, grain being the birds' staple winter diet. This belt stretches in a triangle from Lethbridge to Brooks, south to Medicine Hat and on down to Wild Horse, along the Montana border, up through Cardston and back to Lethbridge. There are isolated areas elsewhere where pheasants can be found, but the deep south is the pheasant Mecca of Alberta.

Pheasants eat grain where it is available or seeds of various plants and rose hips, and they like to pick up grit from roads nd trails. On the prairies where gravel oads are sometimes relatively scarce, have seen them fly almost a mile in the early morning to get their grit. They have a relatively small crop, and it doesn't take long to fill it up with grain. Look for feeding pheasants throughout the day because they can be out and about at any time during the day even though the prime feeding time is in the morning. After they have fed and watered, they will make their way to the nearest cover to bed down for the morning and during midday, venturing forth to feed again late in the day.

The best time to hunt them is after they have bedded down, particularly if you are hunting with a dog, because they will have left a good scent trail for your trusty bird dog to follow. Or, sans man's best friend, team up with a friend or two and slowly walk through available cover. Be sure to stop every so often and wait for a minute or so. This break in your walking has an unnerving effect on pheasants and will often flush them out.

A pheasant is a big bird and is actually quite slow on the wing when first airborne. The trick is to let them rise to their cruising altitude, wait until they level off and then squeeze off a shot. I have used a 20-gauge shotgun for pheasants for many years and have never felt undergunned. Size 6 shot is my favourite for late season hunts, and size 7 ½ shot for early season birds, which tend to flush close. I've taken several doubles, and even a few triples when the season allowed for three birds daily, with my outfit. One of the main reasons for my success; however, is that I have used shotguns with an improved cylinder or skeet barrel. Pheasants are almost always closer than you think they are, and most people tend to shoot too soon before the shotgun pattern can open up. Give the birds a bit of a chance to put on some distance before you start shooting.

Pheasants are gregarious birds and when you find one, others will usually be nearby. Late in the season they can congregate in

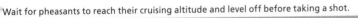

Wait for pheasants to reach their cruising altitude and level off before taking a shot.

Late season pheasant bag made easier with tracking snow

large flocks under some circumstances. What happens is that early winter storms will cause them to bunch up in the best available cover. In the good old days, I saw literally dozens of birds in one patch of cover on several occasions. I remember once when one of my old hunting partners and I flushed what must have been close to 100 birds from a stand of trees in the prairies, and we did not take a single one. The birds rose in such numbers, with hens and cocks mixed together, that it wasn't safe to take a shot because hens were protected. While this doesn't occur often, you will still find them in fairly large congregations where there is good habitat.

Early in the morning is a good time to look for birds feeding in grain fields, near the edge of cover. Always make sure that you have permission to hunt, and respect the owners when on private or leased land. If you ask for permission, there is a good chance that you will be allowed to hunt pheasants as well as other upland birds. If you have never been on a pheasant hunt, you don't know what you're missing!

Donna Martin with a Red Deer River pheasant

Ruffed grouse displaying its plumage during the mating season

The Ruffed Grouse

• A 20-gauge shotgun is recommended, with 7½ shot loads; also 12-gauge shotguns, though, as well as a 410 Bore. All of these gauges are suitable, but the 410 Bore isn't practical for wing shots. Use 7½ shot for these latter gauges.

• Starting in 2016, the season for ruffed grouse was extended in WMUs 102–402, 412–544, 404–410, 841, 936, 728 and 730 (Camp Wainwright) until January 15 from the previous closing date of November 30 to provide additional hunting opportunities.

• There are no tags for any species of grouse in Alberta.

• A #7½ game load is acceptable.

The Elusive Ruffed Grouse: Targeting Bush Bombers

Ruffed grouse are one of Alberta's most abundant game birds, found throughout the foothills, mountains, boreal forest and aspen parkland (the interface between our grasslands and the northern forests). They are most common in the aspen parklands and boreal forests. Ruffed grouse are also present in the Cypress Hills, in southeastern Alberta, as a relic population. They are creatures of aspen stands throughout their range, found never far from these deciduous trees. Their abundance rises and falls in cycles, which have not been very noticeable over the past couple of decades.

Of all of our upland birds, the ruffed grouse is one of the hardest to take on the wing, primarily because of the thick cover they call home. Generally, you'll only have time for one shot, so make it count.

These grouse get their name from a black or reddish-brown ruff of feathers surrounding their neck. Adult ruffed grouse are about 17 inches long. They are a delicacy but must be kept moist when cooking because they are very lean.

It's not uncommon to hear ruffed grouse before you see them. When you're afield, listen for their soft purring and clucking—always a giveaway that they're nearby. One of the most colourful of Alberta's upland birds they have mottled grey feathers streaked with shades of reddish-brown; a barred, fan-shaped tail, which also occasionally comes in a red colour "phase"; and are topped with a tufted crest on their heads. Despite their striking and beautiful coloration, they are well camouflaged and are difficult to spot in the autumn, even when in the open. They have a peculiar bobbing gait as they move about the forest floor, ducking and weaving around like a boxer, often purring as they move along, darting from one place to another. Males have favourite logs that they use as perches.

Ruffed grouse are omnivores, eating both vegetation and insects, but they depend on willow and poplar buds during the winter. They feed on berries, fruits, seeds, buds and clover, which is a favourite food item where available, along with wild rose hips. I've found that ruffed grouse will feed throughout the day but don't like to get their feathers wet when there is heavy dew in the morning. They also tend to stay put after a rain. They can be hunted from sunrise until sunset, and the better areas to try are forest trails in large stands of aspen, especially along the edges, which tend to

Ruffed grouse are creatures of the aspen forest.

Ruffed grouse have striking markings and blend in well with the forest background.

be productive sources of food. As the season wears on; however, look for them roosting in aspen branches during the evening and early morning, out of reach of ground predators and sometimes in groups of several birds. They have feathered feet and can move easily over snow. During inclement weather they'll create a burrow in the snow to wait out storms. Although ruffed grouse are generally solitary birds, it's not uncommon to find family groups in September and pairs in October.

Regardless of where you are hunting ruffed grouse, you're likely going to have to cover a lot of ground in search of birds. Unless they're at the peak of their cycle, the concentration is usually only about one bird per 5 acres in the best aspen habitat, while each bird may have a home range of a quarter section of land (160 acres). In a day's hunt, during which I may cover some 10 to 15 kilometres of bush trails, if I encounter 8 to 10 birds, I consider that an

excellent day. If I shoot 2 or 3 of these birds, I feel as if I've done well. By way of an example, according to government statistics, in 1995 the average daily bag per hunter for all WMUs in Alberta was 0.3 ruffed grouse, whereas it rose to 0.6 birds in 2000. No recent data are available; however, the most recent success rates are available online at My Wild Alberta.

It's important to walk slowly along trails or the edges of clearings when hunting ruffed grouse. Take your time. Look. Listen. Be prepared for a shot, holding your gun in the ready position, which is easier said than done when you're out for the better part of a day.

I find it best to wait until the leaves have started to fall before I venture out on ruffed grouse hunts because it's almost impossible to take grouse on the wing if the trees are in leaf. If possible, when a bird takes flight, wait until after its wings stop beating and it starts its glide before taking

Ruffed grouse are very challenging to shoot on the wing.

your best shot. Once it lifts off, the bird will gain some altitude and then level off in a glide; this is the best time to connect.

One of the side benefits of hunting ruffed grouse during September and October is that the hunter gets an opportunity to scout for big game animals and to get in shape for the rigours of a late-season big game hunt. I've learned a lot about the habits of big game animals while out hunting ruffed grouse, which has paid dividends later on in the season, for example, which game trails are being used by various big game animals; where rubs and white-tailed deer scrapes are located; and where elk and moose are herded up and bedding. Hunting ruffed grouse has made me a better big game hunter.

An improved cylinder choke can be deadly on ruffed grouse, but skeet or modified barrels and even full chokes have their places depending on the time of the year.

What's probably more important is having a shotgun that shoulders easily (with a short barrel) to pick up on a bird and quickly get a lead, if necessary. I never worry about trees and branches being in

———⟨•••⟩———

Grouse will be "locally" abundant.

–Ken Lungle, former Provincial Game Bird Specialist for Alberta. The intent of that statement was that you will likely find grouse wherever some decent habitat remains.

———⟨•••⟩———

the way when I pull the trigger; patterns are a lot larger than you might think, and some pellets will always find their way to the target if you've got the lead down right. Just remember: "put the bead on the beak," and follow through with your swing for best results. It's rare to get off a second shot, even with an autoloader, and even rarer to get a double on ruffed grouse.

While it's great if you can get into a shooter's stance with your left foot forward (if you're a right-handed shot), you'll often have to shoot off balance and try to make the best of it. Not unlike the cackle of a cock pheasant, the sound of beating ruffed grouse wings when they take flight tends to unnerve even the most experienced hunters.

Don't despair if you miss your first shot; it's often possible to follow-up on missed birds and get a second shot after they've landed. Take up the chase, and try to flush them a second time.

I focus on prime ruffed grouse territory to locate the maximum number of birds, and when I'm in the hotspots, I try to locate birds before they spot me, with my gun in the ready position. Even then, I probably get off a shot at only about half of the birds that I encounter and miss half of them. That's par for the course on a typical ruffed grouse hunt. Targeting bush bombers is challenging but can be very rewarding!

Snow hole and wing tracks of a grouse as it burst out of the snow when approached

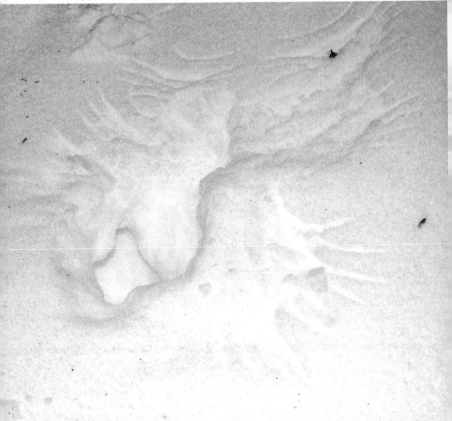

Male sharp-tailed grouse in a strutting position, displaying its plumage during the mating season

Sharp-tailed Grouse

- Alberta has a conservative season on sharp-tailed grouse that extends from October 1 to 31 in WMUs 102–216, 252–256, 300–314, 334, 400–402, 518–520, 524, 525, 528–542, 936. There is a special season in WMUs 728 and 730 (Camp Wainwright) from September 3 to 5.

- The daily limit at the time of publication was 5 birds with a possession limit of 15.

- There are no tags for any grouse in Alberta.

- Either a 20-gauge or 12-gauge shotgun is recommended, preferably with an improved cylinder choke.

- A game load between #6 and #7½ shot size is acceptable.

Hunting Sharp-tailed Grouse

It's hard to top sharp-tailed grouse hunting because of the nature of these birds when hunted with a dog. I always try to hunt into the wind, which makes it easier for a hunting dog to pick up what must be their pungent scent because a pointer can pick it up at a considerable distance. These grouse also tend to fly into the wind if given an opportunity, which makes it a bit easier to take a bead on them as they fly away.

Quite simply, sharp-tailed grouse are most obliging as an upland bird, holding well to a pointer, usually flushing one at a time, not scaring your pants off with cackles or the flutter of wings when they burst from their cover and not being terribly difficult to bring down. Without a good hunting dog, however, all bets are off. The odds are in favour of the sharp-tails. However, they can be spotted from afar and then stalked for shot opportunities.

Hunting Dogs

I was privileged to own a fine dog, Stubs, that I bought from a late friend, Gerry Thompson. Stubs was every bit the consummate hunting dog. He lived to hunt. It was his purpose in life. Even after suffering two anterior cruciate knee surgeries, he went on his last pheasant hunt, on the Milk River Ridge, where we bagged some wily roosters. It was just the two of us, and it was our last hunt together. He collapsed at the end of the day, and I packed him in my arms back to my vehicle. One of the saddest days of my life was when he passed away.

Sharp-tailed grouse often frequent the interface between native prairie and agricultural crops.

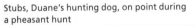

Stubs, Duane's hunting dog, on point during a pheasant hunt

Without question, some of the best spots to hunt sharp-tailed grouse are located along the interface of agriculture fields and native habitat where they can find grain and cover in close proximity. A hunting dog can pick up their scent and either point or flush any birds in the area. Listen for the peculiar guttural chattering sound they make when they flush and burst from cover.

Some of the better habitat for sharp-tailed grouse is in southern Alberta where protected sage grouse also range, so it's important to be certain of your target before you pull the trigger. It is illegal to shoot sage grouse, which are endangered. Also, government surveys continue to indicate that some hunters are shooting sharp-tailed grouse out of season or in closed areas. Some hunters do not realize that the season closes on October 31 when they're deer hunting in November, and that the season is not open throughout the whole province. It is important to check the Alberta Guide to Hunting Regulations for areas that are closed to hunting sharp-tailed grouse. Large parts of Alberta are closed to hunting them, and it is incumbent on hunters to ensure they're in compliance with current regulations and hunt these grouse only in season. I've encountered hunters in eastern Alberta during November big game hunts, for example, who did not realize that the season for sharp-tailed grouse closed on October 31.

You'll put on a lot of miles during most sharp-tailed grouse hunts because their distribution tends to be spotty, so be sure to wear durable hiking boots. These birds tend to stay in flocks, so be prepared for some fast and furious action when you do run into them. As I mentioned earlier, they tend to rise in singles (not as a flock), so take a good bead on each bird as it flushes. Then wait for a second, third and so on to flush. Toward the end of the season it's not unusual to see them roosting in aspen trees, which is probably a defence mechanism to avoid ground predators such as coyotes and foxes.

Sharp-tailed grouse have dark meat and are fine table fare, especially when taken in agricultural areas, but they're not as highly regarded as ruffed grouse, which are considered tops among upland birds.

Prime sharp-tailed grouse habitat in eastern Alberta. Hunt the aspen fringes to locate birds.

It's not often that you'll see three gobblers and one hen.

Turkey

- Use a 12-gauge shotgun with a premium turkey load. Aim for the vital area in the head and neck. Back in the day, BB shot was recommended with a full choke, but times have changed as have turkey loads.

- Choke selection will depend on the nature of the hunt, with a full choke recommended for long-range shots and modified or improved cylinder for close-range shots.

- The season on Merriam's Turkey is subject to a draw with a daily and possession limit of one bird. Only the following WMUs are open to hunting turkeys in Alberta: 300–308, 400, 402.

- The open season is from March 1 to May 31.

Turkey Hunting Woes

It was 1997, and another turkey season had come and gone. Five years had passed since my first turkey hunt, and I still didn't have a gobbler to show for my efforts. As I belted along a gravel road toward Claresholm and on my way back home, my thoughts turned to what had gone wrong. Gordon Lightfoot sang "Early Morning Rain" on 66 CFR out of Calgary as a dust plume spread out half a mile behind my truck. The Porcupine Hills faded out of sight in my rear-view mirror. No more hard ground to sleep on until my next camping trip. That was something positive!

At least the weather had been decent on that trip. Not like the first year I hunted turkeys when I got snowed out, blown out and rained out. I thought my first turkey hunt would be easily done, and I'd have no problems tagging a bird. A week before the season opened, I called up a big gobbler not 10 minutes after I started scouting in the Porcupine Hills. This would be like shooting fish in a barrel, or so I thought. Except that I didn't hear another gobble until the final trip out that year when a wise old tom gave me the slip, after I thought I had him patterned for sure. I was wrong. Something spooked him at the last minute, and he disappeared into thin air. Who said that turkeys were the dumbest birds in the world?

Maybe I hadn't mastered the basic calls. The experts claim there are dozens of turkey calls. That's right; turkeys have 26 different "vocalizations!" It wasn't as though I hadn't listened to calling tapes and practiced them until my wife finally escorted me from the house. You name it—diaphragm calls, box calls, slate calls—I tried them all.

I watched videos on turkey hunting and attended a government-sponsored turkey-hunting seminar. I read books, manuals on how to hunt turkeys and magazine articles on turkey hunting. I bought a new camouflage outfit complete with gloves and face mask. I talked to wildlife biologists and game wardens about turkeys.

Turkeys have dozens of different calls, and it's important to practice basic calls if you hope to call in a gobbler.

pored over topographic maps, looking for hidden turkey valleys and scoured the Porcupine Hills for turkey sign. I was surprised that the turkey hunting fraternity had such an encyclopedia of knowledge on the market. I mean, you could earn a PhD in turkey hunting and still have a lot to learn.

Hunting turkeys is supposed to be simple. First, you scout for turkey tracks. I wouldn't have believed it, but their tracks are as easy to spot as elephant tracks. Next, look for their droppings. These are really cute! The droppings for males and females are actually quite different, so you know when you're on the trail of a tom. No kidding! The males have a long, skinny dropping shaped like a "J" while hens' feces are shaped like coiled clumps. Then you zero in on good roosting areas, usually along ridge tops. You simply locate the roosting tree and call a tom down to terra firma in the wee hours of the morning. Just a couple of soft yelps are all it takes. Take a bead on the head of a big old tom and pull the trigger. End of story. These are simple tactics.

Lanny Amos' son Logan with a Merriam's turkey

If you plan to hunt turkeys on private land, be sure to get permission well in advance of the opening date to secure a spot.

At least that's what all the books say. The trouble is, there are ridge tops galore in the Porcupine Hills!

There must be several thousands, maybe hundreds of thousands, of potential snags a turkey could pick as a roosting tree in this area. But how do you tell which one is *the* roosting tree? That's a good question, and one I've yet to figure out, though not for a lack of trying. I have put on a couple of hundred miles in my search for this Holy Grail of a roosting tree. Maybe it's just around the corner.

I don't think my turkey calls were that bad. After all, I had a couple of toms show an interest during my first hunt. Not to mention I practically had my head taken off on several occasions by goshawks that thought they were going to dine on fresh turkey after they heard my call and went into attack mode. Now that's exciting, being dive-bombed by a large, fierce hawk! Not for someone with a heart condition, though. I even called up a hunter who was confident he was going to fill his tag on my last trip. He said I sounded like a beautiful young hen.

So what am I going to do differently on my next trip out? Should I hire a turkey-hunting guide? I'm not sure there are any in Alberta. What about turkey decoys, which are supposed to work like hot damn in Kentucky? Maybe I should brush up on some of the 26 calls. The popular literature indicates that there are at least 26 calls I have yet to master. It could be just a little thing like that.

Wild turkey in flight

Wild turkey hen with poults

How smart are these birds anyway? What looked like a big tom walked behind my tent as I did the supper dishes on my last hunt and disappeared in the underbrush before I could take a bead on it. I mean, how would that bird know it was safe to practically stop by for a coffee at the end of the day? They can't be that smart, can they? It beats me.

Now don't get me wrong. I don't want to come across as a poor loser. No sour grapes. I paid my money, and I'll take my chances. Lots of guys get skunked on turkey hunts, practically everybody, from what I can gather. I know that hunting is like a crapshoot. The roll of the dice can go any which way on a given trip. But really, why is it that the gobblers have outsmarted me, not to mention practically every other turkey hunter over the previous several years? Now I think I know why Benjamin Franklin proposed a turkey as the United States national symbol.

Yes, I've got my name in the draw again. I'm working on a new game plan. It's not a grudge match or anything like that. Darn it though, it's tough to show your face in the neighbourhood without a gobbler!

CHAPTER ELEVEN

Waterfowl Hunting

Geese, Ducks, Coots and Snipe

- Open season on Snow or Ross's Geese in specified WMUs is from September 1 to December 16 and March 15 to July 5; daily limit of 50* combined and no possession limit.

- Open season on Canada or white-fronted geese runs from September 1 to December 16 or September 8 to December 21, depending on the WMUs; daily limits of 8* and combined possession limits of 24, also subject to limitations on white-fronted geese.

- Open season on ducks, coots and snipe runs from either September 1 to December 16 or September 8 to December 21 depending on the WMU. The daily limit on ducks is 8* and a possession limit of 24*, subject to limitation on pintails and goldeneye for non-resident aliens. For coots and snipe the daily limit is 8* each and a possession limit of 16* each.

- Generally a 12-gauge shotgun is recommended for waterfowl with an improved cylinder for field shoots over decoys and a full choke for pass shooting (i.e., firing at birds as they fly by).

- 12-gauge shotgun shells with BBB steel shot are recommended for geese, and 12-gauge shotgun shells with #2 steel shot for ducks.

* All limits at the time of publication.

Take 'Em!: Guided Waterfowl Hunting

Every once in a while a hunter might experience what's called an "x-hunt," where everything goes according to plan. That's the kind of hunt my son, Myles, and I enjoyed with Black Dog Outfitters, operating out of Tofield, Alberta, in 2014.

Although I've been on many waterfowl hunts, I'd never been on a guided hunt until our booking with Black Dog Outfitters. Myles and I wanted to experience a professional hunt with trained retrievers, experienced guides and an abundance of waterfowl. It turned out to be a father-son hunt of a lifetime, undoubtedly one of the most exciting hunts I've ever experienced.

Mallards are Alberta's go-to species of duck, tough to shoot and delicious to eat.

Going it alone for waterfowl on the Canadian Prairies is a long shot if you don't know what you're doing. And, even if you've been on many do-it-yourself hunts, they're not the same as a guided hunt with expert guides and highly trained retrievers. A guided trip, where the pros are calling the shots, takes a lot the guesswork out of the equation.

The hunting program at Black Dog Outfitters provides an opportunity for field shoots for Canada geese and ducks (mallards in particular) using a variety of hunting techniques: field shoots from both stand-up and layout (also known as "coffin") blinds, pass shooting over prairie creeks for ducks and shooting beside ponds over decoys for mallards. Our booking featured five varied hunts for ducks and geese over the course of three days.

While most of the geese were Canada geese, there were also some greater white-fronted (specklebelly) geese. And although mallards were the focus of our hunts, we also shot pintails, scaups and teal.

The routine at Black Dog Outfitters starts with an early morning wake-up call well before dawn. After a continental breakfast with lots of hot coffee, clients depart for a field shoot. You might want to bring a small thermos of coffee along if you're a caffeine junkie because there are few coffee shops in rural Alberta. Following the morning shoot, the hunters return to camp for a hearty brunch, and maybe an nap, before departing for a late afternoon and evening shoot. Afterwards they return to camp for a delicious home-cooked dinner with all the fixin's before hitting the sack.

Waterfowl guide checks out a decoy spread with a standup blind in the back ground.

All accommodations were provided in a rustic farmhouse near Holden, which is strategically located in the middle of prime waterfowl territory. Black Dog Outfitters has an arrangement with a local Hutterite colony to professionally clean the birds, which are ready for pickup at the end of your hunt. The birds are in excellent shape, ready for the table. A word of advice: Take a large cooler suitable to bring your limit of waterfowl home. You'll need it. The birds will be fully dressed and packaged according to the law for transport. In our hunting party of 6, our bag for the 5 hunts was 113 ducks and 52 geese (27.5 birds per client).

Standup blinds are great for waterfowl field shoots.

A row of layout blinds lined up side by side for a field shoot

Guides do a lot of advance scouting, so they know where ducks and geese are feeding, mornings and evenings. For field shoots, they'll decide whether stand-up or layout blinds work best. Stand-up blinds facilitate side-by-side stand-up shooting over decoys. Hunters are in a prone position in layout blinds, flat on their backs with their shotguns tucked in between their legs, lying in wait for waterfowl to arrive. Shooters with mobility issues prefer stand-up blinds because layout blinds can be a challenge for some shooters to get in and out of as well as to shoot from.

A shooter is basically lying on their back in a layout blind until the guide shouts, "Take 'em." You have to be an experienced hunter to shoot under these conditions, capable of shooting by reflex. The blinds have a small opening to look through, but that's all. At the guide's call, shooters flip open the covering on their blinds, pick out target birds and open fire on the waterfowl. Each hunter has his or her own layout blind strung out near decoys, parallel to each other, in a row.

The guide positions decoys in front of both stand-up blinds and layout blinds pointing into the direction of the wind. Birds tend to land and take off into the wind, so when they cup their wings to get set for a landing, the guide will give a signal to shoot. Typically, hunters should line up on birds in their quadrant. For example, if you're stationed in a blind on the right side of the row, you should target ducks and geese on the right. The same applies to hunters in the middle and left side of the string of blinds. Flocks will be spread out, and there's no point in shooting at birds other hunters are better positioned to hit. The guide will wait until the birds are in range before calling his signal to shoot. That's when the action heats up!

During field shoots over decoys and pass shoots, the trick is to pick out one particular goose or duck as your target. Swing on the bird until you get the proper lead, and then shoot at it until it falls. Canada geese can sometimes be hard to bring down and may take more than one shot. Focus on individual birds and never flock shoot at waterfowl, or you'll likely get skunked. While 12-gauge shotguns are the norm, 20-gauge shotguns are also okay for ducks but are a little under-gunned for geese. Full chokes are recommended for pass shooting, whereas improved cylinders (or modified chokes) work best over decoys. Pump action, semi-autos and over-under or side-by-side shotguns will all do the job, with auto-loaders being the best bet.

A word of advice to novice hunters: Make sure you get in some target practice at your local gun range in advance of your hunt by

They're flying high today

Phrase used by waterfowl hunters, meaning the birds are out of range because the weather is good; under poor weather waterfowl tend to fly low.

A 12-gauge auto loader is ideal on guided hunts for both ducks and geese.

shooting skeet, not trap. You're paying good money to the outfitter, so be sure you can hit clay targets fairly consistently. Bring the loads recommended by the outfitter and at least one box of shells for each hunt, morning and evening, as a rule of thumb. It's a good idea to have a shell carrying bag that you can tuck away in your blind out of sight of the birds as well as for picking up spent shells after the shoot.

Make absolutely sure you know how to operate your shotgun because action is generally fast and furious, and you shouldn't have any doubts about your equipment. Your gun should be cleaned and in good working order. Ideally, it's a good idea to wear full camouflage clothing and long underwear because temperatures are often near 0°C in the morning during fall shoots, and it's not unusual for frost to be on the ground. A headlamp is a real asset for morning shoots because set ups are always done in the dark. Clients are expected to make minor adjustments to layout blinds by inserting chaff and straw to ensure they blend in with their surroundings. This is often done in the dark.

Myles and Duane Radford with limits of Canada geese taken during their guided hunt

A retriever will be under the command of the guide, who will direct it with hand signals to fetch downed birds. The dog will have its own blind and is trained to stay there until the shooting stops. There's nothing like the sight of a well-trained Labrador retriever bringing a downed Canada goose back to the guide or sniffing out fallen mallards under swaths of grain. These are true working dogs and are excellent retrievers.

I'll never forget the first field shoot for Canada geese out of layout blinds during our guided hunt. The guide called flock after flock into the setup, and action was unbelievable on the large honkers. By 9:00 AM, all six in our hunting party had limited out! Likewise, a morning shoot over decoys for mallards the next day also had a happy ending with similar results. It just doesn't get any better. This was one of the best hunts of my lifetime, one of the most exciting experiences I've enjoyed in the great outdoors.

Raining Birds: Shotgun Hunting Tips for Waterfowl

When I approached Blaine Burns regarding an interview on waterfowl shotgun hunting tips he replied, "It's a good topic as most people don't know squat about gun fit and how important it is. Burns has a lifetime of waterfowl shooting knowledge and experience, and is an expert on the subject. He ought to know the skinny on shotgun hunting tips for waterfowl; he's been the owner/manager of Black Dog Outfitters since 1977, and waterfowl hunting has been a big part of his life since he was a teenager. He owned a sporting clays range for many years, has guided hunters for the past 20 years in Canada and Argentina and has instructed shotgun shooters.

Pick one Canada goose out of a flock and keep shooting at it until it drops. Do not flock shoot.

I first met Burns when he worked for Ducks Unlimited Canada as a biologist and Area Manager for 17 years in Brooks. I asked him how to have a successful waterfowl hunt. Despite my having hunted waterfowl for many years, I was surprised by some of the common sense answers he provided.

Burns says that guns that break open can be a bit of a problem in a layout or stand-up blind, but there are no issues with a pump or semi-automatic shotgun. He also says that shotguns with longer barrels are more efficient for shooting at longer ranges and "not blasting your partner's ears" when shooting out of blinds. Burns claims that a semi-automatic shotgun is probably one of the best for waterfowl hunting, but pumps are also okay. "Camo dressing is probably a bit of overkill," he said. "It's more for consumers than birds." Burns says, "It's important that guns don't shine. In Alberta,

with the prevailing northwest winds, shiny barrels can flare birds that pick up sunlight when landing into the wind."

Regarding chokes, Burns is adamant that improved cylinders work best on decoyed birds because of their wider patterns. However, for pass shooting, patterns need to be tighter, so a modified or full choke would work better, he says.

Burns recommends shooting 3-inch #2 shot for ducks and 3-inch BBB loads for geese—over decoys—but maybe 3 ½-inch length for pass shooting over a longer distance. He says, "1 ⅛ oz is ample shot in most cases. You'll need 1500 feet/second (457 metres/second) velocity for knockdown power when shooting steel shot. Mass times velocity creates the energy delivery necessary to bring down birds."

Burns believes that most brands of shotgun shells are similar, but some brands seem to shoot better in some guns and with different chokes, so he suggests trying different loads to find a brand that works for you.

"I don't know that I've shot enough different brands to really make a good assessment," he said. I asked whether there was much difference among the popular brands, to which he replied, "Not in my mind." When I asked him if he recalled the old bargain basement C.I.L. Canuck shotgun shell loads, which some hunters looked down on, he chuckled. "Well, when you think of a gun's accuracy, it's all about your confidence. If you're confident when you pull a gun up, and you know that you've got a good load, you'll shoot well." He also said that if you pattern different guns, you should develop a better level of confidence in both your shotgun and loads—a point well taken, but seldom done by waterfowlers.

"Lots of people shoot a little differently in terms of how low they get their head down, flat on the barrel, looking down the barrel. You should keep your head down. Some guns shoot a higher percentage of the shot pattern above the gun barrel than below the barrel," Burns said. He says that's just how he shoots, and consequently, he enjoys the same success with the Benelli brand of shotguns. On the other hand, he says when he has a Beretta in his arms, it takes him a while to adjust to it. This is testament to the *caveat emptor* warning—Let the buyer beware—because various models really do shoot differently. Burns says the Beretta shotgun product line seems to be made for people who tend to hold their heads upright more than he does. He says these are just some examples of how shotguns can be different, especially for people who are a little shorter than average or have really long arms. You need to make some adjustments to really shoot a gun well.

Outfitters recommend # 2 shot for ducks.

While marksmen are made, not born, those who shoot well tend to shoulder a gun effortlessly and have good eye-hand coordination. A shotgun should come to your cheek first, then your shoulder. Your cheek should be firmly on the comb of the gunstock, all while your head should be erect. Your dominant eye should be looking down the barrel. The bead should be on the target. In other words, ideally, the gun should fit your body frame and feel natural in the ready position. Burns says that some brands of guns have a better fit for him than others and always have. If your shotgun doesn't have a good fit, you won't be able to find the target easily, lead it properly and squeeze the trigger at the right time.

Burns says that sporting clays provide a good variety of targets for hunters trying to improve their waterfowl shooting skills with higher crossings and/or birds settling in, and then dropping, simulating field conditions. Compared with shooting trap loads, these are quite a bit slower because with steel you have to shorten your leads.

When shooting sporting clays, there are several different stations where the clay targets either cross high in front of a shooter or come towards a shooter at a declining altitude. Trap shooting loads are made of lead and don't travel at as high a velocity as steel shot. Lead shot has been illegal for waterfowl hunting for many years, but shooters still practice with lead shot, which is one reason why it can take a while to make the transition.

A shotgun should shoulder well, and it's important to have your cheek flat on the comb for sighting along the barrel.

A trained retriever is especially important when shooting waterfowl over water to retrieve downed birds.

Burns says when he goes to Argentina, where lead shot is still legal, it takes him a while to adjust because it is slower than steel shot. He has to recalibrate, and when he comes back to Alberta he has to lead birds a little more. "Everybody makes those adjustments fairly quickly," he says.

"Faster loads make most shooters better if they hold on the bird. Unless they're a long way out and crossing, you don't need a whole lot of a lead."

Take 'em!

The command to start shooting from a blind when hunting waterfowl.

According to authorities, most lead shot hunting game loads range from 1150 to 1350 feet per second (350 to 410 metres per second) because lead shot will deform easily and blow patterns. (Lead shot is cylindrical in shape, and because it's soft, it can easily be misshapen and then it won't fly straight.) By comparison, steel shot does not deform; consequently, the velocity can increase without shot deformation and disintegrating patterns. Steel shot hunting loads range from 1265 to 1500 feet per second (385 to 460 metres per second).

I'd suggest that waterfowl hunters should not overthink their shots or they might lose focus, like typing on a keyboard—just do it. If you've studied the keyboard and practiced, you shouldn't have to look at the keys. Similarly, if you don't practice your shotgun shooting skills, you'll be handicapped when it comes time to shoot waterfowl. It is imperative that you practice the fundamentals of using a shotgun until you master them. The best place to achieve that mastery is at a local shooting range.

Burns also agrees that you shouldn't over-analyze your shots, to a point. "You can over-think your shots, but doing more of it [shooting] can help you get better. Don't do any thinking until you're consistently missing the target," he says. Good waterfowl shots are able to quickly pick up their target and point a shotgun in the right direction more or less automatically.

If you find yourself consciously thinking about what you should do, you'll probably miss the shot. Burns says what you must do, though, if you're not consistently on target, is to try to and figure out what's going wrong. For example, are you shooting in front of or behind the target? If so, then make some adjustments in your technique.

When it comes to safety concerns, Burns says, "Your shotgun barrel always needs to be above the bar in a layout blind. The doors of the blind always close over the gun. Never point your barrel across the blind. It should be pointed up at all times. Don't shoot over your partner. Stay in your zone." This is one of the reasons

Author with a limit of mallards shot over decoys

The 12-gauge Browning automatic A5 Stalker does the job on Canada geese.

Burns doesn't like short-barrelled over-and-under and side-by-side shotguns because some hunters keep these types of guns under the bar in a layout blind. He knows of one instance in the Brooks area in southern Alberta where a hunter shot his toe off under these circumstances.

Don't shoot over your partners as a courtesy and for reasons of safety. Their ears will be ringing for days if you don't follow this rule. He says the best hunters he sees come from places like Arkansas, where they are used to hunting in timber and keying in on waterfowl in narrow shooting lanes. He sees this as a matter of being efficient and picking your spots when shooting is tight.

Things typically happen quickly during a waterfowl hunt. You don't have much time to analyze shot opportunities; you must be able to react and take advantage of your chances. Learn to shoot by developing a proper lead, and follow through with your swing. Pick the point where you will insert the muzzle as you make your move. If you're a swing-through shooter, this will be behind the target; if you shoot maintained lead, it will be in front. If pull-away, it will be the target's leading edge. Be sure to keep a hard visual focus on the target, and never flock shoot. This is the most important point, all things considered. Focusing on the target solves many ills on the shooting clays course and in the field. With practice, you'll develop reflex shooting skills where you can execute all the proper steps automatically. To be a consistently good shot with a shotgun, it must shoot where you look.

CHAPTER TWELVE

Bears, Cougars and other Predators

If it is predators you're after, you need not look any further than Alberta where numerous black bears, cougars, wolves, coyotes and foxes roam the wild country.

Black Bears

Alberta is a renowned bear hunting hot spot, with two-bear limits in some WMUs, baiting in specified WMUs only, during fall and spring seasons. Some thriving populations are actually considered "under-hunted" by some biologists.

- Spring seasons typically open April 1 and can run to as late as mid-June in some regions.

- Fall seasons open at the end of August and run until the end of November.

- In Alberta, black bears hibernate through the winter months.

- There's no season on grizzly bears because the Alberta government suspended the hunt in 2006 over fears of dwindling numbers and subsequently declared grizzlies a threatened species in 2010.

- It is illegal to hunt a black bear under the age of one year or a female black bear accompanied to a cub under the age of one year.

- Common calibres for hunting black bear range from the .30 calibres up to the .338 Winchester Magnum.

Alberta's black bears are massive, imposing animals that can reach weights of more than 450 pounds (204 kg) and are found in virtually every forested region of the province. They come in a variety of colour phases, from blond to cinnamon to jet black and everything in between. Black bears are relatively abundant throughout their range.

Black bears are abundant throughout much of Alberta's forested areas.

Cougars

- Resident season for cougars runs from September 1 to December 31.

- Non-resident cougar season runs from December 1 to the last day of February for either sex, with lots of opportunity to bag a cat. Non-resident licences must be purchased through an outfitter-guide. Anyone exporting a cougar to points outside of Alberta must obtain a provincial export permit.

- Archery-only season runs from September 1 to December 31 in WMUS 212 and 248; from November 1 to November 30 in WMU 410; and from December 1 to February 28 in WMU 410.

- Cougars are generally managed on a quota system to prevent over-harvest.

- Some of the more popular and relatively common calibres for cougar hunting are: .25-06, .270 Winchester, 7x57, .280 Remington, 7mm Magnum, .30-30, .300 Savage, .308 Winchester and 30-06.

Cougar sightings are becoming more and more numerous, especially in the boreal forest area in northern Alberta, where they weren't all that common until several years ago. Many cougar guides and resident hunters swear they've never seen as many

Alberta's resident season for cougars runs from September 1 to December 31, and most are taken on guided hunts with dogs.

cougars in Alberta as they have in the past few years. Not only that, cougars have expanded their range following an explosion of deer over the past couple of decades, so they are being seen in places not normally associated with traditional cougar habitat on the prairies, parklands and boreal forest. I've actually seen them as far north as Lesser Slave Lake, which is located far north in the boreal forest. Some males can be brutes, large enough to fill the box of a pickup truck!

Winter weather can be harsh, so hunters must be prepared for sub-zero temperatures and deep snow. Dressing in layers with lightweight boots rated for –25°C is recommended.

Good tracking snow

A phrase used by hunters, meaning there's just enough snow to find the tracks left by game animals, which helps them zero in on their approximate whereabouts.

Wolves, Coyotes and Foxes

- Varmint rifles are preferred for coyotes and foxes.

- Popular calibres for coyotes and foxes are: the .204 Ruger, .223 Remington, .22-250 Remington, and .243 Winchester.

- Wolves are larger animals than coyotes and foxes. For shots less than 200 yards (180 m), recommended calibres are: .223 Remington and .22-250 Remington. Larger calibres could damage the pelts.

Coyotes and wolves are abundant in Alberta; they are at an all-time high and are expanding their range. Some municipalities have issued bounties on wolves because they are so abundant. Many local hunters are taking wolves incidental to other game. Coyotes are so common that during a recent November's deer hunt, I saw a dozen coyotes on a single quarter section of land in the prairies.

While there are some disclaimers that should be reviewed in the hunting regulations, according to the "Alberta Guide to Hunting Regulations" at the time of publication:

Any person who is the owner or occupant of privately owned land or has permission to hunt on said

Coyotes are abundant in Alberta and are usually taken using predator calls.

Wolf numbers are currently healthy in the mountain and boreal regions of Alberta.

land may, without a licence, hunt (but not trap) coyotes and timber wolves on such lands, at all times of the year. A resident may, without a licence, hunt (but not trap) timber wolf from the opening of any big game season in a particular WMU to May 31 or until June 15th in WMUs where black bear seasons are open until June 15th under the most recent hunting regulations.

Although their numbers may fluctuate, coyotes remain locally abundant throughout the province and are common just about everywhere including within the city limits of Calgary and Edmonton. Most coyotes are taken by using predator calls, though spot-and-stalk hunting is also popular. Predator calls can be dynamite, and I've had as many as three coyotes respond at a given time to a call.

Red fox may be hunted without a licence and during all seasons by a resident on privately owned land to which the resident has the right of access.

CHAPTER THIRTEEN

Tracking Wounded Game

Day of Reckoning

During a hunt on a cold November day in 2012, I was a bit surprised to see a 6-point bull elk leave the cover of an aspen stand and start to cross a forest clearing. I knew the bull was in the area, which is why I stayed on stand in the hope that the animal might expose itself. Within seconds after spotting the elk, I'd extended the legs on my rifle's bipod, shouldered the rifle and found the bull in my scope. I settled the crosshairs just behind his shoulders, panning the elk as he quartered away from me in a northerly direction. It was basically a chip shot at a range of about 150 yards. I waited until he stopped, presumably deciding whether to go forward, then I squeezed the trigger. At the sound of the shot the bull collapsed onto its chest. I chambered another round. The bull staggered to its feet, unsteady on its legs, facing away from me with no real shot opportunity. It was hard to believe, but the animal then cantered about 125 yards before turning broadside to look back in my direction. It was all the time I needed. I fired

Tracking wounded game is challenging and requires patience and stealth.

off another round from my .300 WSM calibre rifle sending a 180-grain bullet into its shoulder. Down it went, thrashing its legs in the air, as though in its death throes. To my consternation, however, the bull once again regained its feet and headed back toward the bush, not far from where it originally came out of the aspen stand. Within seconds it had disappeared. Yikes! What the devil happened? Two good shoots, either one of which should have anchored the elk, yet it was gone! All this happened in less than 30 seconds. The silence in the woods was deafening. I shook my head, disappointed the elk was gone.

I've learned from experience that this is not the time to lose your cool. It's important to stay calm, sit tight for a while and then take up the chase. After waiting for 15 minutes, I went to look for the bull's trail. It wasn't long before I found the spot where it had been hit the first time. Shortly afterwards, I found the place where the animal had gone down the second time. It was fairly easy to follow the bull's trail after it regained its footing and headed toward the bush. It was like a crime scene. Splatters of blood were easy to find in the snow, as well as splayed tracks where it slipped in the snow, even though there were tracks from other elk in the area. Then there was a rather large patch of blood on an aspen tree where it left the field, almost like a signpost. About 50 feet inside the stand of aspen the bull lay dead. The first shot had gone through its lungs, the second shot through the shoulder, yet it had still travelled about 350 yards after being hit the first time.

This is a textbook story of tracking wounded big game. Fortunately, it had a happy ending. Not all stories end this way. Using this scenario, let's examine the

Always hold on hair for your first shot and try to make it count.

Search for specks of blood when on the trail of wounded game.

art and science of tracking wounded big game animals and what a hunter should do to ensure similar situations end in a positive way. It's only a matter of time before every hunter has to track a wounded animal. It happens to even the best marksmen.

Actually, on some occasions, it's the "perfect" heart or lung shot that's behind wounded big game gone astray! It may be hard to believe, but it's true. It has happened to me on several occasions with pronghorn antelope, elk, moose, mule deer and white-tailed deer after my quarry seemingly vanished, even though the shot was fatal.

What you do and don't do in the aftermath of a shot is crucial and may well have a bearing on whether you find that wounded animal, either dead or in its death throes. This is a time for cool heads, thoughtful

follow-up tactics and contingency plans in case things go awry.

After the Shooting Stops

After you stop shooting, keep your eye on the prize and mentally mark the location where you think the animal was hit. Then, if it runs away instead of falling dead in its tracks, you'll have an idea of where to start your search. Note any key landmarks. Try to recall whether you heard the characteristic "thud" sound of a bullet from a high-powered rifle hitting a big game animal or just the crack of a rifle, such as when it is fired at a paper target. Did the animal fall on its chest or side? Did it stagger? Did it run downhill, or did it hunch over before taking off? If it hunched over it was probably a gut shot, or perhaps shot through the liver, just back of the lungs. Gut shot animals are the worst to track because there's seldom much of a blood trail, and the animals can be quite mobile because they don't necessarily go into shock. Animals shot through the liver can sometimes travel several hundred yards before dying and may not leave much of a blood trail either.

Focus on what actually happened once the shooting stopped, and reconstruct the events until they're clear in your mind before you begin your search. And wait at least 10 to 15 minutes before taking up the search (more on this later).

Go to where the animal was standing when you took your first shot and look for evidence that it was hit. Try to find blood splatters, hair dislodged by a bullet or splayed tracks that characterize an animal losing its footing from the shock of the bullet. If you do find any of these signs, mark the spot by making a cross in the snow or a landmark with branches or rocks on the ground if there's no snow.

This is a key step for beginning your search for a wounded animal. Act as you would if you were investigating a crime scene; you don't want to destroy any evidence, so be careful and systematic.

The Search

You'll know the general direction a wounded animal headed if you were paying attention, so look for clues as you take up the search from the spot where the animal was shot, assuming you found this spot by using key landmarks nearby. You should be able to find it without too much trouble. Here are some tips to follow in your search:

- Walk slowly.

- If you are hunting with a partner or partners, be quiet. Don't talk unless you have to. Use hand signals to communicate.

- Be prepared for a follow-up shot; have a round in the chamber of your rifle.

The last elk I shot left this splatch of blood on a tree.

———<•••>———

*What passes for "ethical"
hunting varies widely with
the locality.*

–Carl Hunt, Edson biologist
and big game hunter

———<•••>———

- Turn the power down on variable scopes in case you have to make a hasty follow-up shot.

- Listen for the sound of a falling animal or an animal crashing through the bush. In other words, be on high alert; you don't want to screw up what might be your only opportunity for a killing shot under tough circumstances.

- If there's snow on the ground, don't walk in the footprints of the animal you're trailing. Walk off to the side of the footprints so you don't destroy any forensic signs in your search.

- Wounded animals watch their back tracks; they're wired after being hit. You'll be surprised how often a wounded animal will jump sideways to throw a hunter off its trail, especially deer. You may have to backtrack if you lose the trail to find where an animal jumped sideways.

- If there's no snow on the ground, go slowly and keep an eye on the ground

and in front of you and peripherally. Watch out of the corner of your eye for signs of your quarry. There may not be a steady trail of blood; rather it will be spotty and may be on grass, shrubs and trees. Pay attention at all times, and don't take anything for granted.

Key Clues

If the animal has only a flesh wound, the loss of blood will be even and slow, and the blood will be bright red. There probably won't be a lot of blood on the trail. If you hit a vein with your shot, there will be a steady slow flow of dark red blood. If you hit an artery, there will be signs of spurting blood, a pulsating flow, bright red in colour and generally lots of blood to follow.

If an animal heads downhill, it was likely hit hard, but not always. I once shot a 6-point bull elk as it was walking uphill through a logged area at a range of about 150 yards. The bullet went through both lungs, but the animal showed no sign whatsoever of being hit. It didn't fall, stagger or break its stride and travelled another 100 yards before falling dead. I found no blood trail, and only by systematically searching imaginary grids did I eventually find the elk, by its smell no less. Elk, in particular, have a pungent smell during the rut, so keep this in mind during your days afield.

If an animal has been mortally wounded, it will likely bed down within a few hundred yards of being hit. This is why it's critical to go slowly, always look ahead and try to spot a bedded animal so you're ready for a shot. If you have hunting partners, work out a plan so they flank you as you go forward in case they have to help make the killing shot. Deer, in particular, will usually head for the thickest bush in their home range. It's where they feel safe.

Why Wait to Take Up the Search?

If you hit a big game animal in a vital area, it will bleed to death in short order. However, you won't know the circumstances under which the animal has disappeared, so assume it has been mortally wounded and don't rush the chase. If you frighten it when it's on its deathbed, the animal could take off again in an adrenalin rush and perhaps disappear forever. Hemorrhaging keeps the brain, heart, liver, lungs and kidneys from receiving the flow of blood they need to function. If there's a hemorrhage, the animal will bleed out after losing consciousness. It will not have full cognitive capacity under these circumstances but will be disoriented and will not necessarily recognize danger when you catch up with it. This is where camouflage clothing comes in handy. It's hard enough for big game to spot a hunter in camouflage clothing when the animal is fully alert, but it's much harder when the animal is in a state of shock as a result of loss of blood. The animal will likely be lethargic, confused and unresponsive. If an artery was severed, bleeding generally occurs quickly, though in some cases the bleeding might spasm and close down partially. Typically, in the case of an injured artery, blood spurts out with each pump of the heart. Venous bleeding is usually slower, described as "oozing." Either way, loss of too much blood eventually causes cardiac arrhythmia, which leads to a heart attack and the animal dies, often within a few minutes at most.

Those "Perfect" Shots

I'm from the old school of hunters and aim just behind the shoulder of an animal for a lung shot so as not to waste any meat.

Be sure to always follow up on your shots at big game animals.

Animals shot in the lungs will leave a bright, frothy blood trail as on the mouth of this deer.

Another school of hunters prefers shoulder shots to immobilize big game and cause shock and massive bleeding especially with magnum rifles. If an animal is shot through either the heart or lungs, it will often travel 75 to 100 yards or more before dying. It's these "perfect" shots that are often the cause of consternation, but they are a fact of life for hunters.

I recall another elk hunt where I surprised a 5-point bull feeding in a forest clearing at sunrise. As soon as I saw the elk, it bolted, charging toward the forest. I knew I'd only have time for one shot. I quickly estimated the range, led the animal and fired. It was running broadside and, as it later turned out, was 230 yards distant when the bullet went through its heart and on through the far shoulder. The elk didn't so much as falter after being shot; it disappeared in the bush. I found it dead about 75 yards away from where it had been when I shot it. I was confident in my shooting ability and familiar with my rifle and making running shots, so I couldn't see how I could have missed this shot on such a large animal. It took me a while to find signs of a hit, then take up the trail and locate the dead elk, but sure enough, it turned out to be a clean kill as I initially suspected.

Duane Radford looking through a spotting scope for bighorn sheep

Cardinal Rules of Shooting

Try to follow the cardinal rules of shooting when hunting big game:

• Adhere to the old cliché, "always hold on hair," for your first shot. Don't shoot over the animal's back.

• Make your first shot count. It's usually the best opportunity you'll have so make the most of it.

• Use a rest or a bipod for your rifle to ensure a minimum of shake.

• Get your breathing under control before you squeeze the trigger.

• Practice at the range before you go hunting so you're confident in your shooting ability.

• Use the proper calibre for the game you're hunting so you're not under-gunned.

• And most importantly, always follow-up on your shots and don't take anything for granted.

CHAPTER FOURTEEN

Big Game Taxidermy

The Art & Science

I've dealt with many taxidermists over the years who have passed on various tips about handling big game animals for purposes of taxidermy. I've also had experience with capes of several species of big game animals. However, for this chapter, I decided to go to Brian Dobson of Artistic Taxidermy in Edmonton to get the skinny on big game taxidermy. Brian is an old friend who is a "World, National, Canadian and International Champion" taxidermist, as well as an avid hunter.

Some of the topics I discussed with Brian were:

1. How does a taxidermist create life-like replicas of big game trophies?

2. What steps do they follow?

3. What kind of form should a customer choose, depending on where the trophy will hang in their home, cottage or office: left/right turn; sweep; straight ahead; sneak? Forms come with a left or right turn of the head, straight ahead

Brian Dobson puts finishing touches on a white-tailed buck.

(with no turn of the head) or what's called a "sneak" with the neck turned downward in the form of a crouch.

4. What should you do to ensure that you don't damage the cape, horns or antlers before they reach a taxidermist?

5. How should you handle a cape in the field if you don't feel confident skinning it out?

6. If the cape is damaged, can it be replaced and what will this cost?

7. What's the range of costs for various big game mounts in today's markets?

No detail is too small for a top taxidermist. From the time he receives a raw head or cape and antlers (or horns), Brian takes the following steps:

1. Flesh out the cape, i.e., remove all excess meat and fat.

2. Wash the cape to rid it of blood and dirt to restore its lustre.

3. Saw the horns off the skull plate so they'll fit properly on a form.

4. Have the hide tanned.

5. Select the right size form for the size of the head.

6. Shape the form, if necessary, to match the likeness of the animal.

7. Properly set the eyes on the form.

8. Paint the nostrils and eyelids so they are lifelike.

9. Position the ears.

10. Comb and smooth the cape so it looks natural.

The Cape

Brian says that it's important not to cut too far up in the brisket area (in between the legs) once an animal is downed and after it has been gutted and cleaned.

"Stop just behind the shoulder," Brian says. "Once you get it home or in the garage and you want to take the cape off, the easiest way is to cut right around behind the front shoulders and roll the cape toward the jaw line and disconnect the head [by cutting through the neck]." This process can also be done in the field when an animal is on the ground or back at the vehicle if you have a portable winch and can hoist it off the ground.

Brian suggests, "Take the cape and antlers, intact, to a taxidermist." He says that if a hunter is experienced, they can skin out the head and disconnect the ear butts. But he cautions, "Ninety-nine percent of hunters don't know how to do this properly, so it's best to bring in the head and cape intact at that stage."

Trophy mule deer (right turn, shoulder mount)

Brian Dobson checking a white-tailed deer form in his Edmonton studio

If a hunter can't bring in the head right away, it should be frozen as soon as possible to prevent the cape from spoiling. During autumn, when on an extended hunt, Brian recommends keeping the head and cape out of sunlight and storing it in a cool area by a creek if a hunter can't get it out for a few days. If it's warm; however, it is important to get it to a taxidermist within a day or two to prevent the hair from slipping.

Get the cape off the carcass as soon as possible to cool the cape down, because the meat will keep the cape warm, which also leads to hair slippage. "We use 3-inch blade Victornox or Henkel paring knives that can be purchased in places that sell trapper supplies or at knife shops," said Brian. These are generally inexpensive 3.5- or 4-inch long knives. You don't need a fancy or expensive knife to cape an animal, but it's always a good idea to keep them sharp.

It's important to use care when skinning the cape to avoid knife cuts, which damage the hair by cutting off the ends. These cuts are difficult to hide and generally cannot be repaired. Most small nicks and cuts can be repaired, and there is no extra charge for this kind of repair work.

If a cape is damaged, it can be replaced. Brian says, "If you're looking at replacing a deer cape, it could cost between $25 and

$75, depending on the size of the neck and head." Elk and moose capes run from $100 to $200 on average. Most taxidermists have surplus capes in stock. "We charge the customer whatever we pay for the cape," said Brian. Big game capes may be legally purchased by a taxidermist from a hunter who wishes to sell them and resold to someone who has a damaged cape but wishes to mount horns or antlers from a legally taken game animal.

It's important that hunters carry water, paper towels or cloths to clean capes of blood. "For any animal that has white hair, particularly antelope or mountain goats, it's best to keep the blood off the hair. These animals have hollow hair, and once the blood soaks in, it's a lot harder to get it out," he said. A tannery or taxidermist might otherwise have to do some bleaching, and this can affect the life of the hair. "Stick some paper towel in the mouth and nostril openings, and remove any blood from the cape with water on a paper towel." Brian tries to wash any blood off capes in a sink and dry them off before they're salted and sent to a commercial tannery. It's best to get them as clean as possible.

Trophy pronghorn antelope with heart-shaped horns

The Horns

If you're doing a horn mount for antelope, it's essential to remove the horn sheath from the core by running a knife between the core and sheath. The fat and grease has to be cleaned from the core of the horns otherwise it will smell, and bugs will get inside. Once the fat and grease in a horn sheath have been boiled off and dried, the clean antelope horns can be reattached to the skull plate with Bondo (autobody fiberglass filler). Baking soda added to the water will help the cleaning process when boiling the skull plate.

Choosing the Right Form

"It's necessary to start with up-to-date forms to create life-like mounts," says Brian. "Nowadays, taxidermy forms have come long ways, and there's a minimal amount of clay work and alterations required. There's a wide variety of forms on today's market, and they're a lot easier to use. The most important thing, though, is that you have to know what an animal looks like, or what you want it look like, before you even put the hide on. This has to do with the detailing of the clay work around the eyes and nose. You have to

Brian Dobson adjusting mule deer antlers on a form (right turn, shoulder)

have it in your mind exactly what you want it to look like. You can't just put the hide on the form with some glue and think you're going to make it look life-like. Basically, once I've done my clay work and put the hide on the form, I know what the animal should look like. Eye expressions, ears and positioning of ear butts are what make a life-like mount."

Customers should choose the type of form for their big game mount with care, considering exactly where they plan to display their trophy. Both the heights at which the mount will be hung and the size of the antlers come into play.

"For a wider rack, I'd suggest more of a semi-sneak pose," says Brian "but if they're a taller rack, then I'd go for an upright pose." If the antlers have a strong side, he would usually turn that side toward the wall, for example, if one side is heavier or has more points. "That's the side that you would see a little bit better. If there are drop tines or kickers, they might look better pulled away from the wall." If there was something wrong with the cape, such as a scar on one side, he says you might want to turn it away from the main viewing position. Most taxidermists will give a hunter advice on what style of mount will work best for their particular circumstances.

Mounted cock pheasant

In the winter, Brian notes that many hunters put their deer carcass in the back of their trucks during sub-zero weather, and the blood bleeds into the hair from the mouth and freezes to the floor. When they get home, they grab the deer and pull it out with loss of hair frozen to the truck bed—a common mistake. This kind of damage cannot be repaired.

Dragging a deer carcass behind a quad for long distances can also damage the hide, ruining a cape. Brian says, "Take some extra care of the cape if you think you're going to have an animal mounted." Leave the rest to the pros! Also take care to protect antlers and horns from rubbing against hard objects or surfaces on the way home.

If you plan to have an upland bird taxidermized, it's a good idea to stuff some cotton balls in its beak so blood doesn't get on the feathers. Also, it's a good idea to fashion some newspaper into the shape of a cone with some masking tape, then put the bird put inside to protect it from any damage.

CHAPTER FIFTEEN

Field Dressing and Cooking Your Bounty

Handling the Carcass

"The fun ends after the shot!" is a universal joke among hunters. That's when the job of field dressing a big game animal starts and subsequently getting the carcass back to your vehicle for the trip home, or to a butcher shop, for processing. This saying is always in the back of my mind whenever I go hunting. It's also something I think about before I even consider a stalk or pulling the trigger.

I've had too many bad experiences that have made me wary about shooting big game in an awkward spot, especially during warm weather. Probably one of the most extreme cases occurred when I shot a cow elk in WMU 300 north of Waterton Lakes National Park on September 6, 1988, during the eruption of Mount St. Helens in the state of Washington when volcanic ash blanketed much of southern Alberta. In addition to the ash and warm weather (25° + C), my hunting partner and I had to contend with literally thousands of yellowjacket wasps while we field dressed and quartered the elk. Miraculously, I was stung only once!

Shooting an animal is not always the tough part of hunting. Getting it out, especially in one piece, often is. You might be able to drag it out yourself or haul it out using a horse. You could also use a snowmobile, OHV or a trail bike to drag it out whole. It's almost impossible to drag an elk or moose; however, on dry ground any great distance without ruining the meat even with two (or more) strong men. If you can't

Getting an elk ready for de-boning

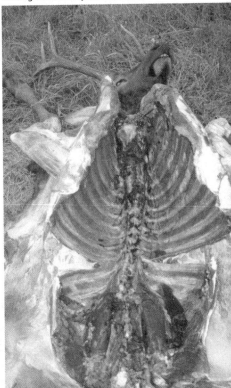

get the carcass out in one piece, you're faced with a few options: a pack job, taking it out one quarter (or half) at a time (e.g., on your back or dragging it on a sled), or de-boning it and packing the meat out in game bags.

I've had some tough situations, wishing I'd passed up taking an animal or suffered regrets that my hunting partner(s) had pulled the trigger because I wasn't properly prepared for the task at hand. I'd like to share my experiences on how I currently handle such challenges in this chapter and what a hunter should do in similar situations.

One of the first things I do each day before I start hunting is decide whether to hold out for a trophy animal or take any legal animal for the table, depending on how

a hunt or my hunting season is going. That way, I don't have to second guess myself if a shot opportunity arises because I've already made up my mind. I rarely think twice about taking a shot at legal big game animals when they're in accessible places. I've found through experience that such chances are few and far between. If weather conditions are ideal, go for it, but there's nothing worse than having to haul an animal out when the weather turns bad. Depending on the time of the season and the abundance of game, you may want to hedge your bets and take an animal early if the chance presents itself. I've dressed big game when temperatures were −25°C with more than two feet of snow on the ground. I speak from experience when I say that the job is not fun under these circumstances! Warm weather isn't the only problem.

Deer being hauled to vehicle using a Jet Sled

Make sure you have a plan to get a big game animal from the field to the trailhead.

The best time to shoot a big game animal is in the early morning; you'll have all day to field dress the animal and get it back to camp or the trailhead. I'm always leery about shooting big game in the late afternoon or evening. If you wound an animal, tracking it in poor light can be difficult. Also, it's much harder to field dress an animal, half it or quarter it, and get it out in the dark. It is not a good idea to leave a downed animal in the field overnight. On the prairies, coyotes will almost certainly find the carcass, and you may find only a grease spot where it lay the next morning. If bears are present, there's always a danger one will claim the animal, particularly if there is any amount of wind to carry the scent.

Tools for Field Dressing Your Kill

Here's what I always put in my daypack to field dress an animal:

- A sharp knife that has both skinning and hide cutter blades to make surgical cuts in the hide and abdomen. This knife also should also have a bone-cutting blade.

- A sharpening stone.

- A Wyoming saw with both bone and wood blades to cut through the pelvis and sternum, and to cut a tree (if necessary) as a back-up to the knife.

- Some ¼-inch rope to tie the legs apart and keep them out of the way, and for other purposes.

- Ziploc plastic bags for the heart and the liver.

- A small towel for clean-up

- A tarp if there's no snow on the ground, to keep the carcass off the ground.

Tips on Field Dressing

After you tag the animal, start by field dressing it. This involves removing the internal organs to start the cooling process and prevent spoilage of meat due to body heat.

Here are some tips on field dressing your animal:

- Usually it isn't necessary to bleed big game animals, particularly if their internal organs and digestive tract are removed soon after being shot.

- Use a hide cutter blade to cut through the hide and abdominal muscles from the crotch to the throat, being careful not to puncture the intestines or rumen.

- Avoid getting any hair in the body cavity.

- Start by making a small incision in the abdomen with a skinning blade.

- Finish the job with a hide cutter blade. A hide cutter blade won't puncture the internal organs and is also great for skinning out the legs.

- Loosen the organs in the body cavity by cutting all connective tissue, including the diaphragm (cut all the way around it).

- After cutting through the pelvis with a meat saw, cut around the vent in the rump, being careful not to puncture the

You'll need proper tools to field dress a large animal such as a moose.

There's no such thing as a small moose; they're all huge.

–Duane Radford after helping field dress and skin an enormous cow weighing close to half a ton that his son, Myles, shot.

- At this stage, I normally cut off the front legs at the knee joint and saw through the back legs below the knee joint. Some hunters prefer to leave the legs on, but if you do, it's important to carefully cut off the large metatarsal glands on the hind legs of deer, in particular, so they don't taint the meat.

- Turn the carcasses of game animals over if you have to leave them in the field for a while otherwise magpies, ravens, eagles and coyotes will peck at the meat, or start eating the hindquarters.

- Rapid cooling is important. If the animal is large (e.g., elk or moose), skin and quarter it as soon as possible. Smaller animals (e.g., deer, bighorn sheep and pronghorn antelope) should also be

Pack frame and deer quarters. Be prepared to pack out deer during hunts on Alberta's prairies.

large intestine. You may wish to tie off the vent with a string to prevent body wastes from spilling onto the meat when you remove the insides.

- Reach inside the throat and cut off the windpipe. Get a good grip on the windpipe and pull backward, using your free hand to cut any connective tissue holding the heart and lungs to the side of the body wall.

- Still holding the windpipe (you may need both hands), pull out all of the internal organs.

- After an animal is drained of blood, clean the body cavity with a damp cloth and trim any damaged meat.

- Wipe the insides with a dry cloth or paper towel to prevent meat spoilage.

skinned as quickly as possible but don't have to be quartered.

• To halve an animal, cut through the backbone with a meat saw.

• Quarter each half by cutting between the second and third last ribs, and through the backbone. A tarp comes in handy to keep the carcass off the ground and to set the quarters aside.

If you shoot a moose or an elk then have to return to the trailhead for a pack board, game carrier or OHV to haul it out and you will be gone for several hours, be sure to cut through the hide in the neck right down to the spine to cool the meat. Otherwise, the meat will spoil because the hide in this area on an elk or moose is so thick it will retain heat even when snow is on the ground.

Skinning the hide off a big game animal speeds up the cooling process and prevents meat spoilage, so I take the hide off as soon as possible. Removing the hide is particularly important on antelope hunts when warm weather is common because pronghorns have hollow hair, which is a great insulator. Bighorn sheep also have very well insulated hides.

To skin animals in the field, I use a portable Quick Winch mentioned in an earlier chapter that fits into the trailer hitch on my truck to lift a carcass off the ground, which makes it a lot easier to cut the hide off. Next, I usually cover the carcass with a meat sock. After it has cooled, I put it in a plastic Jet Sled or tarp, depending on its size, in the back of my truck for the trip home.

It's important to skin a big game animal as soon as is practical to cool the meat and prevent it from spoiling especially when the weather is warm.

While the fun may end after the shot, concerns about field dressing big game animals and getting the meat into your freezer in top-notch shape can be alleviated with proper planning and care of the carcass.

Aging Big Game Animals

In 1973, research was done on aging field-dressed carcasses of six bull and six cow elk at the University of Wyoming meat laboratory, each split, one side skinned immediately, and all aged two weeks at 3˚C (38˚F), except for a loin sample which was removed for tenderness tests. Weight losses and bacterial growth on the carcasses were recorded during aging. After aging, one side of each carcass was butchered into retail cuts, and the other side was separated into bone, fat and lean meat. Loin roasts were saved for flavour and tenderness tests. Detailed tests were done to measure moisture, fat, protein and ash content of ground meat samples, and these samples were also tested for bacteria. On average, about 5.45 hours elapsed between the time of kill and delivery of the carcasses to the University of Wyoming meat laboratory. The bull elk ranged in age from 1.5 to 9.5 years and the cows from 2.5 to 5.5 years.

Following are the key findings:

- The hide side of each elk carcass cooled at a slower rate than the skinned side.

- If the elk sides had not been hung to allow good air circulation, the cooling rates would have been much slower.

- Splitting the backbone, especially between the shoulders, and propping the carcass open, also speeds up chilling.

- The hide-on sides lost 6.2 pounds of moisture over the aging period, while the skinned sides lost 8 pounds over the aging period.

A quick winch makes it easy to skin a deer even during the early season.

I carry some water in a plastic container to clean the carcass and wash my hands of blood. Allow some room for expansion of water because it may freeze if temperatures are below zero! Use paper towels to clean the outside of the carcass of blood and hair and dispose of them in a heavy-duty plastic bag. Do not litter. Take your garbage home!

- The hide prevented some mould and bacterial growth on the outside surface of the carcass and prevented the lean meat from becoming dark and dry.

- Consequently, waste from trimming dried and darkened lean meat was lower from the hide side.

- Many of the disadvantages of aging for two weeks can actually be avoided by aging for one week. In the case of cow elk, one week of aging probably would have been sufficient from a tenderness standpoint. Meat from bull elk did not benefit as much from aging as cow elk. After aging two weeks, meat from the bull elk was still considerably tougher than from the cows; however, bull elk should normally be aged for two weeks for acceptable tenderness.

- Leaving the hide on or removing it during aging did not affect tenderness or flavour of the meat when the elk carcasses were chilled rapidly. Even on relatively cool days, facilities to speed up chilling of an elk carcass are beneficial because the meat can sour unless there's good air circulation around the carcass.

- Aging elk meat is not necessary if the meat is to be ground or made into sausage. Cooking pot roasts or stews will render it tender without aging.

Following are some common sense tips based on the research done in 1973 that are recommended for elk that would also apply to handling any big game carcass after the kill until the meat goes into the freezer. Although some are given above they bear repeating:

- Gut the animal as soon as it's dead, and properly bleed it by cutting the throat, if necessary.

- Lift the carcass to drain blood, and wash the body cavity with clean water. Dry with towels.

- The carcass should be hung or laid on top of rocks or logs to allow for air circulation and cooling.

- The field-dressed carcass can be moved immediately after the kill without chilling. However, under ideal conditions the carcass should be taken directly to a cooler where it can be skinned and chilled rapidly. Where this is not possible, the hot carcass should be hung in camp.

- If the nights in camp are below freezing, skinning is not recommended because the skin does protect the carcass from dirt and insects.

- If the nights are above freezing, skinning will be necessary to prevent spoilage.

- In warm weather it is strongly recommended, when possible, to take the carcass to a cooler on the day of the kill.

- If the carcass is skinned, use cheesecloth or light cotton bags to keep it clean, minimize drying out and protect the meat from insects.

- Ensure the internal temperature of the meat is cooled to 4°C (40°F) or below within 24 hours to prevent spoilage.

- Butcher cow and bull elk carcasses 7 and 14 days after the kill, respectively. Do not age elk if shot during warm weather and not chilled quickly, if the animal was badly stressed by running a long way, for example, prior to the kill, if gunshot areas are bad or if the animal was less than a year old.

- Wrap all cuts in good quality freezer paper or vacuum wrap and store at 0°C (32°F) or below.

You can keep prime cuts separate from meat destined for ground meat or sausage and age it in a container in a cooler for one or two weeks if the animal is obviously old. Generally speaking, one week of aging should be adequate for females, 2 weeks for males; it's not necessary to age a young animal.

"Aging" is defined as "the practice of holding carcasses or cuts at temperatures from 1° to 3°C (34° to 37°F)," in the Wyoming research while enzymes function to break down some of the complex proteins found in muscle tissue. Quick aging of beef is done commercially by holding it at a temperature of 17° to 18°C (62° to 65°F) for two to three days under relatively high humidity to prevent dehydration.

Aging carcasses with little or no fat is not recommended by meat specialists because of excessive weight loss and surface discoloration of lean meat, and since quick aging has occurred when the carcass could not be chilled at 1°C (34°F) after the kill.

Some of the key research recommendations which are applicable to Alberta are as follows:

- Antelope carcasses should be cut and wrapped for the freezer within three days of the kill; short aging helps prevent a liver-like or mushy texture sometimes otherwise found in antelope meat.

- Deer, bighorn sheep, mountain goat, cow elk and moose carcasses should be cut about 7 days after the kill. If they've been

Field-dressed deer. Keep the brisket spread to cool the meat.

Cold shortening is caused by rapid chilling of a big game animal.

held at higher temperatures above 4°C (39°F) the meat should be cut before 7 days.

- Bull elk and moose carcasses should be cut after a 14-day aging period at 1° to 3°C (34° to 37°F) when animals are mature.

Cold Shortening

Alberta hunters should be aware of "cold shortening," which can result in tough meat. This phenomenon is a result of the rapid cooling of lean meat at temperatures below 10°C (50°F). I'd never heard of "cold shortening" until a friend of mine, Perry McCormick, brought it to my attention.

Perry later sent me an e-mail in which he elaborated on the subject: "I was a believer in cooling meat as fast as possible until I had two bad experiences of 'doing the right thing.' My experience was with two young bull moose shot near Oyen, Alberta—both were shot without stress with lethal shots. Both should have been perfect as both were aged in a controlled environment for 14 to 21 days. Both animals were skinned and hung in cold weather within an hour of being shot, and both spent the rest of the day in cheesecloth in an open half ton for the remainder of the day; neither froze, but both were nice and cold. The temperature was somewhere in the low single digits or low minus digits the day of the kills." To his chagrin, Perry found that the meat was tough on both animals. In cold weather Perry now leaves the skin on to cool his meat at a slower rate. He says the meat is tender and adds, according to the definition of "cold shortening," this condition may be specific to bulls as they are by nature quite lean post rut.

Cold shortening is caused by the rapid chilling of carcasses immediately after slaughter, before the glycogen in the muscle has been converted to lactic acid. With glycogen still present as an energy source, the cold temperature induces an irreversible contraction of the muscle (i.e., the actin and myosin filaments shorten). Cold shortening causes meat to be as much as five times tougher than normal. This condition occurs in lean carcasses that have higher proportions of red muscle fibres and very little exterior fat covering. Without the fat covering as insulation, the muscles can cool too quickly causing them to toughen.

I try not to chill carcasses quickly if the temperature is near zero. Once the hide is off, they're put in a large polypropylene sled in the back of my truck and covered with a tarp to keep them from freezing before they're butchered. The box of my pickup is covered with a partially insulated shell. So far, I haven't experienced any problems with cold shortening when I've handled the meat this way in cold weather.

From Field to Table

Wild game meat is fit for a king if it's handled well in the field and properly cooked in the kitchen. I'll preface these requirements with a quote from Susan (Sue) Kane-Doyle who is Canada's outdoor recipe queen. She's a dean of fish and wild game recipes columnists on the national scene, a veteran of some 30 years as "cooking" columnist in *Ontario Out of Doors* magazine. In terms of cooking fowl and wild game, Sue says, "As with all cooking, fresh is best. And for the outdoorsmen, what gets ruined in the field cannot be made better in the kitchen." Proper care and handling of fowl and wild game is absolutely essential to ensure optimum table quality. If your wild fowl and big game tastes "gamey," it's most likely because it wasn't properly cared for in the field, aged and/or butchered.

Antelope Tenderloin with Chokecherry Syrup

Keep shot grouse, partridge, pheasants and waterfowl out of the sun. Dress them as soon as practical, definitely as soon as you return home from your hunt by removing their internal organs and digestive tracts. Fowl is highly subject to freezer burn. It should be eaten as soon as possible, no longer than three or four months after being frozen to ensure optimal eating quality.

Ensure your fowl and wild game is completely thawed once it's out of the freezer. Wash it clean of any blood, pat dry with a paper towel and trim of any fat or connective tissue. Fat from wild game has a strong, unpleasant taste and is best trimmed from edible meat prior to being frozen.

In the kitchen, job one is to cook wild game slowly at a low heat because it's a lean, low fat meat, otherwise it will be dry and chewy. You can compensate for lean meat by using marinades or slow-cooking techniques, and by choosing recipes that help retain moisture in the meat. The same rules apply to fowl, which also tends to be lean and on the dry side.

There are various cooking techniques, such as braising and/or using a slow cooker that should be considered when cooking wild game, especially cuts from mature animals that may need to be tenderized, even after being aged for one to two weeks.

Braising is a combination cooking method that uses both moist and dry heat. Typically, the meat is first seared at a relatively high temperature, seasoned and then finished in a covered pot or skillet with a variable amount of liquid, which keeps the meat tender and flavourful. Braising meat is often referred to as pot-roasting although some authors make a distinction between the two methods based on whether additional liquid is added.

Pot roasts are always a sure-fire way to cook wild game.

Marinated Grouse Breasts

You really can't go wrong with a venison pot roast, one of my favourite recipes for game meat. When I prepare a 3- to 4- pound (1.4 to 1.8 kg) venison roast, I typically cook it in a sealed oven roaster at 350°F for two hours. I never cook a venison roast without first searing it on all sides often at the same time that I'm sautéing some white Spanish onions. I then add beef broth or onion soup mix and veggies. To oven roast 2- to 3-pound (0.9 to ¼ kg) loins, roast them at 400°F for half an hour, after first searing them.

If there's anything I've learned cooking all manner of wild game and fowl it has been to "keep the lid" on things. Seriously! Get in the habit of cooking wild fowl and game in skillets and roasters that have tight fitting lids. When using an oven roaster, seal the lid with a layer of aluminum foil to keep the moisture inside the container, ditto for casseroles featuring game. This isn't necessary if you're cooking meatloaf, ground meat patties or meatballs in the oven because they usually contain a lot of

moisture as part of the recipe, or they're basted with sauces to keep them moist.

I generally sear fowl and game in butter instead of olive oil because olive oil has a lower burn or smoke point compared with vegetable oils, which I'll use occasionally.

If it's to be grilled on a barbeque, then it's a good idea to marinate game, searing it initially at a relatively high heat then subsequently grilling it at a low heat until done. I often marinate roasts for 24 hours or longer. Marinades tenderize meat as well as enhance the flavour. The standard ratio for marinades is one part vinegar or wine to three parts canola or olive oil, with spices to your liking. My go-to spices and herbs are celery seed, cloves, bay leaves, dill seed, thyme, parsley, oregano or marjoram, Italian seasoning and rosemary. I use at least a ½ teaspoon of two or three given spices to two cups of marinade. Place the meat inside a Ziploc plastic bag, add the marinade, slosh it around and refrigerate for several hours or preferably overnight.

Flemish Venison Pot Roast

Another great way to season game meat is to use rubs on steaks prior to cooking. Apply the rub several hours ahead of time so they set up and flavour the meat. Typically, rubs feature spices such as paprika, cayenne pepper, garlic or onion seasoning, sea salt and black pepper. You can make your own rubs to taste with your favourite seasonings, no problem.

Because the meat of wild game is lean, it's best prepared as pot roasts or chili, stews or casseroles, or with marinades for steaks and kebabs, and not simply fried in a skillet. Frying tends to dry out the meat, unless it is done as a Swiss steak or with gobs of butter and onions.

Remember: If game is not cooked at a relatively low heat, it will be tough and chewy.

But it is okay to serve a game steak rare or medium rare, depending on your preference; some people prefer it done this way.

Also take care when you're cooking a wild fowl or game. Plan ahead and get all your ingredients lined up before you start. Give yourself enough time to not only properly prepare the meal but to cook it without feeling rushed so you're not in a hurry and make mistakes.

Wild game cuisine is a distinctly Canadian style of cooking that dates back to our roots as a nation. It has evolved into a high-end epicurean feature on the menus of many fine dining rooms in Alberta and elsewhere.

CHAPTER SIXTEEN

Bowhunting

Bowhunting

The Alberta Bow Hunting Association is now the key lobby group for bow hunters in Alberta. This association was established in 1956. Initially, its primary goal was to legalize bow hunting, which happened in 1957. The Alberta Bow Hunting Association has successfully lobbied for and obtained approval for many progressive bowhunting laws since it was formed.

In 1974, the Alberta government instituted a bowhunting license to better enumerate the number of bow hunters in the province.

Bowhunting has become a popular activity since it was legalized because it is challenging and basically adds another season to the one for rifle hunting. Further, as an added bonus, the archery season is scheduled before the rifle season when the weather is usually more pleasant and game less disturbed. Typically, it runs from one to two months before the start of the general rifle season, adding a lot of opportunity for archers. For these reasons, skilled bow hunters are often successful. Also, tremendous improvements have been made to bow hunting gear and equipment over

Lanny Amos took this prime antelope buck hunting with a blind by using a decoy to lure it within bow range.

the years and archery hunting techniques so with proper training and mentoring success rates have continued to increase. There's even a module on "Bow Hunting" in the provincial Conservation Education Program, which is now available online and is mandatory for first time hunters.

While many bow hunters put away their bow when the rifle season starts, that does not denigrate their commitment to bow hunting.

Because bow hunting regulations are detailed and rather complicated, the following excerpt is provided from the "Alberta Guide to Hunting Regulations" for purposes of clarity and to ensure legislative compliance by bow hunters, at the time this book was published. (Note: The following applies to bowhunting other than with a cross-bow.)

Neophyte bow hunters are taught bow hunting basics in Alberta's Conservation Education Program.

Except for the hunting of black bear, coyote, cougar or wolf under the circumstances as outlined under "Access for Control of Livestock Predation," a Bowhunting Permit is required by anyone who hunts big game, game bird, wolf or coyote with a bow and arrow. Bowhunters with appropriate general or special licences may hunt during the general seasons, archery-only seasons and primitive weapon seasons. A Bowhunting Permit is required in combination with a big game licence. In some areas of the province, hunters require special licences to hunt certain species of big game and should read the season tables. A bowhunter who obtains an Antlered Moose Special Licence, Antlerless Moose Special Licence, Calf Moose Special Licence, Antlered Mule Deer Special Licence, Antlerless Mule Deer Special Licence, Antlered

White-tailed Deer Special Licence, Antlerless White-tailed Deer Special Licence, Antlered Elk Special Licence, Antlerless Elk Special Licence or Landowner Special Licence may, if an early archery season is offered, hunt under the authority of that licence during the archery season but only in the WMU specified on the licence and only for the type and species of animal for which the licence was issued. Holders of a Landowner Special Licence are subject to the terms/conditions of their licence. Bowhunters are reminded that, in some situations, archery-only seasons for some species may be in progress at the same time as primitive weapon and rifle seasons for other species in the same WMU.

Persons hunting big game must use an authorized bow and an authorized arrow. An authorized bow is one that is held, drawn and released by muscular power and has a draw weight of not less than 18 kg (40 lb.). This is the number of kilograms (pounds) required to draw an arrow of 71 cm (28 in.) to its head. An authorized arrow is one that is not less than 61 cm (24 in.) in length that has a tip that bears a head that is not intentionally designed to resist being withdrawn after it has penetrated an object. Furthermore, it must either have a solid, sharp cutting head of at least ⅞ inch in width, or a head that, when the arrow impacts, opens to present sharp cutting edges at least ⅞ inch in width.

Hunters are asked to remove their tree stands at the end of the hunting seasons unless permission has been granted by the landholder to do otherwise.

There are special regulations for hunting with a cross bow in the "Alberta Game Hunting Regulations" that should be reviewed as they are different than those regulating bowhunting.

It should also be noted that Alberta has some bow hunting only zones, such as WMU 248 surrounding Edmonton, which has produced some huge white-tailed bucks and WMU 212, which surrounds Calgary. Because most of the land is privately owned in both of these Wildlife Management Units it is important for archers to obtain permission to hunt. WMU 410 is another special area set aside for archers also known as the Canmore Bow Zone located adjacent to Banff National Park.

The Pope and Young Club, located in Chatfield, Minnesota, is one of North America's leading bowhunting and conservation organizations and maintains official records of game animals taken with a bow and arrow. Its mission is:

> *To ensure bowhunting for future generations by preserving and promoting its heritage and values.*

To be eligible for entry into the Pope and Young Club's Records Program, an animal must meet or exceed the corresponding minimum score requirement for that species category whose minimum scores are lower than those of the Boone and Crocket Club records but still quite respectably high. Two of Alberta's top 10 white-tailed deer have been taken by bow hunters.

Bowhunter at dawn, scoping

Becoming a Complete Hunter

It takes many years of experience to become what I would call a "complete" hunter—an outdoorsman who's at home in the woods and fully capable of hunting a wide variety of game birds and animals.

What does it take to round off a hunter so that they can function independently, and how important are mentors in helping them achieve this status? Where do the long-established hunter education programs fit into the equation, as well as membership in sportsman's clubs, practice at the local gun range, development of interpersonal skills to get along with landowners and so on? When does a hunter reach that stage when they're an equal partner in the hunting party, and how do they get to this level?

In this chapter, I'll outline what I see as the evolution of a hunter based on my personal experiences and those of the members of my hunting fraternity, including my son, Myles, who's been hunting for almost 25 years. I'll never forget his first hunting trip for sharp-tailed grouse when our German shorthair pointer (Stubs) went on point, and Myles calmly took a brace of sharpies on his first two shots! It didn't happen by accident. Myles had practiced shooting trap long before his inaugural hunt for upland birds. He knew what to

expect when the birds flushed, how to get on target then follow through on his lead before pulling the trigger.

Let me start by saying that becoming a complete hunter never really stops; it is a lifelong learning process. However, there are many waypoints that mark a hunter's progress during the various stages. When I was a kid, hunter training

Hunter education course practice shooting gets hunters started on the right foot.

In 1964–65 Alberta's hunter education program began, and the first training manual was published. Well over one million students have graduated from this program since it was initiated, a truly remarkable milestone. In my opinion, the inception of a formal hunter education program marked a key turning point in support of students becoming complete hunters. For the first time there was an education program that provided some structure to hunter training on a wide range of topics:

1. Role of the Hunter

2. Hunting Ethics

3. Wildlife Management and Conservation

4. Wildlife Identification

5. Clothing and Equipment

6. Firearms

7. Bow Hunting

8. Survival

9. Field Techniques

10. First Aid

11. Hypothermia

12. Legal Responsibilities

Prior to the inception of hunter education programs, hunter training had no structure; consequently, the goal of becoming a complete hunter was hard to achieve. When these programs were subsequently mandated by legislation before a first-time hunter could obtain a hunting licence, the stage was set with a level playing field. Graduates of hunter education programs got started in the right direction, and with some mentoring and field experience, they were able to fast track their learning curve.

Another key stimulus in the development of a complete hunter has been the proliferation of Canadian publications (with

Hunters should practice gun safety at all times in their pursuit of becoming complete hunters.

was pretty rudimentary. My neighbor, Ted Amos, taught me some lessons I'll never forget; however, and constantly stressed the importance of safe gun handling. To make a point, once Ted and his son Dennis and I were on a hunting trip, and he took a shot with his 30-06 Husqvarna through a derelict telephone pole. Sparks flew. Flames and smoke erupted. There was a bullet hole clear through the pole. Dennis and I got the message. Be careful with guns! We were also told to never point a gun towards a person and not to touch the trigger unless we intended to fire a shot at a target. Ted also stressed the importance of always knowing your backstop because bullets from a high-powered rifle travel more than a mile. Safe gun handling was always paramount in our minds.

Hunters should be prepared to hunt under a variety of conditions, including often brutal late winter.

a focus on Canadian hunts and hunting product lines) of which there are several outstanding magazines. If you read the popular literature you will become a more complete hunter because you will continue your outdoor education and be aware of new hunting strategies and key products that will make your hunts all that more successful.

While I don't consider myself a tech-hunter, I would not leave home without certain products, such as two-way radios or a range finder, which were unheard of when I first started hunting. There are many additional hunting products that have hit the market over the years that have made hunting much more enjoyable. When I first started hunting, bipods weren't even on the market (neither were shooting sticks). Bipods are a relatively new hunting product. I wouldn't leave home without one today. They make a skilled marksman an even better shot and are invaluable when hunting certain big game animals such as pronghorn antelope and prairie deer.

To say that the Internet is playing a key role in developing more complete hunters would be a gross understatement. The Internet is the modern information highway and is growing in importance each and every day. Websites contain valuable information on everything from hunting tips, new hunting products and ballistic tables to local weather forecasts for your hunting territory.

The proliferation of various outdoor websites and internet forums such as the Alberta Outdoorsmen Forum are going a long way to keep hunters better educated and informed. Likewise, social media is playing an important role in becoming a complete hunter by enabling like-minded people to stay connected.

Hunters who belong to local fish and game clubs also have a leg up on those who don't because they'll benefit from information sharing which pays dividends when it comes to better understanding of where and when to hunt, and what pitfalls to avoid. If you want to get the inside track on prime hunting territory by getting patched up with some of the very best hunters in your community, sign up as a member of your local sportsman's organization. You will meet many great outdoorsmen who have a wealth of knowledge about hunting and Alberta's great outdoors. Many fish and game associations provide range privileges to their members. Hunting clubs have members who are knowledgeable about sighting in rifles, a must-do requirement before going on a hunting trip. They can provide coaching on shooting skills for both shotguns and rifles.

For neophyte hunters, there's no substitute for having a mentor who can show them the ropes in the outdoors. Mentors are a great asset when it comes time to put classroom, published or online information into practice. They can help new hunters better understand where to hunt, when to hunt and how to hunt both bird game and big game. Mentors can also be a great asset in getting permission to hunt on private land. They can also help promote the vital importance of hunting ethics to cast hunting in a positive light to all members of society. Mentors can help new hunters locate signs of big game activity, signs which define the home range of various species whether it be their trails, beds, tracks, hair, droppings, rubs or scrapes. They can ensure neophytes have key hunting tools such as spotting scopes and binoculars, rangefinders and how to use them. When an animal is downed, they can show new hunters how to tag it properly (on the quarter showing evidence of sex), how to field dress big game, de-bone them or quarter them and get them back to a vehicle. Once back at the vehicle, a mentor can show a new hunter how to skin an animal, always a good idea where feasible to cool the meat. They can also provide advice on how to butcher big game, take care of wild fowl and upland birds to ensure the best possible table fare. It's also great to have a mentor when a big game animal is taken to a butcher shop to advise the butcher how it should be cut.

Hunters should check for sign such as deer sheds to undertand their home ranges during their quest to become outdoorsmen.

Neophyte elk hunters would benefit from having a mentor to guide them and take the chase to the elk.

I don't think most hunters realize just how much time and effort is required to be a successful hunter until they've been on several hunts. I'll never forget my first few elk hunts. I really did think that I was chasing a unicorn! I'd be up before dawn, hunt all day usually never even seeing an elk and finally have dinner in the dark. I walked many hard miles each and every day under all kinds of weather, good and bad. If I was lucky, maybe I'd get one chance for a shot at my quarry. If I'd had a mentor, I would have had a much better appreciation just how challenging it was to bag an elk. A mentor would have told me to take to the chase on an elk hunt and be very patient. I would have also realized that you'll earn every elk you shoot, not just the first one. They can be that difficult to hunt.

Hunters do not develop a complete hunting skill set overnight. Oftentimes, it takes years to figure out how to hunt various species successfully. There's no substitute for first-hand knowledge and experience before a hunter can stand on their own. For example, when a shot opportunity at a mature buck presents itself during a snowstorm, all your training and experience has to come into play. If you haven't practiced shooting your rifle at the local range and aren't properly equipped to hunt under less than ideal hunting conditions, there's a good chance you'll blow the shot. If you miss, perhaps you'll go home skunked. That's what it's all about—being prepared to hunt independently and make critical, split second decisions when the chips are down!

Glossary

AFGA: Alberta Fish & Game Association

antlered: in Alberta, "antlered" means a white-tailed deer, mule deer, moose or elk having an antler exceeding 10.2 cm (4 inches) in length

antlerless: in Alberta, "antlerless" means a white-tailed deer, mule deer, moose or elk that is not "antlered" (as defined above)

antlers: one of the branched growths on the head of an adult (usually male) deer, elk or moose that are made of bone and are grown and cast off annually

antler rattling: rubbing and scraping two sets of antlers together to imitate bucks that are sparring, generally used only for white-tailed deer hunting around their rut

ATV: all-terrain vehicle

B&C Club: Boone and Crockett Club

bachelor group: both male elk and moose gather in small to large groups after the rut in secluded areas; occasionally elk will gather in relatively large groups

ballistic coefficient: in mathematical terms, the ratio of a bullet's sectional density to its coefficient of form; practically speaking, basically a measure of how streamlined a bullet is, essentially a measure of air drag

beds and bedding areas: all game animals tend to bed down in secure locations at night and during storms; beds can be found just about anywhere and are sure signs that game animals are present nearby

bedded down: game animal laying down in its bed to rest up

binoculars: field glasses comprised of two telescopes mounted side-by-side and aligned to point in the same direction, allowing a person to use both eyes when viewing distant objects

bipod: two-legged metal support device that's fastened on the fore end of a rifle stock, used to steady it; generally affixed to a collapsible mount

bird dogging: saying used by hunters to describe a white-tailed buck that often has its nose to the ground as it follows the scent of a female deer in heat across country

blood shot meat: meat in the area where a bullet entered and/or exited a big game animal that is tainted by hemorrhaging and should be trimmed from a carcass

Boone and Crockett Club: The Boone and Crockett Club is an American nonprofit organization that advocates fair chase hunting in support of habitat conservation and has maintained official records of all trophy game harvested since 1902; their headquarters are located in Missoula, Montana, United States

bore sighted: a method of adjustment to a rifle scope or iron sights, to align the firearm barrel and sights; generally used to pre-align the sights, which makes zeroing (zero drop at XX distance) much faster; a device called a bore sight or collimator is used to accomplish this rough sighting in process

brace: a pair of something, typically of birds or game animals killed in hunting

braising: derived from the French term "braiser"; describes a method of cooking using both moist and dry heat to keep game birds and venison tender

brass: an unloaded metal cartridge case (spent brass that has been fired can be used several times by handloaders with reloading tools)

bred: as in to mate with (i.e., a doe had bred with a buck to produce a fawn).

brow tines: the first division or set of small antlers (although not only present) off the main beam of deer, elk and moose

browse: food source used by moose, for example, that feed on shrubs like chokecherry, Saskatoon and willow

buck: a male pronghorn antelope, mule deer or white-tailed deer

bugle: the call of a bull (male) elk during the rut

bull: a male elk or moose

boar: a male black or grizzly bear

calibre: the approximate internal diameter of the barrel or the diameter of the projectile it fires, in hundredths or sometimes thousandths of an inch. For example, a ".22 calibre" firearm has a barrel diameter of .22 of an inch. However, when writing firearm calibres the formal cartridge name is used,

therefore, not .270 Winchester, but 270 Winchester

cam-slotted: as in binoculars, means rotating or sliding in a mechanical linkage

Canada goose: a common North American goose with a black head and neck, a white chinstrap and a loud, trumpeting call (or honk)

cape: the hide from the head and shoulders of a big game animal that is tanned for taxidermy purposes

cold shortening: the result of the rapid chilling of carcasses immediately after being shot, before the glycogen in the muscle has been converted to lactic acid that toughens meat; should be avoided

chip shot: hunter slang for a short, easy shot

chokes (shotgun): a tapered constriction of a shotgun barrel's bore at the muzzle end designed to improve performance; the purpose of a choke (e.g., improved cylinder, modified or full) is to shape the spread of the shotgun pellets and optimize range and accuracy

cow: a female big game animal (e.g., cow elk or moose)

CWD: Chronic Wasting Disease; a transmissible, fatal brain disease (i.e. spongiform encephalopathy) of mule deer, white-tailed deer, elk and moose

deer bleat: a call that imitates a bleating female deer, or fawn, used to keep in contact or as a distress call

dies: handloading (reloading) tools designed to size, or resize, new or spent shells while simultaneously removing spent primers and then subsequently seating bullets

doe: a female pronghorn antelope or deer (i.e., mule deer or white-tailed deer)

downwind: because big game animals have a keen sense of smell, it's important to hunt "downwind" of them so they don't smell a hunter; ideally, the wind should be in a hunter's face

double-barreled shotgun: comes in two basic configurations, side-by-side and over-under models, relative to barrel configuration

draw (as in land): a geographical feature characterized by two parallel ridges or spurs with low ground in between them; the area of low ground is the "draw," and it is defined by the spurs surrounding it

droppings: the feces of bird game and big game which can be used to identify different species

drop tine: an antler point or tine that occasionally grows straight down from the main beam on the antlers of a mature white-tailed deer, seldom found on mule deer

elk calls: elk are typically herd animals that use various sounds to communicate with each other (e.g., barking, bugling, chirping and mewling)

ESRD: Alberta Department of Environment and Sustainable Resource Development which was reorganized into Alberta Environment and Parks in 2015

ewe: a female bighorn sheep

feeding craters: elk tend to chomp grasses unevenly when they graze and leave cavities or craters in their foraging sites

five-pointer (5-pointer): as in a white-tailed buck, considered a good trophy deer

field dressing: removing the internal organs from a game animal in the field just after it has been shot to start the cooling process and prevent spoilage of meat due to body heat

field shoot: hunting waterfowl from blinds in fields of grain or peas, for example, using decoys

5Ws: five "Ws"—who, what, where, when and why

flat-shooting rifle: a relative term for a rifle that fires bullets that do not drop as much as other calibres at given distances; a Winchester's 130-grain load zeroed at 100 yards drops 2.7 inches at 200 yards and 10.2 inches at 300 yards; zero a 150-grain Power Point 30-30 bullet at 100 yards and at 300 yards it will drop 32 inches; the key thing is you don't want a bullet to drop in elevation very much if you're shooting at a long distance

flinch (flinching): unwanted body movement associated with the anticipation of sound and recoil from a high-powered rifle (i.e., jerking), which moves the sighting plane off target

flier: a shot that hits wide of a target, usually caused by flinching

four pointer (4-pointer): as in a mule deer buck with four antler points, considered a good trophy deer

game trail: most big game animals follow trails through the forest that can be determined by the tracks left by their hooves

grains: a measurement for the weight of either powder or bullets

ground shrink: a disappointing experience upon discovering that the size of the antlers or horns of a big game animal are smaller than you originally thought they were

group: a cluster of bullet holes in a paper target used to check on the accuracy of a rifle at a gun range

grunt tube: a deer call that imitates a grunting deer, usually a white-tailed buck

gully: a draw, ravine or gorge often used as a travel lane by big game

gut shot: an animal hit with a bullet in the stomach or intestines which is not a killing shot and should be avoided

handloading (reloading): the process of loading firearm cartridges or shotgun shells by assembling the individual components (case/hull, primer, powder and bullet/shot) yourself, rather than purchasing completely assembled, factory-loaded ammunition

hard extraction: a brass casing (i.e., shell that's been fired) or shell that is stuck in the chamber of a rifle which has to be removed by force (e.g., ramming it with a cleaning rod)

herd bull: dominant bull elk with a harem of cows during the rut

hock: the joint in a big game animal's hind leg between the knee and the fetlock, the angle of which points backward

holdover: the distance (at target) by which a rifle scope is aimed higher than the intended point of impact in order to compensate for bullet drop over the distance to the target

hold on hair: a saying that means put your sights on target just behind the shoulder of a big game animal (i.e., "on hair") for your first shot and do not hold over its back if you do not have a range finder but believe it is within the range of your firearm

home range: most game animals have a home range where they spend their lives

horn: a bony part of the skull of certain big game animals that may be shed annually (e.g., pronghorn) or continue to grow annually (e.g., big horn sheep or mountain goat)

gauge: when referring to shotguns all are gauges except the ".410" which is a "bore";

therefore, 12-gauge is correct (with a hyphen) but 410-gauge is not, it should be 410 bore (no hyphen)

Improvement District: Improvement Districts are municipal authorities originally formed by the Government of Alberta in sparsely populated areas where there was neither the population nor the tax base to support and finance a viable local government; there are eight improvement districts in Alberta (i.e., Improvement District No. 4, Waterton; Improvement District No. 9, Banff; Improvement District No. 12, Jasper; Improvement District No. 13, Elk Island; Improvement District No. 24, Wood Buffalo; Improvement District No. 25, Willmore Wilderness; Improvement District No. 349 ; Kananaskis Improvement District)

kicker: abnormal burr or small point on the beam or tines of antlers, used interchangeably with "sticker" in Alberta

layout (coffin) blind: a portable, camouflaged fold-out blind that a hunter can lay down in among stubble to hide from waterfowl

lead shot: shotgun pellets made out of lead

leading a target: sustained and swing-through leads are the two most common methods of leading targets at long distances (e.g., refer to sustained leads and swing-through leads in this glossary for further details)

let your binoculars do the walking: a saying among hunters to use binoculars to locate game rather than walking unnecessarily

limit out: to shoot the legal number of game birds or waterfowl permitted by law, usually defined by either a daily and/or possession (season) limit

mark the spot: experienced hunters "mark" the spot where they shot an animal by using key landmarks so they can find it afterwards; this is critical when trying to locate wounded game in particular

Mauser action: the Mauser bolt action system was introduced in Germany by Paul Mauser and is the most common bolt-action system in the world, being in use in nearly all modern hunting rifles and the majority of military bolt-action rifles until World War II

meat saw: a small, professional grade butcher's saw used to cut through meat, bones and the rib cage

metatarsal gland: a scent gland on deer, elk and moose that is located on the outside of each hind leg just above the dew claw which should not be punctured as part of the field dressing process because it will taint the meat; primarily a concern in deer because of their large size

MOA: a "minute of angle" is an angular measurement in rifle scopes equivalent to $1/60$ of a degree which equates to a spread of approximately one inch at a distance of 100 yards; most scopes incorporate windage and elevation adjustments referenced to MOA; each click of the scope turret is usually $1/4$ MOA change and on some scopes $1/8$ MOA; the point of impact of a bullet is changed by adjusting the windage (i.e., left or right) and elevation (i.e., up or down) MOA on a rifle scope

muzzle: is the front end of rifle/shotgun barrel from which the projectile will exit

non-typical: generally, antlers and horns of game animals are relatively symmetrical but sometimes they're asymmetrical and/or of different shapes (i.e., "non-typical")

OHV: off highway vehicle, also called all-terrain vehicle (ATV)

offhand shot: the most difficult shooting position for fast, urgent shots without the aid of a rest, done simply by bringing a rifle to shoulder, taking aim at a target and then firing

pass shooting: shooting a shotgun from a blind at passing waterfowl

pattern: shotgun pattern testing involves examining evidence for a pattern of holes created by the pellets fired from a shotgun at a paper target; for those unfamiliar with the process it simply means shooting onto a large blank sheet of paper and drawing a 30-inch circle around the densest part of the pattern; next, count the pellet holes inside the circle and then divide by the number of pellets counted in an identical shotshell for a percentage; repeat three times for an average

pinch point: a funnel-like area that animals like to travel, such as a narrow passageway between stands of cover and feeding areas

Pope and Young Club: an American bow hunting organization located in Chatfield, Minnesota, that developed a standardized way of scoring and recording animals harvested by hunters for comparison purposes; Pope and Young records bow harvests

posted land: in Alberta, a landowner can prohibit entry on his or her land by giving oral or written notice or by posting signs prohibiting entry; colloquially, land that has NO HUNTING signs on it
Note: Under Alberta's Petty Trespass Act, entry is prohibited without any notice required on the following kinds of property: privately owned lands (and leased public lands not associated with grazing or cultivation) that are under cultivation, fenced or enclosed by a natural boundary or enclosed in a manner that indicates the landowner's intention to keep people off the premises or animals on the premises.

prong (pronghorn antelope): part of an antelope's horn sheath that is in the shape of a conspicuous pointed prong, which usually points forward, hence the name pronghorn

priming a case: seating a "primer" in a cartridge case; the primer ignites the powder in the case when struck by a firing pin in the bolt of a rifle or shotgun

pull-away lead: mount the shotgun so the muzzle is on the leading edge of a bird's beak, and pull away from the target, shooting when the gap looks right

pump action (slide-action) firearm: a forend can be moved forward and backward in order to eject a spent round of ammunition and to chamber a fresh one

pushing bush: a deer and/or moose (in particular) party hunting technique; normally 2 to 3 hunters move through stands (usually isolated) of bush to alert animals and drive them into the open on the sides of the stand where other hunters are posted in a shooting position

raghorn: an elk with less than five points, typically having two to four points

ram: a male bighorn sheep

RAP: Report-A-Poacher program; in Alberta to report suspected poaching, or serious public land abuse, call the toll-free Report A Poacher line at 1-800-642-3800 or visit alberta.ca/report-poacher

RCMP: Royal Canadian Mounted Police; Canada's national police force

reflex shooting: also known as "point shooting," is a form of instinctive aiming, firing, and shooting a firearm quickly and accurately that does not rely on the use of the sights in close quarters; a skill developed after much practice so that a shooter executes all the skills automatically

ridge top (ridgeline): the height of land between two valleys

rub: defined by an area on a branch of a tree worn off by a deer, elk or moose to mark their territory and polish antlers

ruffies: slang for ruffed grouse (not "ruffled" grouse)

ruminates: (of a ruminant) to chew the cud (i.e., partly digested food that's returned from the first stomach of ruminants to the mouth for further chewing)

rump patch: area on the hind end of a big game animal that may be of different colour than the hide (e.g., white on big horn sheep and mule deer, tan on elk), which is flared to warn other animals of approaching danger

rut: the big game mating season when males breed females

satellite bulls: bull elk that are subordinate to a herd (dominant) bull during the rut

scat: the droppings (feces) of black bears and grizzlies that can be huge

scouting: going afield to look for game and game sign usually prior to actually hunting them

seating bullets: process where a bullet is fitted ("seated") in the neck of a brass casing by using a handloading (reloading) die and crimped as part of the process so it won't fall out of the casing

semi-automatic (self-loading) firearm: a firearm that fires a bullet or shotgun pellets each time the trigger is pulled and also performs all steps necessary to prepare it to discharge again, providing that cartridges remain in the firearm's magazine

shed antlers: antlers of deer, elk and moose are shed each winter, as well as the horn sheaths of pronghorn antelope

skunked: didn't bag anything

six pointer (6-pointer): bull elk with six points, considered a trophy

spiker: a bull elk with no antlers off the main antler beam

scrape: typically made by white-tailed deer, these are areas on the ground that are noticeably "scraped" by bucks with their hooves and antlers down to bare earth; also marked by their urine (and that of receptive does) as territorial sign posts

shed antler: during the winter each year, antlers of deer, elk and moose fall off the heads of males of these species of ungulates

shooter: slang for a legal big game animal of exceptional size

sow: a female black or grizzly bear

spent brass: empty cartridge cases that have been shot one or more times

spot and stalk: a form of hunting, beginning with "spotting" an animal and then "stalking" it to get within shooting range

spotting scope: a lightweight portable telescope usually mounted on a tripod or window mount that's used for distant wildlife spotting and viewing

stand: a location where a hunter situates himself/herself to watch for game, sometimes called a "ground blind"

standing shot: shooting at an animal that is not moving (i.e., standing still)

stalk: stalk (or to put on a "stalk") means to pursue or approach prey, quarry, etc., stealthily and quietly so as not to disturb it or alert it to your presence

stand-up blind: a camouflaged blind that hunters can stand up in during field shoots for waterfowl

steel shot: shotgun pellets made out of steel; mandatory for waterfowl hunting

sticker: abnormal burr or small point on the beam or tines of antlers, used interchangeably with "kicker" in Alberta

still hunting: a form of hunting, by travelling slowly through a forest, quietly, often one step at a time, in search of game animals

sustained lead: estimate the length of the lead necessary to hit the target and maintain that lead as you swing with the target, fire and continue the swing

SRD: formerly the Alberta Department of Sustainable Resource Development, which was reorganized into the department of Alberta Environment and Sustainable Resource Development

swing-through lead: point your firearm at a moving target and swing with it; increase the speed of the gun so that the muzzle passes the target and then fire; i.e., literally "swing through" the target and fire at a blank space in front of the target

tagged: slang for putting a tag (i.e., licence) on a game animal

take 'em: a command from a waterfowl guide or lead hunter to other hunters in a party during a field shoot to start shooting at waterfowl that are within shotgun range

tine: a branch off the main beam of an elk or deer's antlers

tracks: all ungulates leave distinctive footprints with their hooves on the ground or in snow that can be used to identify them

trigger creep: any movement of the trigger that doesn't result in the release of the sear; good triggers have no detectable creep which minimizes flinching

wall-hanger: slang for a legal big game animal of exceptional size

wallow: wetted (usually) area used by male elk and moose, in particular, during the mating season to cool off, mark their presence with urine and body scents to attract females; also, possibly used to cool body temperatures

weapon: under Alberta's Wildlife Act, a weapon is defined as a firearm or any other device that propels a projectile by means of an explosive spring, air, gas, string, wire or elastic material or any combination of these things

white-fronted (specklebelly) goose: "white-fronted" or specklebelly geese are noted for a patch of white feathers or "front" immediately behind the bill of adult birds; they are medium-sized geese, most weighing 4 to 6 pounds, slender and agile on the wing; the chest and breast are greyish with dark brown to black blotches and bars on the breast, giving them the nickname "specklebelly"

white-tail flag: a white-tailed "flag" refers to their distinctive, large white tail that is raised and moved like a flag when alarmed

Wildlife Management Unit (WMU): the province of Alberta is divided into a series of Wildlife Management Units (WMUs), areas that are based on legally defined geographical boundaries; wildlife within the boundaries of each WMU is managed by the Ministry of Environment and Parks (AEP) according to the regulations established in Alberta's Wildlife Act.

WMU(s): Wildlife Management Unit(s)

WIN: a 10-digit Wildlife Identification Number used to identify Alberta anglers and hunters; all anglers and hunters must purchase a WIN card before purchasing any licence, wildlife certificate or draw application; the same card is used to purchase both hunting and fishing licences; a WIN card looks like a credit card and confirms a hunter's eligibility for a licence

ungulate: ultimately, any animal with "hooves" including white-tailed and mule deer, moose, elk, bison, caribou, pronghorn antelope, mountain goats, and bighorn sheep

venison: collectively, meat from bison, antelope, deer, elk and moose

zero your scope: sighting in a rifle scope so it is centred on a target usually at 100 or 225 yards

x-hunt: a hunt where everything goes right and according to plan

Notes on Sources

Landowner maps are variously titled "Map Book" or "Road System and Ownership Maps" and are available for all counties, municipal districts and the Special Area in Alberta from municipal offices.

The Alberta Conservation Association publishes an annual *Alberta Discovery Guide* magazine and provides a free App that features all key conservation sites, including those belonging to Ducks Unlimited Canada and the Alberta Fish & Game Association.

Further Reading

Anonymous. *2015 Edition Alberta's Professional Outfitter.* Edmonton, Alberta: 2015.

Anonymous. *Management Plan for Mule Deer in Alberta.* Edmonton, Alberta: Forestry, Lands and Wildlife, Fish and Wildlife Division, 1989.

Alberta Wildlife Records—*Official Records of the Alberta Fish and Game Association, Second Edition* 1963–2001. Edmonton, Alberta: Alberta Fish & Game Association, 2003.

Alberta Wildlife Records—*Official Records of the Alberta Fish and Game Association Third Edition* 1963–2010. Edmonton, Alberta: Alberta Fish & Game Association, 2011.

Field, Ray A., F.C. Smith, and W.G. Hepworth. *The Elk Carcass.* University of Wyoming, 1973.

Field, Ray A. *Aging Big Game.* University of Wyoming, 1977.

LeMay, R.M. *Field Dressing Your Big Game.* Editions R.M. LeMay, 2005.

Meredith, Don, Duane S. Radford. *Conservation, Pride and Passion—The Alberta Fish and Game Association.* Edmonton, Alberta: The Edmonton Journal, 2008.

Nesbitt, William H. and Phillip L. Wright. *Measuring and Scoring North American Big Game Trophies.* The Boone and Crockett Club, 1985.

Nosler Reloading Guide, 5th Edition. Nosler Bullets for Sportsmen, 2002.

Radford, Duane. *From the Field to the Table: Fish and Wild Game Recipes.* Edmonton, Alberta: Sports Scene Publications Inc., 2006.

Thornberry, Russell. *Trophy Deer of Alberta.* Greenhorn Publishing Limited, 1982.

Websites

Alberta Conservation Association: http://www.ab-conservation.com/

Alberta Bow Hunter's Association: http://www.bowhunters.ca/

Alberta Fish & Game Association: http://www.afga.org/

Alberta Hunter Education Instructor's Association: http://www.aheia.com/

Alberta Outdoorsmen Magazine: http://www.albertaoutdoorsmen.ca/

Alberta Professional Outfitter's Society: https://www.apos.ab.ca/

Cold Shortening: https://www.britannica.com/topic/cold-shortening

Ducks Unlimited Canada Alberta: http://www.ducks.ca/places/alberta/

How to Field Dress a Big Game Animal (Brian Makowecki): https://youtu.be/sCQpdBDl9XI

Map Town: http://www.maptown.com/Alberta_County_and_Municipal_District_Maps_s/2326.htm

Hunting for Tomorrow Foundation: http://www.huntingfortomorrow.com/

My Wild Alberta: http://mywildalberta.com/

About the Author

Duane S. Radford is a native of Bellevue, Alberta and currently lives in Edmonton, Alberta. He is a national award-winning writer and photographer whose articles and photographs have appeared in many outdoor publications and newspapers in Canada and the United States.

He has authored 800+ magazine articles and recipes as well as four award-winning books: *Fish & Wild Game Recipes* (2006), *Conservation Pride and Passion the Alberta Fish and Game Association 1908–2008* (2008), which he co-authored with Don Meredith; *The Cowboy Way* (2014) and *The Canadian Cowboy Cookbook* (2014), which he co-authored with Jean Paré and Gregory Lepine. He also co-edited a book with Ross H. Shickler, *Fishing Northern Canada for Lake Trout, Grayling and Arctic Char* (2015). He co-authored *Rodeo Roundup* with Wendy Pirk (2016) and authored *Canadian Fly Fishing: Hot Spots & Essentials* (2017).

Duane is a Past President of the Outdoor Writers of Canada (OWC). He received the Pete McGillen Award from the OWC in 2017, its highest award. He is a member of the Alberta Fish & Game Association and represents this organization on the Antelope Creek Ranch Management Committee. Duane retired as the director of Alberta's fisheries management branch in 2002 where he worked as a regional director, regional fisheries biologist, and fishery scientist for Alberta's Fish and Wildlife Division. He is certified as a Fisheries Scientist by the American Fisheries Society, has represented Alberta on the National Recreational Fishery Awards Committee and was Vice Chairman of this committee which sun-setted in 2017. He is a honourary member of the Great Plains Fishery Workers Association. He was bestowed an Alberta Order of the Bighorn Award as a member of the Bow Habitat Station Core Committee in 1998, Alberta's foremost conservation award.